Learning jQuery 1.3

Better Interaction Design and Web Development with Simple JavaScript Techniques

Jonathan Chaffer

Karl Swedberg

BIRMINGHAM - MUMBAI

Learning jQuery 1.3

First published: February 2009

Production Reference: 1040209

Published by Packt Publishing Ltd.
32 Lincoln Road
Olton
Birmingham, B27 6PA, UK.

ISBN 978-1-847196-70-5

www.packtpub.com

Cover Image by Karl Swedberg (karl@englishrules.com)

Credits

Authors

Jonathan Chaffer

Karl Swedberg

Reviewers

Akash Mehta

Dave Methvin

Mike Alsup

Senior Acquisition Editor

Douglas Paterson

Development Editor

Usha Iyer

Technical Editor

John Antony

Editorial Team Leader

Akshara Aware

Production Editorial Manager

Abhijeet Deobhakta

Project Team Leader

Lata Basantani

Project Coordinator

Leena Purkait

Indexer

Rekha Nair

Proofreader

Jeff Orloff

Production Coordinator

Aparna Bhagat

Cover Work

Aparna Bhagat

Foreword

I feel honored knowing that Karl Swedberg and Jonathan Chaffer undertook the task of writing Learning jQuery. As the first book about jQuery, it set the standard that other jQuery — and, really, other JavaScript books in general — have tried to match. It's consistently been one of the top selling JavaScript books since its release, in no small part due to its quality and attention to detail.

I'm especially pleased that it was Karl and Jonathan who wrote the book since I already knew them so well and knew that they would be perfect for the job. Being part of the core jQuery team, I've had the opportunity to come to know Karl quite well over the past couple years, and especially within the context of his book writing effort. Looking at the end result, it's clear that his skills as both a developer and a former English teacher were perfectly designed for this singular task.

I've also had the opportunity to meet both of them in person, a rare occurrence in the world of distributed Open Source projects, and they continue to be upstanding members of the jQuery community.

The jQuery library is used by so many different people in the jQuery community. The community is full of designers, developers, people who have experience programming, and those who don't. Even within the jQuery team, we have people from all backgrounds providing their feedback on the direction of the project. There is one thing that is common across all of jQuery's users, though: We are a community of developers and designers who want JavaScript development to be made simple.

It's almost a cliché, at this point, to say that an open source project is community-oriented, or that a project wants to focus on helping new users get started. But it's not just an empty gesture for jQuery; it's the liquid-oxygen fuel for the project. We actually have more people in the jQuery team dedicated to managing the jQuery community, writing documentation, or writing plugins than actually maintaining the core code base. While the health of the library is incredibly important, the community surrounding that code is the difference between a floundering, mediocre project and one that will match and exceed your every need.

How we run the project, and how you use the code, is fundamentally very different from most open source projects — and most JavaScript libraries. The jQuery project and community is incredibly knowledgeable; we understand what makes jQuery a different programming experience and do our best to pass that knowledge on to fellow users.

The jQuery community isn't something that you can read about to understand; it's something that you actually have to participate in for it to fully sink in. I hope that you'll have the opportunity to partake in it. Come join us in our forums, mailing lists, and blogs and let us help guide you through the experience of getting to know jQuery better.

For me, jQuery is much more than a block of code. It's the sum total of experiences that have transpired over the years in order to make the library happen. The considerable ups and downs, the struggle of development together with the excitement of seeing it grow and succeed. Growing close with its users and fellow team members, understanding them and trying to grow and adapt.

When I first saw this book talk about jQuery and discuss it like a unified tool, as opposed to the experiences that it's come to encapsulate for me, I was both taken aback and excited. Seeing how others learn, understand, and mold jQuery to fit them is much of what makes the project so exhilarating.

I'm not the only one who enjoys jQuery on a level that is far different from a normal tool-user relationship. I don't know if I can properly encapsulate why this is, but I've seen it time and time again — the singular moment when a user's face lights up with the realization of just how much jQuery will help them.

There is a specific moment where it just clicks for a jQuery user, when they realize that this tool that they were using was in fact much, much more than just a simple tool all along — and suddenly their understanding of how to write dynamic web applications completely shifts. It's an incredible thing, and absolutely my favorite part of the jQuery project.

I hope you'll have the opportunity to experience this sensation as well.

John Resig
Creator of jQuery

About the Authors

Jonathan Chaffer is the Chief Technology Officer of Structure Interactive, an interactive agency located in Grand Rapids, Michigan. There, he oversees web development projects using a wide range of technologies, and continues to collaborate on day-to-day programming tasks as well.

In the open-source community, Jonathan has been very active in the Drupal CMS project, which has adopted jQuery as its JavaScript framework of choice. He is the creator of the Content Construction Kit, a popular module for managing structured content on Drupal sites. He is responsible for major overhauls of Drupal's menu system and developer API reference.

Jonathan lives in Grand Rapids with his wife, Jennifer.

I would like to thank Jenny for her tireless enthusiasm and support, Karl for the motivation to continue writing when the spirit is weak, and the Ars Technica community for constant inspiration toward technical excellence.

Karl Swedberg is a web developer at Fusionary Media in Grand Rapids, Michigan, where he spends much of his time implementing design with a focus on "web standards"—semantic HTML, well-mannered CSS, and unobtrusive JavaScript. A member of the jQuery Project Team and an active contributor to the jQuery discussion list, Karl has presented at workshops and conferences and provided corporate training in Europe and North America.

Before his current love affair with web development, Karl worked as a copy editor, a high-school English teacher, and a coffee house owner. His fascination with technology began in the early 1990s when he worked at Microsoft in Redmond, Washington, and it has continued unabated ever since.

Karl would rather be spending time with his wife, Sara, and his two children, Benjamin and Lucia.

I wish to thank my wife, Sara, for her steadfast love and support. Thanks also to my two delightful children, Benjamin and Lucia. Jonathan Chaffer has my deepest respect for his programming expertise and my gratitude for his willingness to write this book with me.

Many thanks to John Resig for creating the world's greatest JavaScript library and for fostering an amazing community around it. Thanks also to the folks at Packt Publishing, the technical reviewers of this book, the jQuery Cabal, and the many others who have provided help and inspiration along the way.

About the Reviewers

Akash Mehta is a web application developer, technical writer and business consultant based in Brisbane, Australia. His past projects include brochure websites, e-learning solutions and information systems. He has written web development articles for several of publishers in print and online, is a regular speaker at local conferences, and contributes to prominent PHP blogs.

As a student, Akash maintained PHP web applications and built user interfaces using the jQuery toolkit. While pursuing a degree in both commerce and IT, Akash develops web applications on PHP and Python platforms. After hours, he organizes his local PHP user group.

Akash develops applications on a wide range of open source libraries. His toolbox includes a number of application frameworks, including the Zend Framework, CakePHP and Django; Javascript frameworks like jQuery, Prototype and Mootools, platforms such as Adobe Flash/Flex, and the MySQL and SQLite database engines.

Currently, Akash provides freelance technical writing and web development through his website, `http://bitmeta.org`.

Dave Methvin has more than 25 years of software development experience in both the Windows and Unix environments. His early career focused on embedded software in the fields of robotics, telecommunications, and medicine. Later, he moved to PC-based software projects using C/C++ and web technologies.

Dave also has more than 20 years of experience in computer journalism. He was Executive Editor at PC Tech Journal and Windows Magazine, covering PC and Internet issues; his how-to columns on JavaScript offered some of the first cut-and-paste solutions to common web page problems. He was also a co-author of the book "Networking Windows NT" (John Wiley & Sons, 1997).

Currently, Dave is Chief Technology Officer at PC Pitstop, a web site that helps users fix and optimize the performance of their computers. He is also active in the jQuery community.

Mike Alsup has been involved with the jQuery project since near its inception and has contributed many popular plugins to the community. He is an active participant in the jQuery Google Group where he frequently provides support to new jQuery users.

Mike lives in upstate NY with his wife, Diane, and their triplet teenage sons. He is a Senior Software Developer at Click Commerce, Inc. where he focuses on Java, Swing, and web application development.

His jQuery plugins can be found at `http://jquery.malsup.com/`

Table of Contents

Preface

It began as a labor of love back in 2005 by John Resig, a JavaScript wunderkind who now works for the Mozilla Corporation. Inspired by pioneers in the field such as Dean Edwards and Simon Willison, Resig put together a set of functions to make it easy to programmatically find elements on a web page and assign behaviors to them. By the time he first publicly announced his project in January 2006, he had added DOM modification and basic animations. He gave it the name jQuery to emphasize the central role of finding, or "querying," parts of a web page and acting on them with JavaScript. In the few short years since then, jQuery has grown in its feature set, improved in its performance, and gained widespread adoption by some of the most popular sites on the Internet. While Resig remains the lead developer of the project, jQuery has blossomed, in true open-source fashion, to the point where it now boasts a core team of top-notch JavaScript developers, as well as a vibrant community of thousands of developers.

The jQuery JavaScript Library can enhance your websites regardless of your background. It provides a wide range of features, an easy-to-learn syntax, and robust cross-platform compatibility in a single compact file. What's more, hundreds of plug-ins have been developed to extend jQuery's functionality, making it an essential tool for nearly every client-side scripting occasion.

Learning jQuery provides a gentle introduction to jQuery concepts, allowing you to add interactions and animations to your pages—even if previous attempts at writing JavaScript have left you baffled. This book guides you past the pitfalls associated with AJAX, events, effects, and advanced JavaScript language features, and provides you with a brief reference to the jQuery library to return to again and again.

What this book covers

In Chapter 1 you'll get your feet wet with the jQuery JavaScript library. The chapter begins with a description of jQuery and what it can do for you. It walks you through downloading and setting up the library, as well as writing your first script.

In *Chapter 2* you'll learn how to use jQuery's selector expressions and DOM traversal methods to find elements on the page, wherever they may be. You'll use jQuery to apply styling to a diverse set of page elements, sometimes in a way that pure CSS cannot.

In *Chapter 3* you'll use jQuery's event-handling mechanism to fire off behaviors when browser events occur. You'll see how jQuery makes it easy to attach events to elements unobtrusively, even before the page finishes loading. And, you'll be introduced to more advanced topics, such as event bubbling, delegation, and namespacing.

In *Chapter 4* you'll be introduced to jQuery's animation techniques and see how to hide, show, and move page elements with effects that are both useful and pleasing to the eye.

In *Chapter 5* you'll learn how to change your page on command. This chapter will teach you how to alter the very structure of an HTML document, as well as its content, on the fly.

In *Chapter 6* you'll discover the many ways in which jQuery makes it easy to access server-side functionality without resorting to clunky page refreshes.

In the next three chapters (7, 8, and 9) you'll work through several real-world examples, pulling together what you've learned in previous chapters and creating robust jQuery solutions to common problems.

In *Chapter 7*, "Table Manipulation," you'll sort, sift, and style information to create beautiful and functional data layouts.

In *Chapter 8*, "Forms with Function," you'll master the finer points of client-side validation, design an adaptive form layout, and implement interactive client-server form features such as autocompletion.

In *Chapter 9*, "Shufflers and Rotators," you'll enhance the beauty and utility of page elements by showing them in more manageable chunks. You'll make information fly in and out of view both on its own and under user control.

Chapters 10 and 11 take you beyond the core jQuery methods to explore third-party extensions to the library, and show you various ways you can extend the library yourself.

In *Chapter 10*, "Using Plug-ins," you'll examine the Form plug-in and the official collection of user interface plug-ins known as jQuery UI. You'll also learn where to find many other popular jQuery plug-ins and see what they can do for you.

In *Chapter 11*, "Developing Plug-ins," you'll learn how to take advantage of jQuery's impressive extension capabilities to develop your own plug-ins from the ground up. You'll create your own utility functions, add jQuery object methods, write custom selector expressions, and more.

In Appendix A, "Online Resources," you'll find recommendations for a handful of informative websites on a wide range of topics related to jQuery, JavaScript, and web development in general.

In Appendix B, "Development Tools," you'll discover a number of useful third-party programs and utilities for editing and debugging jQuery code within your personal development environment.

In *Appendix C*, "JavaScript Closures," you'll gain a solid understanding of closures—what they are and how you can use them to your advantage.

In *Appendix D*, "Quick Reference," you'll get a glimpse of the entire jQuery library, including every one of its methods and selector expressions. Its easy-to-scan format is perfect for those moments when you know what you want to do, but you're just unsure about the right method name or selector.

What you need for this book

In order to both write and run the code demonstrated in this book, you need the following:

- A basic text editor.
- A modern web browser such as Mozilla Firefox, Apple Safari, or Microsoft Internet Explorer.
- The jQuery source file, version 1.3.1 or later, which can be downloaded from `http://jquery.com/`.

Additionally, to run the AJAX examples in *Chapter 6*, you will need a PHP-enabled server.

Who is this book for

This book is for web designers who want to create interactive elements for their designs, and for developers who want to create the best user interface for their web applications. Basic JavaScript programming knowledge is required. You will need to know the basics of HTML and CSS, and should be comfortable with the syntax of JavaScript. No knowledge of jQuery is assumed, nor is experience with any other JavaScript libraries required.

Conventions

In this book, you will find a number of styles of text that distinguish between different kinds of information. Here are some examples of these styles, and an explanation of their meaning.

Code words in text are shown as follows: "We can include other contexts through the use of the `include` directive."

A block of code will be set as follows:

```html
<html>
  <head>
    <title>the title</title>
  </head>
  <body>
    <div>
      <p>This is a paragraph.</p>
      <p>This is another paragraph.</p>
      <p>This is yet another paragraph.</p>
    </div>
  </body>
</html>
```

When we wish to draw your attention to a particular part of a code block, the relevant lines or items will be made bold:

```javascript
$(document).ready(function() {
  $('a[href^=mailto:]').addClass('mailto');
  $('a[href$=.pdf]').addClass('pdflink');
  $('a[href^=http][href*=henry]')
    .addClass('henrylink');
});
```

Any command-line input and output is written as follows:

```
outerFn():
Outer function
Inner function
```

New terms and **important words** are introduced in a bold-type font. Words that you see on the screen, in menus or dialog boxes for example, appear in our text like this: "Note the PDF icon to the right of the **Hamlet** link, the envelope icon next to the **email** link, and the white background and black border around the **Henry V** link.".

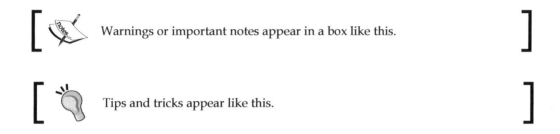

Warnings or important notes appear in a box like this.

Tips and tricks appear like this.

Reader feedback

Feedback from our readers is always welcome. Let us know what you think about this book, what you liked or may have disliked. Reader feedback is important for us to develop titles that you really get the most out of.

To send us general feedback, simply drop an email to feedback@packtpub.com, making sure to mention the book title in the subject of your message.

If there is a book that you need and would like to see us publish, please send us a note in the **SUGGEST A TITLE** form on www.packtpub.com or email suggest@packtpub.com.

If there is a topic that you have expertise in and you are interested in either writing or contributing to a book, see our author guide on www.packtpub.com/authors.

Customer support

Now that you are the proud owner of a Packt book, we have a number of things to help you to get the most from your purchase.

Downloading the example code for the book

Visit `http://www.packtpub.com/files/code/6705_Code.zip` to directly download the example code.

The downloadable files contain instructions on how to use them.

Errata

Although we have taken every care to ensure the accuracy of our contents, mistakes do happen. If you find a mistake in one of our books—maybe a mistake in text or code—we would be grateful if you would report this to us. By doing this you can save other readers from frustration, and help to improve subsequent versions of this book. If you find any errata, report them by visiting `http://www.packtpub.com/support`, selecting your book, clicking on the **let us know** link, and entering the details of your errata. Once your errata are verified, your submission will be accepted and the errata added to the list of existing errata. The existing errata can be viewed by selecting your title from `http://www.packtpub.com/support`.

Piracy

Piracy of copyright material on the Internet is an ongoing problem across all media. At Packt, we take the protection of our copyright and licenses very seriously. If you come across any illegal copies of our works in any form on the Internet, please provide the location address or website name immediately so we can pursue a remedy.

Please contact us at `copyright@packtpub.com` with a link to the suspected pirated material.

We appreciate your help in protecting our authors, and our ability to bring you valuable content.

Questions

You can contact us at `questions@packtpub.com` if you are having a problem with some aspect of the book, and we will do our best to address it.

1
Getting Started

Today's World Wide Web is a dynamic environment, and its users set a high bar for both style and function of sites. To build interesting, interactive sites, developers are turning to JavaScript libraries such as jQuery to automate common tasks and simplify complicated ones. One reason the jQuery library is a popular choice is its ability to assist in a wide range of tasks.

It can seem challenging to know where to begin because jQuery performs so many different functions. Yet, there is a coherence and symmetry to the design of the library; most of its concepts are borrowed from the structure of **HTML** and **Cascading Style Sheets (CSS)**. The library's design lends itself to a quick start for designers with little programming experience since many web developers have more experience with these technologies than they do with JavaScript. In fact, in this opening chapter we'll write a functioning jQuery program in just three lines of code. On the other hand, experienced programmers will also be aided by this conceptual consistency, as we'll see in the later, more advanced chapters.

So let's look at what jQuery can do for us.

What jQuery does

The jQuery library provides a general-purpose abstraction layer for common web scripting, and is therefore useful in almost every scripting situation. Its extensible nature means that we could never cover all possible uses and functions in a single book, as plugins are constantly being developed to add new abilities. The core features, though, address the following needs:

- **Access elements in a document**. Without a JavaScript library, many lines of code must be written to traverse the **Document Object Model (DOM)** tree, and locate specific portions of an HTML document's structure. A robust and efficient selector mechanism is offered in jQuery for retrieving the exact piece of the document that is to be inspected or manipulated.

- **Modify the appearance of a web page**. CSS offers a powerful method of influencing the way a document is rendered, but it falls short when web browsers do not all support the same standards. With jQuery, developers can bridge this gap, relying on the same standards support across all browsers. In addition, jQuery can change the classes or individual style properties applied to a portion of the document even after the page has been rendered.

- **Alter the content of a document**. Not limited to mere cosmetic changes, jQuery can modify the content of a document itself with a few keystrokes. Text can be changed, images can be inserted or swapped, lists can be reordered, or the entire structure of the HTML can be rewritten and extended—all with a single easy-to-use **Application Programming Interface (API)**.

- **Respond to a user's interaction**. Even the most elaborate and powerful behaviors are not useful if we can't control when they take place. The jQuery library offers an elegant way to intercept a wide variety of events, such as a user clicking on a link, without the need to clutter the HTML code itself with event handlers. At the same time, its event-handling API removes browser inconsistencies that often plague web developers.

- **Animate changes being made to a document**. To effectively implement such interactive behaviors, a designer must also provide visual feedback to the user. The jQuery library facilitates this by providing an array of effects such as fades and wipes, as well as a toolkit for crafting new ones.

- **Retrieve information from a server without refreshing a page**. This code pattern has become known as **Asynchronous JavaScript And XML (AJAX)**, and assists web developers in crafting a responsive, feature-rich site. The jQuery library removes the browser-specific complexity from this process, allowing developers to focus on the server-end functionality.

- **Simplify common JavaScript tasks**. In addition to all of the document-specific features of jQuery, the library provides enhancements to basic JavaScript constructs such as iteration and array manipulation.

Why jQuery works well

With the recent resurgence of interest in dynamic HTML comes a proliferation of JavaScript frameworks. Some are specialized, focusing on just one or two of the above tasks. Others attempt to catalog every possible behavior and animation, and serve these all up pre-packaged. To maintain the wide range of features outlined above while remaining compact, jQuery employs several strategies:

- **Leverage knowledge of CSS**. By basing the mechanism for locating page elements on **CSS selectors**, jQuery inherits a terse yet legible way of expressing a document's structure. The jQuery library becomes an entry point for designers who want to add behaviors to their pages because a prerequisite for doing professional web development is knowledge of CSS syntax.

- **Support extensions**. In order to avoid "feature creep", jQuery relegates special-case uses to **plugins**. The method for creating new plugins is simple and well-documented, which has spurred the development of a wide variety of inventive and useful modules. Even most of the features in the basic jQuery download are internally realized through the plugin architecture, and can be removed if desired, yielding an even smaller library.

- **Abstract away browser quirks**. An unfortunate reality of web development is that each browser has its own set of deviations from published standards. A significant portion of any web application can be relegated to handling features differently on each platform. While the ever-evolving browser landscape makes a perfectly browser-neutral code base impossible for some advanced features, jQuery adds an **abstraction layer** that normalizes the common tasks, reducing the size of code, and tremendously simplifying it.

- **Always work with sets**. When we instruct jQuery, *Find all elements with the class* `collapsible` *and hide them*, there is no need to loop through each returned element. Instead, methods such as `.hide()` are designed to automatically work on sets of objects instead of individual ones. This technique, called **implicit iteration**, means that many looping constructs become unnecessary, shortening code considerably.

- **Allow multiple actions in one line**. To avoid overuse of temporary variables or wasteful repetition, jQuery employs a programming pattern called **chaining** for the majority of its methods. This means that the result of most operations on an object is the object itself, ready for the next action to be applied to it.

These strategies have kept the jQuery package slim—under 20 KB compressed—while at the same time providing techniques for keeping our custom code that uses the library compact, as well.

The elegance of the library comes about partly by design, and partly due to the evolutionary process spurred by the vibrant community that has sprung up around the project. Users of jQuery gather to discuss not only the development of plugins, but also enhancements to the core library. Appendix A details many of the community resources available to jQuery developers.

Despite all of the efforts required to engineer such a flexible and robust system, the end product is free for all to use. This open-source project is dually licensed under the **GNU Public License** (appropriate for inclusion in many other open-source projects) and the **MIT License** (to facilitate use of jQuery within proprietary software).

History of the jQuery project

This book covers the functionality and syntax of **jQuery 1.3.x**, the latest version at the time of writing. The premise behind the library—providing an easy way to find elements on a web page and manipulating them—has not changed over the course of its development, but some syntax details and features have. This brief overview of the project history describes the most significant changes from version to version.

- **Public Development Phase**: John Resig first made mention of an improvement on Prototype's "Behaviour" library in August of 2005. This new framework was formally released as **jQuery** on January 14, 2006.

- **jQuery 1.0** (August 2006): This, the first stable release of the library, already had robust support for CSS selectors, event handling, and AJAX interaction.

- **jQuery 1.1** (January 2007): This release streamlined the API considerably. Many rarely-used methods were combined, reducing the number of methods to learn and document.

- **jQuery 1.1.3** (July 2007): This minor release contained massive speed improvements for jQuery's selector engine. From this version on, jQuery's performance would compare favorably to its fellow JavaScript libraries such as Prototype, Mootools, and Dojo.

- **jQuery 1.2** (September 2007): **XPath** syntax for selecting elements was removed in this release, as it had become redundant with the CSS syntax. Effect customization became much more flexible in this release, and plugin development became easier with the addition of **namespaced events**.

- **jQuery UI** (September 2007): This new plugin suite was announced to replace the popular but aging Interface plugin. A rich collection of prefabricated widgets was included, as well as a set of tools for building sophisticated elements such as drag-and-drop interfaces.

- **jQuery 1.2.6** (May 2008): The functionality of Brandon Aaron's popular **Dimensions** plugin was brought into the main library.

- **jQuery 1.3 (January 2009)**: A major overhaul of the selector engine (**Sizzle**) provided a huge boost to the library's performance. **Event delegation** became formally supported.

Release notes for older jQuery versions can be found on the project's web site at `http://docs.jquery.com/History_of_jQuery`.

Our first jQuery-powered web page

Now that we have covered the range of features available to us with jQuery, we can examine how to put the library into action.

Downloading jQuery

The **official jQuery website** (`http://jquery.com/`) is always the most up-to-date resource for code and news related to the library. To get started, we need a copy of jQuery, which can be downloaded right from the home page of the site. Several versions of jQuery may be available at any given moment; the most appropriate for us as site developers will be the latest uncompressed version of the library. This can be replaced with a compressed version in production environments.

No installation is required. To use jQuery, we just need to place it on our site in a public location. Since JavaScript is an interpreted language, there is no compilation or build phase to worry about. Whenever we need a page to have jQuery available, we will simply refer to the file's location from the HTML document.

Setting up the HTML document

There are three pieces to most examples of jQuery usage: the HTML document itself, CSS files to style it, and JavaScript files to act on it. For our first example, we'll use a page with a book excerpt that has a number of classes applied to portions of it.

```
<!DOCTYPE html PUBLIC "-//W3C//DTD XHTML 1.0 Transitional//EN"
  "http://www.w3.org/TR/xhtml1/DTD/xhtml1-transitional.dtd">

<html xmlns="http://www.w3.org/1999/xhtml"
    xml:lang="en" lang="en">
  <head>
    <meta http-equiv="Content-Type"
      content="text/html; charset=utf-8"/>

    <title>Through the Looking-Glass</title>

    <link rel="stylesheet" href="alice.css"
      type="text/css" media="screen" />

    <script src="jquery.js" type="text/javascript"></script>
```

```
      <script src="alice.js" type="text/javascript"></script>
    </head>

  <body>
    <h1>Through the Looking-Glass</h1>
    <div class="author">by Lewis Carroll</div>

    <div class="chapter" id="chapter-1">
      <h2 class="chapter-title">1. Looking-Glass House</h2>
      <p>There was a book lying near Alice on the table,
        and while she sat watching the White King (for she
        was still a little anxious about him, and had the
        ink all ready to throw over him, in case he fainted
        again), she turned over the leaves, to find some
        part that she could read, <span class="spoken">
        "&mdash;for it's all in some language I don't know,"
        </span> she said to herself.</p>
      <p>It was like this.</p>
      <div class="poem">
        <h3 class="poem-title">YKCOWREBBAJ</h3>
        <div class="poem-stanza">
          <div>sevot yhtils eht dna ,gillirb sawT'</div>
          <div>;ebaw eht ni elbmig dna eryg diD</div>
          <div>,sevogorob eht erew ysmim llA</div>
          <div>.ebargtuo shtar emom eht dnA</div>
        </div>
      </div>
      <p>She puzzled over this for some time, but at last
        a bright thought struck her. <span class="spoken">
        "Why, it's a Looking-glass book, of course! And if
        I hold it up to a glass, the words will all go the
        right way again."</span></p>
      <p>This was the poem that Alice read.</p>
      <div class="poem">
        <h3 class="poem-title">JABBERWOCKY</h3>
        <div class="poem-stanza">
          <div>'Twas brillig, and the slithy toves</div>
          <div>Did gyre and gimble in the wabe;</div>
          <div>All mimsy were the borogoves,</div>
          <div>And the mome raths outgrabe.</div>
        </div>
      </div>
    </div>
  </body>
</html>
```

The actual layout of files on the server does not matter. References from one file to another just need to be adjusted to match the organization we choose. In most examples in this book, we will use relative paths to reference files (../images/foo.png) rather than absolute paths (/images/foo.png). This will allow the code to run locally without the need for a web server.

Immediately following the normal HTML preamble, the stylesheet is loaded. For this example, we'll use a spartan one.

```css
body {
    font: 62.5% Arial, Verdana, sans-serif;
}
h1 {
    font-size: 2.5em;
    margin-bottom: 0;
}
h2 {
    font-size: 1.3em;
    margin-bottom: .5em;
}
h3 {
    font-size: 1.1em;
    margin-bottom: 0;
}
.poem {
    margin: 0 2em;
}
.highlight {
    font-style: italic;
    border: 1px solid #888;
    padding: 0.5em;
    margin: 0.5em 0;
    background-color: #ffc;
}
```

After the stylesheet is referenced, the JavaScript files are included. It is important that the script tag for the jQuery library be placed *before* the tag for our custom scripts; otherwise, the jQuery framework will not be available when our code attempts to reference it.

Throughout the rest of this book, only the relevant portions of HTML and CSS files will be printed. The files in their entirety are available from the book's companion website `http://book.learningjquery.com` or from the publisher's website `http://www.packtpub.com/support`.

Now we have a page that looks like this:

Through the Looking-Glass

by Lewis Carroll

1. Looking-Glass House

There was a book lying near Alice on the table, and while she sat watching the White King (for she was still a little anxious about him, and had the ink all ready to throw over him, in case he fainted again), she turned over the leaves, to find some part that she could read, "—for it's all in some language I don't know," she said to herself.

It was like this.

YKCOWREBBAJ

sevot yhtils eht dna ,gillirb sawT'
;ebaw eht ni elbmig dna eryg diD
,sevogorob eht erew ysmim llA
.ebargtuo shtar emom eht dnA

She puzzled over this for some time, but at last a bright thought struck her. "Why, it's a Looking-glass book, of course! And if I hold it up to a glass, the words will all go the right way again."

This was the poem that Alice read.

JABBERWOCKY

'Twas brillig, and the slithy toves
Did gyre and gimble in the wabe;
All mimsy were the borogoves,
And the mome raths outgrabe.

We will use jQuery to apply a new style to the poem text.

 This example is to demonstrate a simple use of jQuery. In real-world situations, this type of styling could be performed purely with CSS.

Adding jQuery

Our custom code will go in the second, currently empty, JavaScript file, which we included from the HTML using `<script src="alice.js" type="text/javascript"></script>`. For this example, we only need three lines of code:

```
$(document).ready(function() {
  $('.poem-stanza').addClass('highlight');
});
```

Finding the poem text

The fundamental operation in jQuery is selecting a part of the document. This is done with the `$()` construct. Typically, it takes a string as a parameter, which can contain any CSS selector expression. In this case, we wish to find all parts of the document that have the `poem-stanza` class applied to them, so the selector is very simple. However, we will cover much more sophisticated options through the course of the book. We will step through the different ways of locating parts of a document in Chapter 2.

The `$()` function is actually a factory for the **jQuery object**, which is the basic building block we will be working with from now on. The jQuery object encapsulates zero or more DOM elements, and allows us to interact with them in many different ways. In this case, we wish to modify the appearance of these parts of the page, and we will accomplish this by changing the classes applied to the poem text.

Injecting the new class

The `.addClass()` method, like most jQuery methods, is named self-descriptively; it applies a CSS class to the part of the page that we have selected. Its only parameter is the name of the class to add. This method, and its counterpart, `.removeClass()`, will allow us to easily observe jQuery in action as we explore the different selector expressions available to us. For now, our example simply adds the `highlight` class, which our stylesheet has defined as italicized text with a border.

Note that no iteration is necessary to add the class to all the poem stanzas. As we discussed, jQuery uses **implicit iteration** within methods such as `.addClass()`, so a single function call is all it takes to alter all of the selected parts of the document.

Executing the code

Taken together, `$()` and `.addClass()` are enough for us to accomplish our goal of changing the appearance of the poem text. However, if this line of code is inserted alone in the document header, it will have no effect. JavaScript code is generally run as soon as it is encountered in the browser, and at the time the header is being processed, no HTML is yet present to style. We need to delay the execution of the code until after the DOM is available for our use.

The traditional mechanism for controlling when JavaScript code is run is to call the code from within **event handlers**. Many handlers are available for user-initiated events, such as mouse clicks and key presses. If we did not have jQuery available for our use, we would need to rely on the `onload` handler, which fires after the page (along with all of its images) has been rendered. To trigger our code from the `onload` event, we would place the code inside a function:

```
function highlightPoemStanzas() {
  $('.poem-stanza').addClass('highlight');
}
```

Then we would attach the function to the event by modifying the HTML `<body>` tag to reference it:

```
<body onload="highlightPoemStanzas();">
```

This causes our code to run after the page is completely loaded.

There are drawbacks to this approach. We altered the HTML itself to effect this behavior change. This tight coupling of structure and function clutters the code, possibly requiring the same function calls to be repeated over many different pages, or in the case of other events such as mouse clicks, over every instance of an element on a page. Adding new behaviors would then require alterations in multiple places, increasing the opportunity for error and complicating parallel workflows for designers and programmers.

To avoid this pitfall, jQuery allows us to schedule function calls for firing once the DOM is loaded—without waiting for images—with the `$(document).ready()` construct. With our function defined as above, we can write:

```
$(document).ready(highlightPoemStanzas);
```

This technique does not require any HTML modifications. Instead, the behavior is attached entirely from within the JavaScript file. We will learn how to respond to other types of **events**, divorcing their effects from the HTML structure as well, in Chapter 3.

This incarnation is still slightly wasteful, though, because the function `highlightPoemStanzas()` is defined only to be used immediately, and exactly once. This means that we have used an identifier in the global namespace of functions that we have to remember not to use again, and for little gain. JavaScript, like some other programming languages, has a way around this inefficiency called **anonymous functions** (sometimes also called **lambda functions**). Using anonymous functions, we can write the code as it was originally presented:

```
$(document).ready(function() {
  $('.poem-stanza').addClass('highlight');
});
```

By using the `function` keyword without a function name, we define a function exactly where it is needed, and not before. This removes clutter and brings us down to three lines of JavaScript. This idiom is extremely convenient in jQuery code, as many methods take a function as an argument and such functions are rarely reusable.

When this syntax is used to define an anonymous function within the body of another function, a **closure** can be created. This is an advanced and powerful concept, but should be understood when making extensive use of nested function definitions as it can have unintended consequences and ramifications on memory use. This topic is discussed fully in Appendix C.

The finished product

Now that our JavaScript is in place, the page looks like this:

Through the Looking-Glass
by Lewis Carroll

1. Looking-Glass House

There was a book lying near Alice on the table, and while she sat watching the White King (for she was still a little anxious about him, and had the ink all ready to throw over him, in case he fainted again), she turned over the leaves, to find some part that she could read, "—for it's all in some language I don't know," she said to herself.

It was like this.

YKCOWREBBAJ

sevot yhtils eht dna ,gillirb sawT'
;ebaw eht ni elbmig dna eryg diD
,sevogorob eht erew ysmim llA
.ebargtuo shtar emom eht dnA

She puzzled over this for some time, but at last a bright thought struck her. "Why, it's a Looking-glass book, of course! And if I hold it up to a glass, the words will all go the right way again."

This was the poem that Alice read.

JABBERWOCKY

'Twas brillig, and the slithy toves
Did gyre and gimble in the wabe;
All mimsy were the borogoves,
And the mome raths outgrabe.

The poem stanzas are now italicized and enclosed in boxes, as specified by the `alice.css` stylesheet, due to the insertion of the `highlight` class by the JavaScript code.

Summary

We now have an idea of why a developer would choose to use a JavaScript framework rather than writing all code from scratch, even for the most basic tasks. We also have seen some of the ways in which jQuery excels as a framework, and why we might choose it over other options. We also know in general which tasks jQuery makes easier.

In this chapter, we have learned how to make jQuery available to JavaScript code on our web page, use the $() factory function to locate a part of the page that has a given class, call .addClass() to apply additional styling to this part of the page, and invoke $(document).ready() to cause this code to execute upon the loading of the page.

The simple example we have been using demonstrates how jQuery works, but is not very useful in real-world situations. In the next chapter, we will expand on the code here by exploring jQuery's sophisticated selector language, finding practical uses for this technique.

2
Selectors

The jQuery library harnesses the power of Cascading Style Sheets (CSS) selectors to let us quickly and easily access elements or groups of elements in the Document Object Model (DOM). In this chapter, we will explore a few of these selectors, as well as jQuery's own **custom selectors**. We'll also look at jQuery's **DOM traversal methods** that provide even greater flexibility for getting what we want.

The Document Object Model

One of the most powerful aspects of jQuery is its ability to make selecting elements in the DOM easy. The Document Object Model is a family-tree structure of sorts. HTML, like other markup languages, uses this model to describe the relationships of things on a page. When we refer to these relationships, we use the same terminology that we use when referring to family relationships—parents, children, and so on. A simple example can help us understand how the family tree metaphor applies to a document:

```
<html>
  <head>
    <title>the title</title>
  </head>
  <body>
    <div>
      <p>This is a paragraph.</p>
      <p>This is another paragraph.</p>
      <p>This is yet another paragraph.</p>
    </div>
  </body>
</html>
```

Here, `<html>` is the **ancestor** of all the other elements; in other words, all the other elements are **descendants** of `<html>`. The `<head>` and `<body>` elements are not only descendants, but **children** of `<html>`, as well. Likewise, in addition to being the ancestor of `<head>` and `<body>`, `<html>` is also their **parent**. The `<p>` elements are children (and descendants) of `<div>`, descendants of `<body>` and `<html>`, and **siblings** of each other. For information on how to visualize the family-tree structure of the DOM using third-party software, see Appendix B.

An important point to note before we begin is that the resulting set of elements from selectors and methods is always wrapped in a jQuery object. These jQuery objects are very easy to work with when we want to actually do something with the things that we find on a page. We can easily bind **events** to these objects and add slick **effects** to them, as well as **chain** multiple modifications or effects together. Nevertheless, jQuery objects are different from regular DOM elements or node lists, and as such do not necessarily provide the same methods and properties for some tasks. In the final part of this chapter, therefore, we will look at ways to access the DOM elements that are wrapped in a jQuery object.

The $() factory function

No matter which type of selector we want to use in jQuery, we always start with the dollar sign and parentheses: `$()`. Just about anything that can be used in a stylesheet can also be wrapped in quotation marks and placed inside the parentheses, allowing us to apply jQuery methods to the matched set of elements.

Making jQuery Play Well with Other JavaScript Libraries

In jQuery, the dollar sign `$` is simply an "alias" for `jQuery`. Conflicts could arise if more than one of these libraries were being used in a given page because a `$()` function is very common in JavaScript libraries. We can avoid such conflicts by replacing every instance of `$` with `jQuery` in our custom jQuery code. Additional solutions to this problem are addressed in Chapter 10.

Three building blocks of these selectors are **tag name**, **ID**, and **class**. They can be used either on their own or in combination with other selectors. Here is an example of what each of these three selectors looks like on its own:

Selector	CSS	jQuery	Description
Tag name	p	$('p')	Selects all paragraphs in the document
ID	#some-id	$('#some-id')	Selects the single element in the document that has an ID of some-id
Class	.some-class	$('.some-class')	Selects all elements in the document that have a class of some-class

As mentioned in Chapter 1, when we attach methods to the $() factory function, the elements wrapped in the jQuery object are looped through automatically and implicitly. Therefore, we can usually avoid **explicit iteration**, such as a `for` loop, that is so often required in DOM scripting.

Now that we have covered the basics, we're ready to start exploring some more powerful uses of selectors.

CSS selectors

The jQuery library supports nearly all of the selectors included in CSS specifications 1 through 3, as outlined on the *World Wide Web Consortium*'s site: `http://www.w3.org/Style/CSS/#specs`. This support allows developers to enhance their websites without worrying about which browsers (particularly Internet Explorer 6) might not understand advanced selectors, as long as the browsers have JavaScript enabled.

 Responsible jQuery developers should always apply the concepts of **progressive enhancement** and **graceful degradation** to their code, ensuring that a page will render as accurately, even if not as beautifully, with JavaScript disabled as it does with JavaScript turned on. We will continue to explore these concepts throughout the book.

To begin learning how jQuery works with CSS selectors, we'll use a structure that appears on many websites, often for navigation—the nested, unordered list.

```
<ul id="selected-plays">
  <li>Comedies
    <ul>
      <li><a href="/asyoulikeit/">As You Like It</a></li>
      <li>All's Well That Ends Well</li>
      <li>A Midsummer Night's Dream</li>
      <li>Twelfth Night</li>
    </ul>
  </li>
  <li>Tragedies
```

```
<ul>
  <li><a href="hamlet.pdf">Hamlet</a></li>
  <li>Macbeth</li>
  <li>Romeo and Juliet</li>
</ul>
</li>
<li>Histories
  <ul>
    <li>Henry IV (<a href="mailto:henryiv@king.co.uk">email</a>)
      <ul>
        <li>Part I</li>
        <li>Part II</li>
      </ul>
    <li><a href="http://www.shakespeare.co.uk/henryv.htm">
                                    Henry V</a></li>
    <li>Richard II</li>
  </ul>
</li>
</ul>
```

Notice that the first `<ul>` has an ID of `selected-plays`, but none of the `<li>` tags have a class associated with them. Without any styles applied, the list looks like this:

- Comedies
  - As You Like It
  - All's Well That Ends Well
  - A Midsummer Night's Dream
  - Twelfth Night
- Tragedies
  - Hamlet
  - Macbeth
  - Romeo and Juliet
- Histories
  - Henry IV (email)
    - Part I
    - Part II
  - Henry V
  - Richard II

The nested list appears as we would expect it to—a set of bulleted items arranged vertically and indented according to their level.

Styling list-item levels

Lets suppose that we want the top-level items, and *only* the top-level items, to be arranged horizontally. We can start by defining a `horizontal` class in the stylesheet:

```
.horizontal {
  float: left;
  list-style: none;
  margin: 10px;
}
```

The `horizontal` class floats the element to the left of the one following it, removes the bullet from it if it's a list item, and adds a 10 pixel margin on all sides of it.

Rather than attaching the `horizontal` class directly in our HTML, we'll add it dynamically to the top-level list items only—**Comedies**, **Tragedies**, and **Histories**—to demonstrate jQuery's use of selectors:

```
$(document).ready(function() {
  $('#selected-plays > li').addClass('horizontal');
});
```

As discussed in Chapter 1, we begin the jQuery code with the `$(document).ready()` wrapper, that runs as soon as the DOM has loaded.

The second line uses the **child combinator** (>) to add the `horizontal` class to all top-level items only. In effect, the selector inside the `$()` function is saying, *find each list item* (`li`) *that is a child* (>) *of the element with an ID of* `selected-plays` (`#selected-plays`).

With the class now applied, our nested list looks like this:

Comedies
  - As You Like It
  - All's Well That Ends Well
  - A Midsummer Night's Dream
  - Twelfth Night

Tragedies
  - Hamlet
  - Macbeth
  - Romeo and Juliet

Histories
  - Henry IV (email)
    - Part I
    - Part II
  - Henry V
  - Richard II

Styling all of the other items—those that are *not* in the top level—can be done in a number of ways. Since we have already applied the `horizontal` class to the top-level items, one way to select all sub-level items is to use a **negation pseudo-class** to identify all list items that do *not* have a class of `horizontal`. Note the addition of the third line of code:

```
$(document).ready(function() {
  $('#selected-plays > li').addClass('horizontal');
  $('#selected-plays li:not(.horizontal)').addClass('sub-level');
});
```

This time we are selecting every list item (`li`) that:

1. Is a descendant of the element with an ID of `selected-plays` (`#selected-plays`)

2. Does not have a class of `horizontal` (`:not(.horizontal)`)

When we add the `sub-level` class to these items, they receive the shaded background defined in the stylesheet. Now the nested list looks like this:

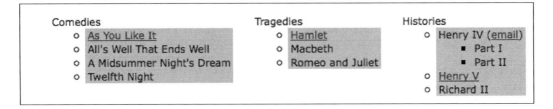

Attribute selectors

Attribute selectors are a particularly helpful subset of CSS selectors. They allow us to specify an element by one of its HTML properties, such as a link's `title` attribute or an image's `alt` attribute. For example, to select all images that have an `alt` attribute, we write the following:

```
$('img[alt]')
```

In versions prior to 1.2, jQuery used **XML Path Language (XPath)** syntax for its attribute selectors and included a handful of other XPath selectors. While these basic XPath selectors have since been removed from the core jQuery library, they are still available as a plugin:
`http://plugins.jquery.com/project/xpath/`

Styling links

Attribute selectors accept a wildcard syntax inspired by regular expressions for identifying the value at the beginning (^) or ending ($) of a string. They can also take an asterisk (*) to indicate the value at an arbitrary position within a string or an exclamation mark to indicate a negated value.

Let's say we want to have different styles for different types of links. We first define the styles in our stylesheet:

```
a {
   color: #00c;
}
a.mailto {
   background: url(images/mail.png) no-repeat right top;
   padding-right: 18px;
}
a.pdflink {
   background: url(images/pdf.png) no-repeat right top;
   padding-right: 18px;
}
a.henrylink {
   background-color: #fff;
   padding: 2px;
   border: 1px solid #000;
}
```

Then, we add the three classes—`mailto`, `pdflink`, and `henrylink`—to the appropriate links using jQuery.

To add a class for all email links, we construct a selector that looks for all anchor elements (a) with an `href` attribute (`[href`) that begins with `mailto:` (`^=mailto:]`), as follows:

```
$(document).ready(function() {
   $('a[href^=mailto:]').addClass('mailto');
});
```

To add a class for all links to PDF files, we use the dollar sign rather than the caret symbol. This is because we're selecting links with an `href` attribute that *ends* with `.pdf`:

```
$(document).ready(function() {
   $('a[href^=mailto:]').addClass('mailto');
   $('a[href$=.pdf]').addClass('pdflink');
});
```

Attribute selectors can be combined as well. We can, for example, add a `henrylink` class for all links with an `href` value that both *starts* with `http` and *contains* `henry` anywhere:

```
$(document).ready(function() {
  $('a[href^=mailto:]').addClass('mailto');
  $('a[href$=.pdf]').addClass('pdflink');
  $('a[href^=http][href*=henry]')
    .addClass('henrylink');
});
```

With the three classes applied to the three types of links, we should see the following:

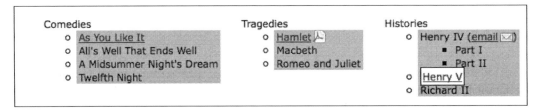

Note the PDF icon to the right of the **Hamlet** link, the envelope icon next to the **email** link, and the white background and black border around the **Henry V** link.

Custom selectors

To the wide variety of CSS selectors, jQuery adds its own custom selectors. Most of the custom selectors allow us to pick certain elements out of a line-up, so to speak. The syntax is the same as the **CSS pseudo-class** syntax, where the selector starts with a colon (:). For example, to select the second item from a matched set of `div` selectors with a class of `horizontal`, we write this:

```
$('div.horizontal:eq(1)')
```

Note that `:eq(1)` selects the second item in the set because JavaScript array numbering is **zero-based**, meaning that it starts with 0. In contrast, CSS is **one-based**, so a CSS selector such as `$('div:nth-child(1)')` would select all `div` selectors that are the first child of their parent (in this case, however, we would probably use `$('div:first-child')` instead).

Styling alternate rows

Two very useful custom selectors in the jQuery library are `:odd` and `:even`. Let's take a look at how we can use one of them for basic table striping, given the following table:

```
<table>
  <tr>
    <td>As You Like It</td>
    <td>Comedy</td>
    <td></td>
  </tr>
  <tr>
    <td>All's Well that Ends Well</td>
    <td>Comedy</td>
    <td>1601</td>
  </tr>
  <tr>
    <td>Hamlet</td>
    <td>Tragedy</td>
    <td>1604</td>
  </tr>
  <tr>
    <td>Macbeth</td>
    <td>Tragedy</td>
    <td>1606</td>
  </tr>
  <tr>
    <td>Romeo and Juliet</td>
    <td>Tragedy</td>
    <td>1595</td>
  </tr>
  <tr>
    <td>Henry IV, Part I</td>
    <td>History</td>
    <td>1596</td>
  </tr>
  <tr>
    <td>Henry V</td>
    <td>History</td>
    <td>1599</td>
  </tr>
</table>
```

Now we can add a style to the stylesheet for all table rows, and use an `alt` class for the even rows:

```
tr {
  background-color: #fff;
}
.alt {
  background-color: #ccc;
}
```

Finally, we write our jQuery code, attaching the class to the even-numbered table rows (`<tr>` tags):

```
$(document).ready(function() {
  $('tr:odd').addClass('alt');
});
```

But wait! Why use the `:odd` selector for even-numbered rows? Well, just as with the `:eq()` selector, the `:odd` and `:even` selectors use JavaScript's native zero-based numbering. Therefore, the first row counts as 0 (even) and the second row counts as 1 (odd), and so on. With this in mind, we can expect our simple bit of code to produce a table that looks like this:

As You Like It	Comedy	
All's Well that Ends Well	Comedy	1601
Hamlet	Tragedy	1604
Macbeth	Tragedy	1606
Romeo and Juliet	Tragedy	1595
Henry IV, Part I	History	1596
Henry V	History	1599

Note that we may see unintended results if there is more than one table on a page. For example, since the last row in this table has a white background, the first row in the next table would have the "alternate" gray background. One way to avoid this type of problem is to use the `:nth-child()` selector instead. This selector can take either a number, `odd`, or `even` as its argument. Notably, however, `:nth-child()` is the only jQuery selector that is one-based. To achieve the same row striping as we did above, and to make it consistent across multiple tables in a document, the code would look like this:

```
$(document).ready(function() {
  $('tr:nth-child(even)').addClass('alt');
});
```

For one final custom-selector touch, let's suppose for some reason we want to highlight any table cell that referred to one of the **Henry** plays. All we have to do—after adding a class to the stylesheet to make the text bold and italicized (`.highlight {font-weight:bold; font-style: italics;}`)—is add a line to our jQuery code, using the `:contains()` selector.

```
$(document).ready(function() {
$('tr:nth-child(even)').addClass('alt');
  $('td:contains(Henry)').addClass('highlight');
});
```

So, now we can see our lovely striped table with the **Henry** plays prominently featured:

As You Like It	Comedy	
All's Well that Ends Well	Comedy	1601
Hamlet	Tragedy	1604
Macbeth	Tragedy	1606
Romeo and Juliet	Tragedy	1595
Henry IV, Part I	History	1596
Henry V	History	1599

It's important to note that the `:contains()` selector is case sensitive. Using `$('td:contains(henry)')` instead, without the uppercase "H," would select no cells.

Admittedly, there are ways to achieve the row striping and text highlighting without jQuery—or any client-side programming, for that matter. Nevertheless, jQuery, along with CSS, is a great alternative for this type of styling in cases where the content is generated dynamically and we don't have access to either the HTML or server-side code.

Form selectors

When working with forms, jQuery's custom selectors can make short work of selecting just the elements we need. The following table describes a handful of these selectors:

Selector	Match
`:text, :checkbox, :radio, :image, :submit, :reset, :password, :file`	Input elements with a type attribute equal to the selector name (excluding the colon). For example, :text selects `<input type="text">`
`:input`	Input, textarea, select, and button elements

Selector	Match
:button	Button elements and input elements with a type attribute equal to button
:enabled	Form elements that are enabled
:disabled	Form elements that are disabled
:checked	Radio buttons or checkboxes that are checked
:selected	Option elements that are selected

As with the other selectors, form selectors can be combined for greater specificity. We can, for example, select all checked radio buttons (but not checkboxes) with `$(':radio:checked')` or select all password inputs and disabled text inputs with `$(':password, :text:disabled')`. Even with custom selectors, we use the same basic principles of CSS to build the list of matched elements.

DOM traversal methods

The jQuery selectors that we have explored so far allow us to select a set of elements as we navigate *across* and *down* the DOM tree and filter the results. If this were the only way to select elements, our options would be quite limited (although, frankly, the selector expressions are robust in their own right, especially when compared to the regular DOM scripting options). There are many occasions when selecting a **parent** or **ancestor** element is essential; that is where jQuery's DOM traversal methods come into play. With these methods at our disposal, we can go up, down, and all around the DOM tree with ease.

Some of the methods have a nearly identical counterpart among the selector expressions. For example, the line we first used to add the alt class, `$('tr:odd').addClass('alt');`, could be rewritten with the `.filter()` method as follows:

```
$('tr').filter(':odd').addClass('alt');
```

For the most part, however, the two ways of selecting elements complement each other. Also, the `.filter()` method in particular has enormous power because it can take a function as its argument. The function allows us to create complex tests for whether elements should be kept in the matched set. Let's suppose, for example, we want to add a class to all external links. jQuery has no selector for this sort of case. Without a filter function, we'd be forced to explicitly loop through each element, testing each one separately. With the following **filter function**, however, we can still rely on jQuery's implicit iteration and keep our code compact:

```
$('a').filter(function() {
  return this.hostname && this.hostname != location.hostname;
}).addClass('external');
```

The second line filters the set of `<a>` elements by two criteria:

1. They must have an `href` attribute with a domain name (`this.hostname`). We use this test to exclude `mailto` links and others of its ilk.

2. The domain name that they link to (again, `this.hostname`) must not match (`!=`) the domain name of the current page (`location.hostname`).

More precisely, the `.filter()` method iterates through the matched set of elements, testing the return value of the function against each one. If the function returns `false`, the element is removed from the matched set. If it returns `true`, the element is kept.

Now let's take a look at our striped table again to see what else is possible with traversal methods.

Styling specific cells

Earlier we added a `highlight` class to all cells containing the text **Henry.** To instead style the cell *next to* each cell containing **Henry**, we can begin with the selector that we have already written, and simply chain the `next()` method to it:

```
$(document).ready(function() {
  $('td:contains(Henry)').next().addClass('highlight');
});
```

The table should now look like this:

As You Like It	Comedy	
All's Well that Ends Well	Comedy	1601
Hamlet	Tragedy	1604
Macbeth	Tragedy	1606
Romeo and Juliet	Tragedy	1595
Henry IV, Part I	*History*	1596
Henry V	*History*	1599

The `.next()` method selects only the very next sibling element. To highlight all of the cells following the one containing **Henry**, we could use the `.nextAll()` method instead.

```
$(document).ready(function() {
  $('td:contains(Henry)').nextAll().addClass('highlight');
});
```

As we might expect, the `.next()` and `.nextAll()` methods have counterparts: `.prev()` and `.prevAll()`. Additionally, `.siblings()` selects all other elements at the same DOM level, regardless of whether they come before or after the previously selected element.

To include the original cell (the one that contains **Henry**) along with the cells that follow, we can add the `.andSelf()` method:

```
$(document).ready(function() {
    $('td:contains(Henry)').nextAll().andSelf().addClass('highlight');
});
```

To be sure, there are a multitude of selector and traversal-method combinations by which we can select the same set of elements. Here, for example, is another way to select every cell in each row where at least one of the cells contains **Henry**:

```
$(document).ready(function() {
    $('td:contains(Henry)').parent().children().addClass('highlight');
});
```

Here, rather than traversing across to sibling elements, we travel up one level in the DOM to the `<tr>` with `.parent()` and then select all of the row's cells with `.children()`.

Chaining

The traversal-method combinations that we have just explored illustrate jQuery's **chaining** capability. It is possible with jQuery to select multiple sets of elements and do multiple things with them, all within a single line of code. This chaining not only helps keep jQuery code concise, but it also can improve a script's performance when the alternative is to re-specify a selector.

It is also possible to break a single line of code into multiple lines for greater readability. For example, a single chained sequence of methods could be written as one line …

```
$('td:contains(Henry)').parent().find('td:eq(1)')
    .addClass('highlight').end().find('td:eq(2)')
                            .addClass('highlight');
```

… or as seven lines …

```
$('td:contains(Henry)') // Find every cell containing "Henry"
.parent() // Select its parent
.find('td:eq(1)') // Find the 2nd descendant cell
.addClass('highlight') // Add the "highlight" class
.end() // Return to the parent of the cell containing "Henry"
.find('td:eq(2)') // Find the 3rd descendant cell
.addClass('highlight'); // Add the "highlight" class
```

Admittedly, the DOM traversal in this example is circuitous to the point of absurdity. We certainly wouldn't recommend using it, as there are clearly simpler, more direct methods at our disposal. The point of the example is simply to demonstrate the tremendous flexibility that chaining affords us.

Chaining can be like speaking a whole paragraph's worth of words in a single breath—it gets the job done quickly, but it can be hard for someone else to understand. Breaking it up into multiple lines and adding judicious comments can save more time in the long run.

Accessing DOM elements

Every selector expression and most jQuery methods return a jQuery object. This is almost always what we want, because of the implicit iteration and chaining capabilities that it affords.

Still, there may be points in our code when we need to access a **DOM element** directly. For example, we may need to make a resulting set of elements available to another JavaScript library. Or we might need to access an element's tag name, which is available as a **property** of the DOM element. For these admittedly rare situations, jQuery provides the .get() method. To access the first DOM element referred to by a jQuery object, we would use .get(0). If the DOM element is needed within a loop, we would use .get(index). So, if we want to know the tag name of an element with id="my-element", we would write:

```
var myTag = $('#my-element').get(0).tagName;
```

For even greater convenience, jQuery provides a shorthand for .get(). Instead of writing the above line, we can use square brackets immediately following the selector:

```
var myTag = $('#my-element')[0].tagName;
```

It's no accident that this syntax looks like an array of DOM elements; using the square brackets is like peeling away the jQuery wrapper to get at the node list, while including the **index** (in this case, 0) is like plucking out a DOM element itself.

Summary

With the techniques that we have covered in this chapter, we should now be able to style top-level and sub-level items in a nested list by using basic **CSS selectors**, apply different styles to different types of links by using **attribute selectors**, add rudimentary striping to a table by using either the **custom jQuery selectors** :odd and :even or the advanced CSS selector :nth-child(), and highlight text within certain table cells by **chaining** jQuery methods.

So far, we have been using the $(document).ready() event to add a class to a matched set of elements. In the next chapter, we'll explore ways in which to add a class in response to a variety of user-initiated events.

3
Events

JavaScript has several built-in ways of reacting to user interaction and other events. To make a page dynamic and responsive, we need to harness this capability so that we can, at the appropriate times, use the jQuery techniques we have learned so far and the other tricks we'll learn later. While we could do this with vanilla JavaScript, jQuery enhances and extends the basic event handling mechanisms to give them a more elegant syntax while at the same time making them more powerful.

Performing tasks on page load

We have already seen how to make jQuery react to the loading of a web page. The `$(document).ready()` event handler can be used to fire off a function's worth of code, but there's a bit more to be said about it.

Timing of code execution

In Chapter 1, we noted that `$(document).ready()` was jQuery's way to perform tasks that were typically triggered by JavaScript's built-in `onload` event. While the two have a similar effect, however, they trigger actions at subtly different times.

The `window.onload` event fires when a document is completely downloaded to the browser. This means that every element on the page is ready to be manipulated by JavaScript, which is a boon for writing featureful code without worrying about load order.

On the other hand, a handler registered using `$(document).ready()` is invoked when the DOM is completely ready for use. This also means that all elements are accessible by our scripts, but does not mean that every associated file has been downloaded. As soon as the HTML has been downloaded and parsed into a DOM tree, the code can run.

To ensure that the page has also been styled before the JavaScript code executes, it is a good practice to place `<link rel="stylesheet">` tags prior to `<script>` tags within the document's `<head>` element.

Consider, for example, a page that presents an image gallery; such a page may have many large images on it, which we can hide, show, move, and otherwise manipulate with jQuery. If we set up our interface using the `onload` event, users will have to wait until each and every image is completely downloaded before they can use the page. Even worse, if behaviors are not yet attached to elements that have default behaviors (such as links), user interactions could produce unintended outcomes. However, when we use `$(document).ready()` for the setup, the interface gets ready to use much earlier with the correct behavior.

Using `$(document).ready()` is almost always preferable to using an `onload` handler, but we need to keep in mind that because supporting files may not have loaded, attributes such as image height and width are not necessarily available at this time. If these are needed, we may at times also choose to implement an `onload` handler (or more likely, use jQuery to set a handler for the `load` event); the two mechanisms can coexist peacefully.

Multiple scripts on one page

The traditional mechanism for registering event handlers through JavaScript (rather than adding handler attributes right in the HTML) is to assign a function to the DOM element's corresponding attribute. For example, suppose we had defined the function:

```
function doStuff() {
  // Perform a task...
}
```

We could then either assign it within our HTML markup:

```
<body onload="doStuff();">
```

Or, we could assign it from within JavaScript code:

```
window.onload = doStuff;
```

Both of these approaches will cause the function to execute when the page is loaded. The advantage of the second is that the behavior is more cleanly separated from the markup.

Note here that when we assign a function as a handler, we use the function name but omit the trailing parentheses. With the parentheses, the function is *called* immediately; without, the name simply *identifies* the function, and can be used to call it later.

With one function, this strategy works quite well. However, suppose we have a second function:

```
function doOtherStuff() {
  // Perform another task...
}
```

We could then attempt to assign this function to run on page load:

```
window.onload = doOtherStuff;
```

However, this assignment trumps the first one. The `.onload` attribute can only store one function reference at a time, so we can't add to the existing behavior.

The `$(document).ready()` mechanism handles this situation gracefully. Each call to the method adds the new function to an internal queue of behaviors; when the page is loaded all of the functions will execute. The functions will run in the order in which they were registered.

To be fair, jQuery doesn't have a monopoly on workarounds to this issue. We can write a JavaScript function that forms a new function that calls the existing `onload` handler, then calls a passed-in handler. This approach, used for example by Simon Willison's `addLoadEvent()`, avoids conflicts between rival handlers like `$(document).ready()` does, but lacks some of the other benefits we have discussed. Browser-specific methods such as `document.addEventListener()` and `document.attachEvent()` offer similar functionality, but jQuery allows us to accomplish this task without concerning ourselves with browser inconsistencies.

Shortcuts for code brevity

The `$(document).ready()` construct is actually calling the `.ready()` method on a jQuery object we've constructed from the `document` DOM element. The `$()` **factory function** provides a shortcut for us as this is a common task. When called with no arguments, the function behaves as though `document` were passed in. This means that instead of:

```
$(document).ready(function() {
  // Our code here...
});
```

we can write:

```
$().ready(function() {
  // Our code here...
});
```

In addition, the factory function can take another function as an argument. When we do this, jQuery performs an implicit call to `.ready()`, so for the same result we can write:

```
$(function() {
  // Our code here...
});
```

While these other syntaxes are shorter, the authors recommend the longer version to make it clearer as to what the code is doing.

Coexisting with other libraries

In some cases, it may prove useful to use more than one JavaScript library on the same page. Since many libraries make use of the $ identifier (since it is short and convenient), we need a way to prevent collisions between these names.

Fortunately, jQuery provides a method called `.noConflict()` to return control of the $ identifier back to other libraries. Typical usage of `.noConflict()` follows the following pattern:

```
<script src="prototype.js" type="text/javascript"></script>
<script src="jquery.js" type="text/javascript"></script>
<script type="text/javascript">
  jQuery.noConflict();
</script>
<script src="myscript.js" type="text/javascript"></script>
```

First, the other library (Prototype in this example) is included. Then, jQuery itself is included, taking over $ for its own use. Next, a call to `.noConflict()` frees up $, so that control of it reverts to the first included library (Prototype). Now in our custom script we can use both libraries—but whenever we need to use a jQuery method, we need to use `jQuery` instead of $ as an identifier.

The `.ready()` method has one more trick up its sleeve to help us in this situation. The callback function we pass to it can take a single parameter: the jQuery object itself. This allows us to effectively rename it without fear of conflicts:

```
jQuery(document).ready(function($) {
  // In here, we can use $ like normal!
});
```

Or, using the shorter syntax we learned above:

```
jQuery(function($) {
  // Code that uses $.
});
```

Simple events

There are many other times apart from the loading of the page at which we might want to perform a task. Just as JavaScript allows us to intercept the page load event with `<body onload="">` or `window.onload`, it provides similar hooks for user-initiated events such as mouse clicks (`onclick`), form fields being modified (`onchange`), and windows changing size (`onresize`). When assigned directly to elements in the DOM, these hooks have similar drawbacks to the ones we outlined for `onload`. Therefore, jQuery offers an improved way of handling these events as well.

A simple style switcher

To illustrate some event handling techniques, suppose we wish to have a single page rendered in several different styles based on user input. We will allow the user to click buttons to toggle between a normal view, a view in which the text is constrained to a narrow column, and a view with large print for the content area.

In a real-world example, a good web citizen will employ the principle of **progressive enhancement** here. The style switcher should either be hidden when JavaScript is unavailable or, better yet, should still function through links to alternative versions of the page. For the purposes of this tutorial, we'll assume that all users have JavaScript turned on.

The HTML markup for the style switcher is as follows:

```
<div id="switcher">
  <h3>Style Switcher</h3>
  <div class="button selected" id="switcher-default">
    Default
  </div>
  <div class="button" id="switcher-narrow">
    Narrow Column
  </div>
  <div class="button" id="switcher-large">
    Large Print
  </div>
</div>
```

Combined with the rest of the page's HTML markup and some basic CSS, we get a page that looks like the following figure:

To begin, we'll make the **Large Print** button operate. We need a bit of CSS to implement our alternative view of the page:

```
body.large .chapter {
  font-size: 1.5em;
}
```

Our goal, then, is to apply the `large` class to the `<body>` tag. This will allow the stylesheet to reformat the page appropriately. Using what we learned in Chapter 2, we already know the statement needed to accomplish this:

```
'body').addClass('large');
```

However, we want this to occur when the button is clicked, not when the page loaded as we have seen so far. To do this, we'll introduce the `.bind()` method. This method allows us to specify any **JavaScript event**, and to attach a **behavior** to it. In this case, the event is called `click`, and the behavior is a function consisting of our one-liner above:

```
$(document).ready(function() {
  $('#switcher-large').bind('click', function() {
    $('body').addClass('large');
  });
});
```

Now when the button gets clicked, our code runs and the text is enlarged as shown in the following figure:

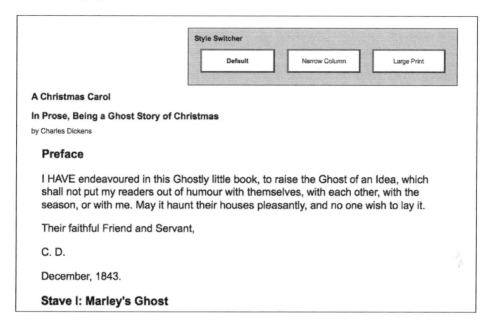

That's all there is to binding an event. The advantages we discussed with the `.ready()` method apply here, as well. Multiple calls to `.bind()` coexist nicely, appending additional behaviors to the same event as necessary.

This is not necessarily the most elegant or efficient way to accomplish this task. As we proceed through this chapter, we will extend and refine this code into something we can be proud of.

Enabling the other buttons

We now have a **Large Print** button that works as advertised, but we need to apply similar handling to the other two buttons (**Default** and **Narrow Column**) to make them perform their tasks. This is straightforward; we use `.bind()` to add a `click` handler to each of them, removing and adding classes as necessary. The new code reads as follows:

```
$(document).ready(function() {
  $('#switcher-default').bind('click', function() {
    $('body').removeClass('narrow');
    $('body').removeClass('large');
  });
  $('#switcher-narrow').bind('click', function() {
```

```
    $('body').addClass('narrow');
    $('body').removeClass('large');
  });
  $('#switcher-large').bind('click', function() {
    $('body').removeClass('narrow');
    $('body').addClass('large');
  });
});
```

This is combined with a CSS rule for the narrow class:

```
body.narrow .chapter {
  width: 400px;
}
```

Now, after clicking the **Narrow Column** button, its corresponding CSS is applied and the text gets laid out differently as shown in the following figure:

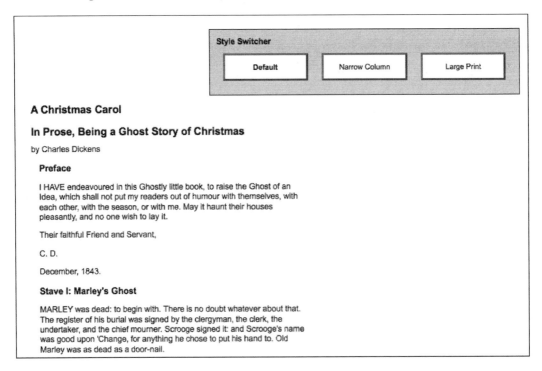

Clicking **Default** removes both class names from the <body> tag, returning the page to its initial rendering.

Event handler context

Our switcher is behaving correctly, but we are not giving the user any feedback about which button is currently active. Our approach for handling this will be to apply the `selected` class to the button when it is clicked, and remove this class from the other buttons. The `selected` class simply makes the button's text bold:

```
.selected {
  font-weight: bold;
}
```

We could accomplish this class modification as we do above, by referring to each button by ID and applying or removing classes as necessary, but instead we'll explore a more elegant and scalable solution that exploits the **context** in which event handlers run.

When any event handler is triggered, the keyword `this` refers to the DOM element to which the behavior was attached. Earlier we noted that the `$()` factory function could take a DOM element as its argument; this is one of the key reasons that facility is available. By writing `$(this)` within the event handler, we create a jQuery object corresponding to the element, and can act on it just as if we had located it with a CSS selector.

With this in mind, we can write:

```
$(this).addClass('selected');
```

Placing this line in each of the three handlers will add the class when a button is clicked. To remove the class from the other buttons, we can take advantage of jQuery's implicit iteration feature, and write:

```
$('#switcher .button').removeClass('selected');
```

This line removes the class from every button inside the style switcher. So, placing these in the correct order, we have the code as:

```
$(document).ready(function() {
  $('#switcher-default').bind('click', function() {
    $('body').removeClass('narrow');
    $('body').removeClass('large');
    $('#switcher .button').removeClass('selected');
    $(this).addClass('selected');
  });
  $('#switcher-narrow').bind('click', function() {
    $('body').addClass('narrow');
    $('body').removeClass('large');
    $('#switcher .button').removeClass('selected');
```

```
      $(this).addClass('selected');
    });
    $('#switcher-large').bind('click', function() {
      $('body').removeClass('narrow');
      $('body').addClass('large');
      $('#switcher .button').removeClass('selected');
      $(this).addClass('selected');
    });
  });
```

Now the style switcher gives appropriate feedback as shown in the following figure:

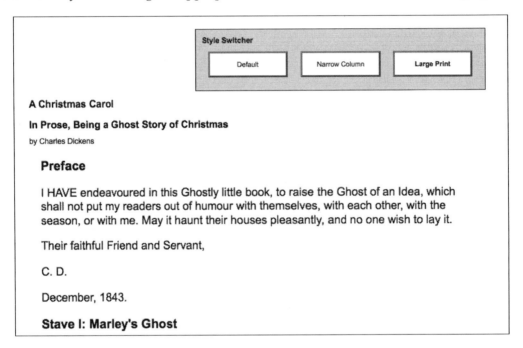

Generalizing the statements by using the handler context allows us to be yet more efficient. We can factor the highlighting routine out into a separate handler, as shown in the following code, because it is the same for all three buttons:

```
$(document).ready(function() {
  $('#switcher-default').bind('click', function() {
    $('body').removeClass('narrow').removeClass('large');
  });
  $('#switcher-narrow').bind('click', function() {
    $('body').addClass('narrow').removeClass('large');
  });
  $('#switcher-large').bind('click', function() {
```

```
        $('body').removeClass('narrow').addClass('large');
    });

    $('#switcher .button').bind('click', function() {
        $('#switcher .button').removeClass('selected');
        $(this).addClass('selected');
    });
});
```

This optimization takes advantage of the three jQuery features we have discussed. First, **implicit iteration** is once again useful when we bind the same `click` handler to each button with a single call to `.bind()`. Second, **behavior queuing** allows us to bind two functions to the same `click` event, without the second overwriting the first. Lastly, we're using jQuery's **chaining** capabilities to collapse the adding and removing of classes into a single line of code each time.

Further consolidation

The code optimization we've just completed is an example of **refactoring**—modifying existing code to perform the same task in a more efficient or elegant way. To explore further refactoring opportunities, let's look at the behaviors we have bound to each button. The `.removeClass()` method's parameter is optional; when omitted, it removes *all* classes from the element. We can streamline our code a bit by exploiting this as follows:

```
$(document).ready(function() {
    $('#switcher-default').bind('click', function() {
        $('body').removeClass();
    });
    $('#switcher-narrow').bind('click', function() {
        $('body').removeClass().addClass('narrow');
    });
    $('#switcher-large').bind('click', function() {
        $('body').removeClass().addClass('large');
    });

    $('#switcher .button').bind('click', function() {
        $('#switcher .button').removeClass('selected');
        $(this).addClass('selected');
    });
});
```

Note that the order of operations has changed a bit to accommodate our more general class removal; we need to execute `.removeClass()` first so that it doesn't undo the `.addClass()` we perform in the same breath.

We can only safely remove all classes because we are in charge of the HTML in this case. When we are writing code for reuse (such as for a plugin), we need to respect any classes that might be present and leave them intact.

Now we are executing some of the same code in each of the buttons' handlers. This can be easily factored out into our general button `click` handler:

```
$(document).ready(function() {
  $('#switcher .button').bind('click', function() {
    $('body').removeClass();
    $('#switcher .button').removeClass('selected');
    $(this).addClass('selected');
  });
  $('#switcher-narrow').bind('click', function() {
    $('body').addClass('narrow');
  });
  $('#switcher-large').bind('click', function() {
    $('body').addClass('large');
  });
});
```

Note that we need to move the general handler above the specific ones now. The `.removeClass()` needs to happen before the `.addClass()`, and we can count on this because jQuery always triggers event handlers in the order in which they were registered.

Finally, we can get rid of the specific handlers entirely by once again exploiting **event context**. Since the context keyword `this` gives us a DOM element rather than a jQuery object, we can use native DOM properties to determine the ID of the element that was clicked. We can thus bind the same handler to all the buttons, and within the handler perform different actions for each button:

```
$(document).ready(function() {
  $('#switcher .button').bind('click', function() {
    $('body').removeClass();
    if (this.id == 'switcher-narrow') {
      $('body').addClass('narrow');
    }
    else if (this.id == 'switcher-large') {
      $('body').addClass('large');
    }
    $('#switcher .button').removeClass('selected');
    $(this).addClass('selected');
  });
});
```

Shorthand events

Binding a handler for an event (like a simple `click` event) is such a common task that jQuery provides an even terser way to accomplish it; **shorthand event methods** work in the same way as their `.bind()` counterparts with a couple fewer keystrokes.

For example, our style switcher could be written using `.click()` instead of `.bind()` as follows:

```
$(document).ready(function() {
  $('#switcher .button').click(function() {
    $('body').removeClass();
    if (this.id == 'switcher-narrow') {
      $('body').addClass('narrow');
    }
    else if (this.id == 'switcher-large') {
      $('body').addClass('large');
    }

    $('#switcher .button').removeClass('selected');
    $(this).addClass('selected');
  });
});
```

Shorthand event methods such as this exist for all standard DOM events:

- blur
- change
- click
- dblclick
- error
- focus
- keydown
- keypress
- keyup
- load
- mousedown
- mousemove
- mouseout
- mouseover
- mouseup

- resize
- scroll
- select
- submit
- unload

Each shortcut method binds a handler to the event with the corresponding name.

Compound events

Most of jQuery's event-handling methods correspond directly to native JavaScript events. A handful, however, are custom handlers added for convenience and cross-browser optimization. One of these, the `.ready()` method, we have discussed in detail already. The `.toggle()` and `.hover()` methods are two more custom event handlers; they are both referred to as **compound event handlers** because they intercept combinations of user actions, and respond to them using more than one function.

Showing and hiding advanced features

Suppose that we wanted to be able to hide our style switcher when it is not needed. One convenient way to hide advanced features is to make them collapsible. We will allow one click on the label to hide the buttons, leaving the label alone. Another click on the label will restore the buttons. We need another class to handle the hidden buttons:

```
.hidden {
  display: none;
}
```

We could implement this feature by storing the current state of the buttons in a variable, and checking its value each time the label is clicked to know whether to add or remove the `hidden` class on the buttons. We could also directly check for the presence of the class on a button, and use this information to decide what to do. Instead, jQuery provides the `.toggle()` method, which performs this housekeeping task for us.

 There are in fact two `.toggle()` methods defined by jQuery. For information on the **effect** method of this name (which is distinguished by different argument types), see: `http://docs.jquery.com/Effects/toggle`

The `.toggle()` event method takes two or more arguments, each of which is a function. The first click on the element causes the first function to execute, the second click triggers the second function, and so forth. Once each function has been invoked, the cycle begins again from the first function. With `.toggle()`, we can implement our collapsible style switcher quite easily:

```
$(document).ready(function() {
  $('#switcher h3').toggle(function() {
    $('#switcher .button').addClass('hidden');
  }, function() {
    $('#switcher .button').removeClass('hidden');
  });
});
```

After the first click, the buttons are all hidden:

And a second click returns them to visibility:

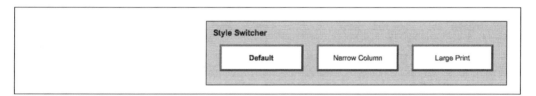

Once again we rely on implicit iteration; this time, to hide all the buttons in one fell swoop without requiring an enclosing element.

For this specific case, jQuery provides another mechanism for the collapsing we are performing. We can use the `.toggleClass()` method to automatically check for the presence of the class before applying or removing it:

```
$(document).ready(function() {
  $('#switcher h3').click(function() {
    $('#switcher .button').toggleClass('hidden');
  });
});
```

In this case, `.toggleClass()` is probably the more elegant solution, but `.toggle()` is a more versatile way to perform two or more different actions in alternation.

Highlighting clickable items

In illustrating the ability of the `click` event to operate on normally non-clickable page elements, we have crafted an interface that gives few hints that the buttons—actually just `<div>` elements—are actually *live* parts of the page, awaiting user interaction. To remedy this, we can give the buttons a rollover state, making it clear that they interact in some way with the mouse:

```
#switcher .hover {
  cursor: pointer;
  background-color: #afa;
}
```

The CSS specification includes a pseudo-class called `:hover`, which allows a stylesheet to affect an element's appearance when the user's mouse cursor hovers over it. In Internet Explorer 6, this capability is restricted to link elements, so we can't use it for other items in cross-browser code. Instead, jQuery allows us to use JavaScript to change an element's styling—and indeed, perform any arbitrary action—both when the mouse cursor enters the element and when it leaves the element.

The `.hover()` method takes two function arguments, just as in our `.toggle()` example above. In this case, the first function will be executed when the mouse cursor enters the selected element, and the second is fired when the cursor leaves. We can modify the classes applied to the buttons at these times to achieve a rollover effect:

```
$(document).ready(function() {
  $('#switcher .button').hover(function() {
    $(this).addClass('hover');
  }, function() {
    $(this).removeClass('hover');
  });
});
```

We once again use implicit iteration and event context for short, simple code. Now when hovering over any button, we see our class applied as shown in the following screenshot:

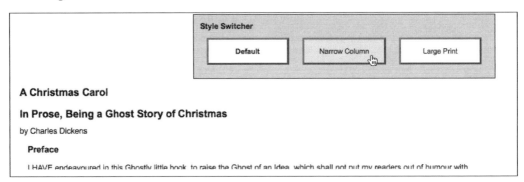

The use of .hover() also means we avoid headaches caused by **event propagation** in JavaScript. To understand this, we need to take a look at how JavaScript decides which element gets to handle a given event.

The journey of an event

When an event occurs on a page, an entire hierarchy of DOM elements gets a chance to handle the event. Consider a page model like this:

```
<div class="foo">
  <span class="bar">
    <a href="http://www.example.com/">
      The quick brown fox jumps over the lazy dog.
    </a>
  </span>
  <p>
    How razorback-jumping frogs can level six piqued gymnasts!
  </p>
</div>
```

We then visualize the code as a set of nested elements as shown in the following figure:

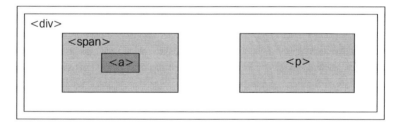

For any event, there are multiple elements that could logically be responsible for reacting. When the link on this page is clicked, for example, the <div>, <span>, and <a> all should get the opportunity to respond to the click. After all, the three are all under the user's mouse cursor at the time. The <p> element, on the other hand, is not part of this interaction at all.

One strategy for allowing multiple elements to respond to a click is called **event capturing**. With event capturing, the event is first given to the most all-encompassing element, and then to successively more specific ones. In our example, this means that first the `<div>` gets passed the event, then the `<span>`, and finally the `<a>`.

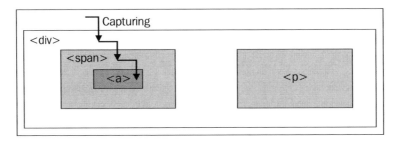

 Technically, in browser implementations of event capturing, specific elements **register** to listen for events that occur among their descendants. The approximation provided here is close enough for our needs.

The opposite strategy is called **event bubbling**. The event gets sent to the most specific element, and after this element has an opportunity to react, the event **bubbles up** to more general elements. In our example, the `<a>` would be handed the event first, and then the `<span>` and `<div>` in that order.

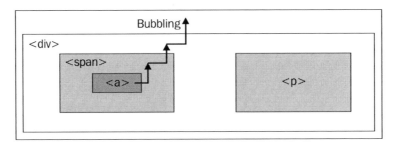

Unsurprisingly, different browser developers originally decided on different models for event propagation. The DOM standard that eventually developed thus specified that both strategies should be used: first the event is **captured** from general elements to specific ones, and then the event **bubbles** back up to the top of the DOM tree. Event handlers can be registered for either part of the process.

Not all browsers have been updated to match this new standard, and in those that support capturing it typically must be specifically enabled. To provide cross-browser consistency, therefore, jQuery always registers event handlers for the bubbling phase of the model. We can always assume that the most specific element will get the first opportunity to respond to any event.

Side effects of event bubbling

Event bubbling can cause unexpected behavior, especially when the wrong element responds to a mouseover or mouseout. Consider a mouseout event handler attached to the <div> in our example. When the user's mouse cursor exits the <div>, the mouseout handler is run as anticipated. Since this is at the top of the hierarchy, no other elements get the event. On the other hand, when the cursor exits the <a> element, a mouseout event is sent to that. This event will then bubble up to the <span> and then to the <div>, firing the same event handler. This bubbling sequence is likely not desired; for the buttons in our style switcher example, it could mean the highlight was turned off prematurely.

The .hover() method is aware of these bubbling issues, and when we use that method to attach events, we can ignore the problems caused by the wrong element getting a mouseover or mouseout event. This makes .hover() a very attractive alternative to binding the individual mouse events.

 If action only needs to be taken when the mouse enters or leaves an element, but not both, we can bind jQuery's mouseenter and mouseleave events, which also circumvent bubbling concerns. These events are paired so often, however, that .hover() is generally the right choice.

The mouseout scenario just described illustrates the need to constrain the scope of an event. While .hover() handles this specific case, we will encounter other situations in which we need to limit an event spatially (preventing the event from being sent to certain elements) or temporally (preventing the event from being sent at certain times).

Altering the journey: the event object

We have already seen one situation in which **event bubbling** can cause problems. To show a case in which .hover() does not help our cause, we'll alter the collapsing behavior we implemented earlier.

Suppose we wish to expand the clickable area that triggers the collapsing or expanding of the style switcher. One way to do this is to move the event handler from the label, <h3>, to its containing <div> element:

```
$(document).ready(function() {
  $('#switcher').click(function() {
    $('#switcher .button').toggleClass('hidden');
  });
});
```

This alteration makes the entire area of the style switcher clickable to toggle its visibility. The downside is that clicking on a button also collapses the style switcher after the style on the content has been altered. This is due to event bubbling; the event is first handled by the buttons, then passed up to the DOM tree until it reaches the `<div id="switcher">`, where our new handler is activated and hides the buttons.

To solve this problem, we need access to the **event object**. This is a JavaScript construct that is passed to each element's event handler when it is invoked. It provides information about the event, such as where the mouse cursor was at the time of the event. It also provides some methods that can be used to affect the progress of the event through the DOM.

To use the event object in our handlers, we only need to add a parameter to the function:

```
$(document).ready(function() {
  $('#switcher').click(function(event) {
    $('#switcher .button').toggleClass('hidden');
  });
});
```

Event targets

Now we have the event object available to us as the variable `event` within our handler. The property `event.target` can be helpful in controlling *where* an event takes effect. This property is a part of the DOM API, but is not implemented in all browsers; jQuery extends the event object as necessary to provide the property in every browser. With `.target`, we can determine which element in the DOM was the first to receive the event—that is, in the case of a `click` event, the actual item clicked on. Remembering that `this` gives us the DOM element handling the event, we can write the following code:

```
$(document).ready(function() {
  $('#switcher').click(function(event) {
    if (event.target == this) {
      $('#switcher .button').toggleClass('hidden');
    }
  });
});
```

This code ensures that the item clicked on was `<div id="switcher">`, not one of its sub-elements. Now clicking on buttons will *not* collapse the style switcher, and clicking on the switcher's background *will*. However, clicking on the label, `<h3>`, now does nothing, because it too is a sub-element. Instead of placing this check here, we can modify the behavior of the buttons to achieve our goals.

Stopping event propagation

The event object provides the `.stopPropagation()` method, which can halt the bubbling process completely for the event. Like `.target`, this method is a plain JavaScript feature, but cannot be safely used across all browsers. As long as we register all of our event handlers using jQuery, though, we can use it with impunity.

We'll remove the `event.target == this` check we just added, and instead add some code in our buttons' `click` handlers:

```
$(document).ready(function() {
  $('#switcher .button').click(function(event) {
    $('body').removeClass();
    if (this.id == 'switcher-narrow') {
      $('body').addClass('narrow');
    }
    else if (this.id == 'switcher-large') {
      $('body').addClass('large');
    }

    $('#switcher .button').removeClass('selected');
    $(this).addClass('selected');
    event.stopPropagation();
  });
});
```

As before, we need to add a parameter to the function we're using as the `click` handler, so we have access to the event object. Then we simply call `event.stopPropagation()` to prevent any other DOM element from responding to the event. Now our click is handled by the buttons, and only the buttons; clicks anywhere else on the style switcher will collapse or expand it.

Default actions

Were our `click` event handler registered on a link element (`<a>`) rather than a generic `<div>`, we would face another problem. When a user clicks on a link, the browser loads a new page. This behavior is not an **event handler** in the same sense as the ones we have been discussing; instead, this is the **default action** for a click on a link element. Similarly, when the *Enter* key is pressed while the user is editing a form, the `submit` event is triggered on the form, but then the form submission actually occurs after this.

If these default actions are undesired, calling `.stopPropagation()` on the event will not help. These actions occur nowhere in the normal flow of event propagation. Instead, the `.preventDefault()` method will serve to stop the event in its tracks before the default action is triggered.

> Calling `.preventDefault()` is often useful after we have done some tests on the environment of the event. For example, during a form submission we might wish to check that required fields are filled in, and prevent the default action only if they are not. We'll see this in action in Chapter 8.

Event propagation and default actions are independent mechanisms; either can be stopped while the other still occurs. If we wish to halt both, we can return `false` from our event handler, which is a shortcut for calling both `.stopPropagation()` and `.preventDefault()` on the event.

Event delegation

Event bubbling isn't always a hindrance; we can often use it to great benefit. One great technique that exploits bubbling is called **event delegation**. With it, we can use an event handler on a single element to do the work of many.

> In jQuery 1.3, a new pair of methods, `.live()` and `.die()`, have been introduced. These methods perform the same tasks as `.bind()` and `.unbind()`, but behind the scenes they use event delegation to gain the benefits we'll describe in this section. Documentation on these methods can be found at: `http://docs.jquery.com/Events/live`

In our example, there are just three `<div class="button">` elements that have attached `click` handlers. But what if there were many? This is more common than one might think. Consider, for example, a large table of information in which each row has an interactive item requiring a `click` handler. Implicit iteration makes assigning all of these `click` handlers easy, but performance can suffer because of the looping being done internally to jQuery, and because of the memory footprint of maintaining all the handlers.

Instead, we can assign a single `click` handler to an ancestor element in the DOM. An uninterrupted `click` event will eventually reach the ancestor due to event bubbling, and we can do our work there.

As an example, let's apply this technique to our style switcher (even though the number of items does not demand the approach). As seen above, we can use the `event.target` property to check what element was under the mouse cursor when the click occurred.

```
$(document).ready(function() {
  $('#switcher').click(function(event) {
    if ($(event.target).is('.button')) {
      $('body').removeClass();
      if (event.target.id == 'switcher-narrow') {
        $('body').addClass('narrow');
      }
      else if (event.target.id == 'switcher-large') {
        $('body').addClass('large');
      }
      $('#switcher .button').removeClass('selected');
      $(event.target).addClass('selected');
      event.stopPropagation();
    }
  });
});
```

We've used a new method here, called `.is()`. This method accepts the **selector expressions** we investigated in the previous chapter, and tests the current jQuery object against the selector. If at least one element in the set is matched by the selector, `.is()` returns true. In this case, `$(event.target).is('.button')` asks whether the element clicked has a class of `button` assigned to it. If so, we proceed with the code from before, with one significant alteration: the keyword `this` now refers to `<div id="switcher">`, so every time we are interested in the clicked button we must now refer to it with `event.target`.

 We can also test for the presence of a class on an element with a shortcut method, `.hasClass()`. The `.is()` method is more flexible, however, and can test any selector expression.

We have an unintentional side-effect from this code, however. When a button is clicked now, the switcher collapses, as it did before we added the call to `.stopPropagation()`. The handler for the switcher visibility toggle is now bound to the same element as the handler for the buttons, so halting the event bubbling does not stop the toggle from being triggered. To sidestep this issue, we can remove the `.stopPropagation()` call and instead add another `.is()` test:

```
$(document).ready(function() {
  $('#switcher').click(function(event) {
    if (!$(event.target).is('.button')) {
      $('#switcher .button').toggleClass('hidden');
    }
  });
});

$(document).ready(function() {
  $('#switcher').click(function(event) {
    if ($(event.target).is('.button')) {
      $('body').removeClass();
      if (event.target.id == 'switcher-narrow') {
        $('body').addClass('narrow');
      }
      else if (event.target.id == 'switcher-large') {
        $('body').addClass('large');
      }
      $('#switcher .button').removeClass('selected');
      $(event.target).addClass('selected');
    }
  });
});
```

This example is a bit overcomplicated for its size, but as the number of elements with event handlers increases, event delegation is the right technique to use.

 Event delegation is also useful in other situations we'll see later, such as when new elements are added by **DOM manipulation** methods (Chapter 5) or **AJAX** routines (Chapter 6).

Removing an event handler

There are times when we will be done with an event handler we previously registered. Perhaps the state of the page has changed such that the action no longer makes sense. It is typically possible to handle this situation with conditional statements inside our event handlers, but it may be more elegant to **unbind** the handler entirely.

Suppose that we want our collapsible style switcher to remain expanded whenever the page is not using the normal style. While the **Narrow Column** or **Large Print** button is selected, clicking the background of the style switcher should do nothing. We can accomplish this by calling the `.unbind()` method to remove the collapsing handler when one of the non-default style switcher buttons is clicked.

```
$(document).ready(function() {
  $('#switcher').click(function(event) {
    if (!$(event.target).is('.button')) {
      $('#switcher .button').toggleClass('hidden');
    }
  });

  $('#switcher-narrow, #switcher-large').click(function() {
    $('#switcher').unbind('click');
  });
});
```

Now when a button such as **Narrow Column** is clicked, the `click` handler on the style switcher `<div>` is removed, and clicking the background of the box no longer collapses it. However, the button doesn't work anymore! It is attached to the `click` event of the style switcher `<div>` as well because we rewrote the button-handling code to use event delegation. This means that when we call `$('#switcher').unbind('click')`, both behaviors are removed.

Event namespacing

We need to make our `.unbind()` call more specific, so that it does not remove both of the `click` handlers we have registered. One way of doing this is to use **event namespacing**. We can introduce additional information when an event is bound that allows us to identify that particular handler later. To use namespacing, we need to return to the non-shorthand method of binding event handlers, the `.bind()` method itself.

The first parameter we pass to `.bind()` is the name of the JavaScript event we want to watch for. We can use a special syntax here, though, that allows us to subcategorize the event.

```
$(document).ready(function() {
  $('#switcher').bind('click.collapse', function(event) {
    if (!$(event.target).is('.button')) {
      $('#switcher .button').toggleClass('hidden');
    }
  });
```

```
$('#switcher-narrow, #switcher-large').click(function() {
  $('#switcher').unbind('click.collapse');
});
});
```

The `.collapse` suffix is invisible to the event handling system; `click` events are handled by this function, just as if we wrote `.bind('click')`. However, the addition of the namespace means that we can unbind just this handler, without affecting the separate `click` handler we wrote for the buttons.

 There are other ways of making our `.unbind()` call more specific, as we will see in a moment. However, event namespacing is a useful tool in our arsenal. It is especially handy in the creation of **plugins**, as we'll see in Chapter 11.

Rebinding events

Now clicking the **Narrow Column** or **Large Print** button causes the style switcher collapsing functionality to be disabled. However, we want the behavior to return when the **Default** button is pressed. To do this, we will need to **rebind** the handler whenever **Default** is clicked.

First, we should give our handler function a name so that we can use it more than once without repeating ourselves:

```
$(document).ready(function() {
  var toggleStyleSwitcher = function(event) {
    if (!$(event.target).is('.button')) {
      $('#switcher .button').toggleClass('hidden');
    }
  };
  $('#switcher').bind('click.collapse', toggleStyleSwitcher);
});
```

Note that we are here using a new syntax for defining a function. Rather than defining the function by leading with the `function` keyword, we assign an **anonymous function** to a **local variable**. This is a stylistic choice to make our event handlers and other function definitions resemble each other more closely; the two syntaxes are functionally equivalent.

Also, recall that `.bind()` takes a **function reference** as its second argument. It is important to remember, when using a named function here, to omit parentheses after the function name; parentheses would cause the function to be *called*, rather than *referenced*.

Now that the function has a name, we can bind it again later without repeating the function definition:

```
$(document).ready(function() {
  var toggleStyleSwitcher = function(event) {
    if (!$(event.target).is('.button')) {
      $('#switcher .button').toggleClass('hidden');
    }
  };

  $('#switcher').bind('click.collapse', toggleStyleSwitcher);

  $('#switcher-narrow, #switcher-large').click(function() {
    $('#switcher').unbind('click.collapse');
  });
  $('#switcher-default').click(function() {
    $('#switcher')
      .bind('click.collapse', toggleStyleSwitcher);
  });
});
```

Now the toggle behavior is bound when the document is loaded, unbound when **Narrow Column** or **Large Print** is clicked, and rebound when **Normal** is clicked after that.

We have sidestepped a potential pitfall here. Remember that when a handler is bound to an event in jQuery, previous handlers remain in effect. This would seem to mean that if **Normal** was clicked multiple times in succession, many copies of the toggleStyleSwitcher handler would be bound, causing strange behavior when the <div> was clicked. Indeed, if we had used anonymous functions throughout our example, this would be the case. But since we gave the function a name and used the same function throughout the code, the behavior is only bound once. The .bind() method will not attach an event handler to an element if it has already been attached.

As another benefit to naming this function, we no longer need to use namespacing. The .unbind() method can take a function as a second argument; in this case, it unbinds only that specific handler.

```
$(document).ready(function() {
  var toggleStyleSwitcher = function(event) {
    if (!$(event.target).is('.button')) {
      $('#switcher .button').toggleClass('hidden');
    }
  };

  $('#switcher').click(toggleStyleSwitcher);
```

```
$('#switcher-narrow, #switcher-large').click(function() {
  $('#switcher').unbind('click', toggleStyleSwitcher);
});
$('#switcher-default').click(function() {
  $('#switcher').click(toggleStyleSwitcher);
});
});
```

A shortcut is also available for the situation in which we want to unbind an event handler immediately after the first time it is triggered. This shortcut, called `.one()`, is used like this:

```
$(document).ready(function() {
  $('#switcher').one('click', toggleStyleSwitcher);
});
```

This would cause the toggle action to occur only once.

Simulating user interaction

At times it is convenient to execute code that we have bound to an event, even if the normal circumstances of the event are not occurring. For example, suppose we wanted our style switcher to begin in its collapsed state. We could accomplish this by hiding buttons from within the stylesheet, or by calling the `.hide()` method from a `$(document).ready()` handler. Another way would be to simulate a click on the style switcher so that the toggling mechanism we've already established is triggered.

The `.trigger()` method allows us to do just this:

```
$(document).ready(function() {
  $('#switcher').trigger('click');
});
```

Now right when the page loads the switcher is collapsed, just as if it had been clicked. If we were hiding content that we wanted people without JavaScript enabled to see, this would be a reasonable way to implement **graceful degradation**.

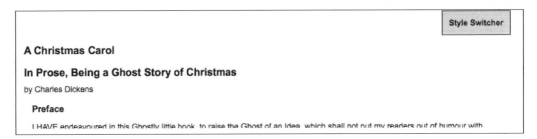

The `.trigger()` method provides the same set of shortcuts that `.bind()` does. When these shortcuts are used with no arguments, the behavior is to trigger the action rather than bind it:

```
$(document).ready(function() {
  $('#switcher').click();
});
```

Keyboard events

As another example, we can add keyboard shortcuts to our style switcher. When the user types the first letter of one of the display styles, we will have the page behave as if the corresponding button were clicked. To implement this feature, we will need to explore **keyboard events**, that behave a bit differently from **mouse events**.

There are two types of keyboard events: those that react to the keyboard directly (`keyup` and `keydown`) and those that react to text input (`keypress`). A single character entry event could correspond to several keys, for example when the *Shift* key in combination with the *X* key creates the capital letter **X**. While the specifics of implementation differ from one browser to the next (unsurprisingly), a safe rule of thumb is as follows: if you want to know what key the user pushed, you should observe the `keyup` or `keydown` event; if you want to know what character ended up on the screen as a result, you should observe the `keypress` event. For this feature, we just want to know when the user presses the *D*, *N*, or *L* key, so we will use `keyup`.

Next, we need to determine which element should watch for the event. This is a little less obvious than with mouse events, where we have an obvious mouse cursor to tell us about the event's target. Instead, the target of a keyboard event is the element that currently has the **keyboard focus**. The element with focus can be changed in several ways, including mouse clicks and presses of the *Tab* key. Not every element can get the focus, either; only items that have default keyboard-driven behaviors such as form fields, links, and elements with a `.tabIndex` property are candidates.

In this case, we don't really care what element has the focus; we want our switcher to work whenever the user presses one of the keys. Event bubbling will once again come in handy, as we can bind our `keyup` event to the `document` element and have assurance that eventually, any key event will bubble up to us.

Finally, we will need to know which key was pressed when our `keyup` handler gets triggered. We can inspect the event object for this. The `.keyCode` property of the event contains an identifier for the key that was pressed, and for alphabetic keys, this identifier is the ASCII value of the uppercase letter. So we can switch on this value and trigger the appropriate button click:

```
$(document).ready(function() {
  $(document).keyup(function(event) {
    switch (String.fromCharCode(event.keyCode)) {
      case 'D':
        $('#switcher-default').click();
        break;
      case 'N':
        $('#switcher-narrow').click();
        break;
      case 'L':
        $('#switcher-large').click();
        break;
    }
  });
});
```

Presses of these three keys now simulate mouse clicks on the buttons—provided that the key event is not interrupted by features such as Firefox's "search for text when I start typing."

As an alternative to using `.trigger()` to simulate this click, let's explore how to factor out code into a function so that more than one handler can call it—in this case, both `click` and `keyup`. While not necessary in this case, this technique can be useful in eliminating code redundancy.

```
$(document).ready(function() {
  // Enable hover effect on the style switcher buttons.
  $('#switcher .button').hover(function() {
    $(this).addClass('hover');
  }, function() {
    $(this).removeClass('hover');
  });

  // Allow the style switcher to expand and collapse.
  var toggleStyleSwitcher = function(event) {
    if (!$(event.target).is('.button')) {
      $('#switcher .button').toggleClass('hidden');
    }
  };
  $('#switcher').click(toggleStyleSwitcher);
```

```javascript
// Simulate a click so we start in a collaped state.
$('#switcher').click();

// The setBodyClass() function changes the page style.
// The style switcher state is also updated.
var setBodyClass = function(className) {
  $('body').removeClass();
  $('body').addClass(className);
  $('#switcher .button').removeClass('selected');
  $('#switcher-' + className).addClass('selected');

  if (className == 'default') {
    $('#switcher').click(toggleStyleSwitcher);
  }
  else {
    $('#switcher').unbind('click', toggleStyleSwitcher);
    $('#switcher .button').removeClass('hidden');
  }
};

// Invoke setBodyClass() when a button is clicked.
$('#switcher').click(function(event) {
  if ($(event.target).is('.button')) {
    if (event.target.id == 'switcher-default') {
      setBodyClass('default');
    }
    if (event.target.id == 'switcher-narrow') {
      setBodyClass('narrow');
    }
    else if (event.target.id == 'switcher-large') {
      setBodyClass('large');
    }
  }
});

// Invoke setBodyClass() when a key is pressed.
$(document).keyup(function(event) {
  switch (String.fromCharCode(event.keyCode)) {
    case 'D':
      setBodyClass('default');
      break;
    case 'N':
      setBodyClass('narrow');
      break;
    case 'L':
      setBodyClass('large');
      break;
  }
});
});
```

Summary

The abilities we've discussed in this chapter allow us to:

- Let multiple JavaScript libraries coexist on a single page using `.noConflict()`.

- Use **mouse event handlers** to react to a user's click on a page element with `.bind()` or `.click()`.

- Observe **event context** to perform different actions depending on the page element clicked, even when the handler is bound to several elements.

- Alternately expand and collapse a page element by using `.toggle()`.

- Highlight page elements under the mouse cursor by using `.hover()`.

- Influence **event propagation** to determine which elements get to respond to an event by using `.stopPropagation()` and `.preventDefault()`.

- Implement **event delegation** to reduce the number of bound event handlers necessary on a page.

- Call `.unbind()` to remove an event handler we're finished with.

- Segregate related event handlers with **event namespacing** so they can be acted on as a group.

- Cause bound event handlers to execute with `.trigger()`.

- Use **keyboard event handlers** to react to a user's key press with `.keyup()`.

Used together, we can use these capabilities to build quite interactive pages. In the next chapter, we'll learn how to provide visual feedback to the user during these interactions.

4
Effects

If actions speak louder than words, then in the JavaScript world, effects make actions speak louder still. With jQuery, we can easily add impact to our actions through a set of simple visual **effects**, and even craft our own, more sophisticated **animations**.

jQuery effects certainly add flair, as is evident when we see elements gradually slide into view instead of appearing all at once. However, they can also provide important usability enhancements that help orient the user when there is some change on a page (especially common in AJAX applications). In this chapter, we will explore a number of these effects and combine them in interesting ways.

Inline CSS modification

Before we jump into the nifty jQuery effects, a quick look at CSS is in order. In previous chapters we have been modifying a document's appearance by defining styles for classes in a separate stylesheet and then adding or removing those classes with jQuery. Typically, this is the preferred process for injecting CSS into HTML because it respects the stylesheet's role in dealing with the presentation of a page. However, there may be times when we need to apply styles that haven't been, or can't easily be, defined in a stylesheet. Fortunately, jQuery offers the `.css()` method for such occasions.

This method acts as both a **getter** and a **setter**. To get the value of a style property, we simply pass the name of the property as a string, like `.css('backgroundColor')`. Multi-word properties can be interpreted by jQuery when hyphenated, as they are in CSS notation (`background-color`), or camel-cased, as they are in DOM notation (`backgroundColor`). For setting style properties, the `.css()` method comes in two flavors—one that takes a single style property and its value and one that takes a **map** of property-value pairs:

```
.css('property','value')
.css({property1: 'value1', 'property-2': 'value2'})
```

Experienced JavaScript developers will recognize these jQuery maps as JavaScript **object literals**.

 Numeric values do not take quotation marks while string values do. However, when using the map notation, quotation marks are not required for property names if they are written in camel-cased DOM notation.

We use the `.css()` method the same way we've been using `.addClass()`—by **chaining** it to a selector and **binding** it to an event. To demonstrate this, we'll return to the style switcher example of Chapter 3, but with different HTML:

```
<div id="switcher">
  <div class="label">Text Size</div>
  <button id="switcher-default">Default</button>
  <button id="switcher-large">Bigger</button>
  <button id="switcher-small">Smaller</button>
</div>
<div class="speech">
  <p>Fourscore and seven years ago our fathers brought forth
     on this continent a new nation, conceived in liberty,
     and dedicated to the proposition that all men are created
     equal.</p>
</div>
```

By linking to a stylesheet with a few basic style rules, the page can initially look like the following screenshot:

In this version of the style switcher, we're using `<button>` elements. Clicking on the **Bigger** and **Smaller** buttons will increase or decrease the text size of `<div class="speech">`, while clicking on the **Default** button will reset `<div class="speech">` to its original text size.

If all we wanted were to change the font size a single time to a predetermined value, we could still use the .addClass() method. But let's suppose that now we want the text to continue increasing or decreasing incrementally each time the respective button is clicked. Although it might be possible to define a separate class for each click and iterate through them, a more straightforward approach would be to compute the new text size each time by getting the current size and increasing it by a set factor (for example, 40%).

Our code will start with the $(document).ready() and $('#switcher-large'). click() event handlers:

```
$(document).ready(function() {
  $('#switcher-large').click(function() {
  });
});
```

Next, the font size can be easily discovered by using the .css() method: $('div. speech').css('fontSize'). However, because the returned value will include a trailing 'px', we'll need to strip that part in order to perform calculations with the value. Also, when we plan to use a jQuery object more than once, it's generally a good idea to **cache** the selector by storing the resulting jQuery object in a variable as well.

```
$(document).ready(function() {
  var $speech = $('div.speech');
  $('#switcher-large').click(function() {
    var num = parseFloat($speech.css('fontSize'), 10);
  });
});
```

The first line inside $(document).ready() now stores a variable for <div class="speech"> itself. Notice the use of a $ in the variable name, $speech. Since $ is a legal character in JavaScript variables, we can use it as a reminder that the variable is storing a jQuery object.

Inside the .click() handler, we use parseFloat() to get the font size property's number only. The parseFloat() function looks at a string from left to right until it encounters a non-numeric character. The string of digits is converted into a floating-point (decimal) number. For example, it would convert the string '12' to the number 12. In addition, it strips non-numeric trailing characters from the string, so '12px' becomes 12 as well. If the string begins with a non-numeric character, parseFloat() returns NaN, which stands for **Not a Number**. The second argument for parseFloat() allows us to ensure that the number is interpreted as base-10 instead of octal or some other representation.

All that's left to do, if we are increasing by 40%, is to multiply num by 1.4 and then set the font size by concatenating num and 'px':

```
$(document).ready(function() {
  var $speech = $('div.speech');
  $('#switcher-large').click(function() {
    var num = parseFloat($speech.css('fontSize'), 10 );
    num *= 1.4;
    $speech.css('fontSize', num + 'px');
  });
});
```

The equation num *= 1.4 is shorthand for num = num * 1.4. We can use the same type of shorthand for the other basic mathematical operations, as well: addition, num += 1.4; subtraction, num -= 1.4; division, num /= 1.4; and modulus (division remainder), num %= 1.4.

Now when a user clicks on the **Bigger** button, the text becomes larger. Another click, and the text becomes larger still, as shown in the following screenshot:

Abraham Lincoln's Gettysburg Address

Text Size
Default Bigger Smaller

Fourscore and seven years ago our fathers brought forth on this continent a new nation, conceived in liberty, and dedicated to the proposition that all men are created equal.

To get the **Smaller** button to decrease the font size, we will divide rather than multiply—num /= 1.4. Better still, we'll combine the two into a single .click() handler on all <button> elements within <div id="switcher">. Then, after finding the numeric value, we can either multiply or divide depending on the ID of the button that was clicked. Here is what that code looks like now:

```
$(document).ready(function() {
  var $speech = $('div.speech');
  $('#switcher button').click(function() {
    var num = parseFloat( $speech.css('fontSize'), 10 );
    if (this.id == 'switcher-large') {
      num *= 1.4;
    } else if (this.id == 'switcher-small') {
```

```
        num /= 1.4;
    }
    $speech.css('fontSize', num + 'px);
  });
});
```

Recall from Chapter 3 that we can access the id property of the DOM element referred to by this, which appears here inside the if and else if statements. Here, it is more efficient to use this than to create a jQuery object just to test the value of a property.

It's also nice to have a way to return the font size to its initial value. To allow the user to do so, we can simply store the font size in a variable immediately when the DOM is ready. We can then use this value whenever the **Default** button is clicked. To handle this click, we could add another else if statement. However, perhaps a switch statement would be more appropriate.

```
$(document).ready(function() {
  var $speech = $('div.speech');
  var defaultSize = $speech.css('fontSize');
  $('#switcher button').click(function() {
    var num = parseFloat( $speech.css('fontSize'), 10 );
    switch (this.id) {
      case 'switcher-large':
        num *= 1.4;
        break;
      case 'switcher-small':
        num /= 1.4;
        break;
      default:
        num = parseFloat(defaultSize, 10);
    }
    $speech.css('fontSize', num + 'px');
  });
});
```

Here we're still checking the value of this.id and changing the font size based on it, but if its value is neither 'switcher-large' nor 'switcher-small' it will default to the initial font size.

Basic hide and show

The basic .hide() and .show() methods, without any parameters, can be thought of as smart shorthand methods for .css('display','string'), where 'string' is the appropriate display value. The effect, as might be expected, is that the matched set of elements will be immediately hidden or shown, with no animation.

The .hide() method sets the **inline style attribute** of the matched set of elements to display:none. The smart part here is that it remembers the value of the display property—typically block or inline—before it was changed to none. Conversely, the .show() method restores the matched set of elements to whatever visible display property they had before display:none was applied.

> For more information about the display property and how its values are visually represented in a web page, visit the Mozilla Developer Center at https://developer.mozilla.org/en/CSS/display/ and view examples at https://developer.mozilla.org/samples/cssref/display.html.

This feature of .show() and .hide() is especially helpful when hiding elements whose default display property is overridden in a stylesheet. For example, the <li> element has the property display:block by default, but we might want to change it to display:inline for a horizontal menu. Fortunately, using the .show() method on a hidden element such as one of these <li> tags would not merely reset it to its default display:block, because that would put the <li> on its own line. Instead, the element is restored to its previous display:inline state, thus preserving the horizontal design.

A quick demonstration of these two methods can be set up by adding a second paragraph and a "read more" link after the first paragraph in the example HTML:

```
<div id="switcher">
  <div class="label">Text Size</div>
  <button id="switcher-default">Default</button>
  <button id="switcher-large">Bigger</button>
  <button id="switcher-small">Smaller</button>
</div>
<div class="speech">
  <p>Fourscore and seven years ago our fathers brought forth
     on this continent a new nation, conceived in liberty,
```

```
        and dedicated to the proposition that all men are
        created equal.
    </p>
    <p>Now we are engaged in a great civil war, testing whether
        that nation, or any nation so conceived and so dedicated,
        can long endure. We are met on a great battlefield of
        that war. We have come to dedicate a portion of that
        field as a final resting-place for those who here gave
        their lives that the nation might live. It is altogether
        fitting and proper that we should do this. But, in a
        larger sense, we cannot dedicate, we cannot consecrate,
        we cannot hallow, this ground.
    </p>
    <a href="#" class="more">read more</a>
</div>
```

When the DOM is ready, the second paragraph is hidden:

```
$(document).ready(function() {
    $('p:eq(1)').hide();
});
```

And the speech looks like the following screenshot:

Then, when the user clicks on **read more** at the end of the first paragraph, that link is hidden and the second paragraph is shown:

```
$(document).ready(function() {
    $('p:eq(1)').hide();
    $('a.more').click(function() {
        $('p:eq(1)').show();
        $(this).hide();
        return false;
    });
});
```

Note the use of `return false` to keep the link from activating its **default action**. Now the speech looks like this:

Text Size
Default   Bigger   Smaller

Fourscore and seven years ago our fathers brought forth on this continent a new nation, conceived in liberty, and dedicated to the proposition that all men are created equal.

Now we are engaged in a great civil war, testing whether that nation, or any nation so conceived and so dedicated, can long endure. We are met on a great battlefield of that war. We have come to dedicate a portion of that field as a final resting-place for those who here gave their lives that the nation might live. It is altogether fitting and proper that we should do this. But, in a larger sense, we cannot dedicate, we cannot consecrate, we cannot hallow, this ground.

The `.hide()` and `.show()` methods are quick and useful, but they aren't very flashy. To add some flair, we can give them a speed.

Effects and speed

When we include a **speed** (or, more precisely, a **duration**) with `.show()` or `.hide()`, it becomes animated—occurring over a specified period of time. The `.hide('speed')` method, for example, decreases an element's height, width, and opacity simultaneously until all three reach zero, at which point the CSS rule `display:none` is applied. The `.show('speed')` method will increase the element's height from top to bottom, width from left to right, and opacity from 0 to 1 until its contents are completely visible.

Speeding in

With any jQuery effect, we can use one of three preset speeds: `'slow'`, `'normal'`, and `'fast'`. Using `.show('slow')` makes the show effect complete in .6 seconds, `.show('normal')` in .4 seconds, and `.show('fast')` in .2 seconds. For even greater precision we can specify a number of milliseconds, for example `.show(850)`. Unlike the speed names, the numbers are not wrapped in quotation marks.

Let's include a speed in our example when showing the second paragraph of Lincoln's **Gettysburg Address**:

```
$(document).ready(function() {
  $('p:eq(1)').hide();
  $('a.more').click(function() {
    $('p:eq(1)').show('slow');
    $(this).hide();
    return false;
  });
});
```

When we capture the paragraph's appearance at roughly halfway through the effect, we see something like the following:

Fourscore and seven years ago our fathers brought forth on this continent a new nation, conceived in liberty, and dedicated to the proposition that all men are created equal.

Now we are engaged in a great civil war, testing whether that nation, or any nation so conceived and so dedicated, can long

Fading in and fading out

While the animated `.show()` and `.hide()` methods are certainly flashy, they may at times be too much of a good thing. Fortunately, jQuery offers a couple other pre-built animations for a more subtle effect. For example, to have the whole paragraph appear just by gradually increasing the opacity, we can use `.fadeIn('slow')` instead:

```
$(document).ready(function() {
  $('p:eq(1)').hide();
  $('a.more').click(function() {
    $('p:eq(1)').fadeIn('slow');
    $(this).hide();
    return false;
  });
});
```

This time when we capture the paragraph's appearance halfway, it's seen as:

Fourscore and seven years ago our fathers brought forth on this continent a new nation, conceived in liberty, and dedicated to the proposition that all men are created equal.

Now we are engaged in a great civil war, testing whether that nation, or any nation so conceived and so dedicated, can long endure. We are met on a great battlefield of that war. We have come to dedicate a portion of that field as a final resting-place for those who here gave their lives that the nation might live. It is altogether fitting and proper that we should do this. But, in a larger sense, we cannot dedicate, we cannot consecrate, we cannot hallow, this ground.

The difference here is that the `.fadeIn()` effect starts by setting the dimensions of the paragraph so that the contents can simply fade into it. To gradually decrease the opacity we can use `.fadeOut()`.

Compound effects

Sometimes we have a need to toggle the visibility of elements, rather than displaying them once as we did in the previous example. Toggling can be achieved by first checking the visibility of the matched elements and then attaching the appropriate method. Using the fade effects again, we can modify the example script to look like this:

```
$(document).ready(function() {
  var $firstPara = $('p:eq(1)');
  $firstPara.hide();
  $('a.more').click(function() {
    if ($firstPara.is(':hidden')) {
      $firstPara.fadeIn('slow');
      $(this).text('read less');
    } else {
      $firstPara.fadeOut('slow');
      $(this).text('read more');
    }
    return false;
  });
});
```

As we did earlier in the chapter, we're **caching** our selector here to avoid repeated DOM traversal. Notice, too, that we're no longer hiding the clicked link; instead, we're changing the its text.

Using an `if else` statement is a perfectly reasonable way to toggle elements' visibility. But with jQuery's **compound effects** we can leave the conditionals out of it (although, in this example, we still need one for the link text). jQuery provides a `.toggle()` method, which acts like `.show()` and `.hide()`, and like them, can be used with a speed argument or without. The other compound method is `.slideToggle()`, which shows or hides elements by gradually increasing or decreasing their height. Here is what the script looks like when we use the `.slideToggle()` method:

```
$(document).ready(function() {
var $firstPara = $('p:eq(1)');
  $firstPara.hide();
  $('a.more').click(function() {
    $firstPara.slideToggle('slow');
    var $link = $(this);
    if ( $link.text() == "read more" ) {
      $link.text('read less');
    } else {
```

```
        $link.text('read more');
    }
    return false;
  });
});
```

This time $(this) would have been repeated, so we're storing it in the $link variable for performance and readability. Also, the conditional statement checks for the text of the link rather than the visibility of the second paragraph, since we're only using it to change the text.

Creating custom animations

In addition to the pre-built effect methods, jQuery provides a powerful
.animate() method that allows us to create our own **custom animations** with fine-grained control. The .animate() method comes in two forms. The first takes up to four arguments:

1. A **map** of style properties and values — similar to the .css() map discussed earlier in this chapter

2. An optional **speed** — which can be one of the preset strings or a number of milliseconds

3. An optional **easing type** — an advanced option discussed in Chapter 10

4. An optional **callback function** — which will be discussed later in this chapter

All together, the four arguments look like this:

```
.animate({property1: 'value1', property2: 'value2'},
  speed, easing, function() {
    alert('The animation is finished.');
  }
);
```

The second form takes two arguments, a **map** of properties and a map of options.

```
.animate({properties}, {options})
```

In effect, the second argument wraps up the second through fourth arguments of the first form into another map, and adds two more options to the mix. When we adjust the line breaks for readability, the second form looks like this:

```
.animate({
  property1: 'value1',
  property2: 'value2'
```

```
}, {
  duration: 'value',
  easing: 'value',
  complete: function() {
    alert('The animation is finished.');
  },
  queue: boolean,
  step: callback
});
```

For now we'll use the first form of the `.animate()` method, but we'll return to the second form later in the chapter when we discuss queuing effects.

Toggling the fade

When we discussed compound effects, did you notice that not all methods have a corresponding method for toggling? That's right: while the sliding methods include `.slideToggle()`, there is no corresponding `.fadeToggle()` to go along with `.fadeIn()` and `.fadeOut()`! The good news is that we can use the `.animate()` method to easily make our own toggling fade animation. Here, we'll replace the `.slideToggle()` line of the previous example with our custom animation:

```
$(document).ready(function() {
  $('p:eq(1)').hide();
  $('a.more').click(function() {
    $('p:eq(1)').animate({opacity: 'toggle'}, 'slow');
    var $link = $(this);
    if ( $link.text() == "read more" ) {
      $link.text('read less');
    } else {
      $link.text('read more');
    }
    return false;
  });
});
```

As the example illustrates, the `.animate()` method provides convenient **shorthand values** for CSS properties — `'show'`, `'hide'`, and `'toggle'` — to ease the way when the shorthand *methods* aren't quite right for the particular task.

Animating multiple properties

With the `.animate()` method, we can modify any combination of properties simultaneously. For example, to create a simultaneous sliding and fading effect when toggling the second paragraph, we simply add the `height` property-value pair to `.animate()`'s properties map:

```
$(document).ready(function() {
  $('p:eq(1)').hide();
  $('a.more').click(function() {
    $('p:eq(1)').animate({
      opacity: 'toggle',
      height: 'toggle'
    },
    'slow');
    var $link = $(this);
    if ( $link.text() == "read more" ) {
      $link.text('read less');
    } else {
      $link.text('read more');
    }
    return false;
  });
});
```

Additionally, we have not only the style properties used for the shorthand effect methods at our disposal, but also other properties such as: `left`, `top`, `fontSize`, `margin`, `padding`, and `borderWidth`. Recall the script to change the text size of the speech paragraphs. We can animate the increase or decrease in size by simply substituting the `.animate()` method for the `.css()` method:

```
$(document).ready(function() {
  var $speech = $('div.speech');
  var defaultSize = $speech.css('fontSize');
  $('#switcher button').click(function() {
    var num = parseFloat( $speech.css('fontSize'), 10 );
    switch (this.id) {
      case 'switcher-large':
        num *= 1.4;
        break;
      case 'switcher-small':
        num /= 1.4;
        break;
      default:
        num = parseFloat(defaultSize, 10);
```

```
        }
        $speech.animate({fontSize: num + 'px'},
                                'slow');
    });
});
```

The extra properties allow us to create much more complex effects, too. We can, for example, move an item from the left side of the page to the right while increasing its height by 20 pixels and changing its border width to 5 pixels.

So, let's do that with the `<div id="switcher">` box. Here is what it looks like before we animate it:

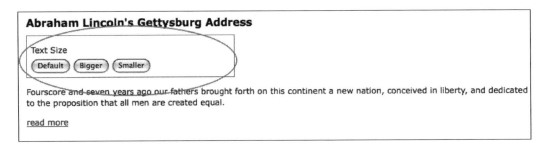

With a flexible-width layout, we need to compute the distance that the box needs to travel before it lines up at the right side of the page. Assuming that the paragraph's width is 100%, we can subtract the **Text Size** box's width from the paragraph's width. While jQuery's `.width()` method would usually come in handy for such calculations, it doesn't factor in the width of the right and left padding or the right and left border. As of jQuery version 1.2.6, though we also have the `.outerWidth()` method at our disposal. This is what we'll use here, to avoid having to add padding and border widths as well. For the sake of this example, we'll trigger the animation by clicking the **Text Size** label, just above the buttons. Here is what the code should look like:

```
$(document).ready(function() {
  $('div.label').click(function() {
    var paraWidth = $('div.speech p').outerWidth();
    var $switcher = $(this).parent();
    var switcherWidth = $switcher.outerWidth();
    $switcher.animate({left: paraWidth - switcherWidth,
            height: '+=20px', borderWidth: '5px'}, 'slow');
  });
});
```

Note that the `height` property has `+=` before the pixel value. This expression, introduced in jQuery 1.2, indicates a **relative value**. So, instead of animating the height to 20 pixels, the height is animated to 20 pixels greater than the current height.

Although this code successfully increases the height of the `<div>` and widens its border, at the moment the `left` position cannot be changed. We still need to enable changing its position in the CSS.

Positioning with CSS

When working with `.animate()`, it's important to keep in mind the limitations that CSS imposes on the elements that we wish to change. For example, adjusting the `left` property will have no effect on the matching elements unless those elements have their CSS position set to `relative` or `absolute`. The default CSS position for all block-level elements is `static`, which accurately describes how those elements will remain if we try to move them without first changing their `position` value.

> For more information on absolute and relative positioning, see Joe Gillespie's article, Absolutely Relative at: `http://www.wpdfd.com/issues/78/absolutely_relative/`

A peek at our stylesheet shows that we have now set `<div id="switcher">` to be relatively positioned:

```
#switcher {
  position: relative;
}
```

With the CSS taken into account, the result of clicking on **Text Size**, when the animation has completed, will look like this:

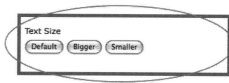

Abraham Lincoln's Gettysburg Address

Text Size
Default   Bigger   Smaller

Fourscore and seven years ago our fathers brought forth on this continent a new nation, conceived in liberty, and dedicated to the proposition that all men are created equal.

read more

Simultaneous versus queued effects

The `.animate()` method, as we've just discovered, is very useful for creating simultaneous effects in a particular set of elements. There may be times, however, when we want to **queue** our effects, having them occur one after the other.

Working with a single set of elements

When applying multiple effects to the same set of elements, **queuing** is easily achieved by chaining those effects. To demonstrate this queuing, we'll again move the **Text Size** box to the right, increase its height and increase its border width. This time, however, we perform the three effects sequentially, simply by placing each in its own `.animate()` method and chaining the three together:

```
$(document).ready(function() {
  $('div.label').click(function() {
    var paraWidth = $('div.speech p').outerWidth();
    var $switcher = $(this).parent();
    var switcherWidth = $switcher.outerWidth();
    $switcher
      .animate({left: paraWidth - switcherWidth},
                                        'slow')
      .animate({height: '+=20px'}, 'slow')
      .animate({borderWidth: '5px'}, 'slow');
  });
});
```

Recall that chaining permits us to keep all three `.animate()` methods on the same line, but here we have indented them and put each on its own line for greater readability.

We can queue any of the jQuery effect methods, not just `.animate()`, by chaining them. We can, for example, queue effects on `<div id="switcher">` in the following order:

1. Fade its opacity to .5 with `.fadeTo()`.
2. Move it to the right with `.animate()`.
3. Fade it back in to full opacity with `.fadeTo()`.
4. Hide it with `.slideUp()`.
5. Show it once more with `.slideDown()`.

All we need to do is chain the effects in the same order in our code:

```
$(document).ready(function() {
    $('div.label').click(function() {
        var paraWidth = $('div.speech p').outerWidth();
        var $switcher = $(this).parent();
        var switcherWidth = $switcher.outerWidth();
        $switcher
            .fadeTo('fast',0.5)
            .animate({
                'left': paraWidth - switcherWidth
            }, 'slow')
            .fadeTo('slow',1.0)
            .slideUp('slow')
            .slideDown('slow');
    });
});
```

But what if we want to move the <div> to the right at the same time as it fades to half opacity? If the two animations were occurring at the same speed, we could simply combine them into a single .animate() method. But in this example, the fade is using the 'fast' speed while the move to the right is using the 'slow' speed. Here is where the second form of the .animate() method comes in handy:

```
$(document).ready(function() {
    $('div.label').click(function() {
        var paraWidth = $('div.speech p').outerWidth();
        var $switcher = $(this).parent();
        var switcherWidth = $switcher.outerWidth();
        $switcher
            .fadeTo('fast',0.5)
            .animate({
                'left': paraWidth - switcherWidth
            }, {duration: 'slow', queue: false})
            .fadeTo('slow',1.0)
            .slideUp('slow')
            .slideDown('slow');
    });
});
```

The second argument, an options map, provides the queue option, which when set to false makes the animation start simultaneously with the previous one.

One final observation about queuing effects on a single set of elements is that queuing does not automatically apply to other, non-effect methods such as .css(). So let's suppose we wanted to change the background color of <div id="switcher"> to red after the .slideUp() but before the slideDown(). We could try doing it like this:

```
$(document).ready(function() {
$('div.label').click(function() {
    var paraWidth = $('div.speech p').outerWidth();
    var $switcher = $(this).parent();
    var switcherWidth = $switcher.outerWidth();
    $switcher
      .fadeTo('fast',0.5)
      .animate({
        'left': paraWidth - switcherWidth
      }, 'slow')
      .fadeTo('slow',1.0)
      .slideUp('slow')
      .css('backgroundColor','#f00')
      .slideDown('slow');
    });
});
```

However, even though the background-changing code is placed at the correct position in the chain, it occurs immediately upon the click.

One way we can add non-effect methods to the queue is to use the appropriately named .queue() method. Here is what it would look like in our example:

```
$(document).ready(function() {
    $('div.label').click(function() {
    var paraWidth = $('div.speech p').outerWidth();
    var $switcher = $(this).parent();
    var switcherWidth = $switcher.outerWidth();
    $switcher
      .fadeTo('fast',0.5)
      .animate({
        'left': paraWidth - switcherWidth
      }, 'slow')
      .fadeTo('slow',1.0)
      .slideUp('slow')
      .queue(function() {
        $switcher
          .css('backgroundColor', '#f00')
          .dequeue();
```

```
    })
      .slideDown('slow');
   });
});
```

When given a **callback function**, as it is here, the `.queue()` method adds the function to the queue of effects for the matched elements. Within the function, we set the background color to red and then add the corollary `.dequeue()` method. Including this `.dequeue()` method allows the animation queue to pick up where it left off and complete the chain with the following `.slideDown('slow')` line. If we hadn't used `.dequeue()`, the animation would have stopped.

> More information and examples for `.queue()` and `.dequeue()` are available at `http://docs.jquery.com/Effects`.

We'll discover another way to queue non-effect methods as we examine effects with multiple sets of elements.

Working with multiple sets of elements

Unlike with a single set of elements, when we apply effects to different sets, they occur at virtually the same time. To see these simultaneous effects in action, we'll slide one paragraph down while sliding another paragraph up. First, we'll add the remaining portion of the Gettysburg Address to the HTML, dividing it into two separate paragraphs:

```
<div id="switcher">
  <div class="label">Text Size</div>
  <button id="switcher-default">Default</button>
  <button id="switcher-large">Bigger</button>
  <button id="switcher-small">Smaller</button>
</div>
<div class="speech">
  <p>Fourscore and seven years ago our fathers brought forth
     on this continent a new nation, conceived in liberty, and
     dedicated to the proposition that all men are created
     equal.
  </p>
  <p>Now we are engaged in a great civil war, testing whether
     that nation, or any nation so conceived and so dedicated,
     can long endure. We are met on a great battlefield of
     that war. We have come to dedicate a portion of that
     field as a final resting-place for those who here gave
```

```
    their lives that the nation might live. It is altogether
    fitting and proper that we should do this. But, in a
    larger sense, we cannot dedicate, we cannot consecrate,
    we cannot hallow, this ground.
</p>
<a href="#" class="more">read more</a>
<p>The brave men, living and dead, who struggled
    here have consecrated it, far above our poor
    power to add or detract. The world will little
    note, nor long remember, what we say here, but it
    can never forget what they did here. It is for us
    the living, rather, to be dedicated here to the
    unfinished work which they who fought here have
    thus far so nobly advanced.
</p>
<p>It is rather for us to be here dedicated to the
    great task remaining before us—that from
    these honored dead we take increased devotion to
    that cause for which they gave the last full
    measure of devotion—that we here highly
    resolve that these dead shall not have died in
    vain—that this nation, under God, shall
    have a new birth of freedom and that government
    of the people, by the people, for the people,
    shall not perish from the earth.
</p>
</div>
```

Next, to help us see what's happening during the effect, we'll give the third paragraph a 1-pixel border and the fourth paragraph a gray background. We'll also hide the fourth paragraph when the DOM is ready:

```
$(document).ready(function() {
  $('p:eq(2)').css('border', '1px solid #333');
  $('p:eq(3)').css('backgroundColor', '#ccc').hide();
});
```

Finally, we'll add the `.click()` method to the third paragraph so that when it is clicked, the third paragraph will slide up (and out of view), while the fourth paragraph slides down (and into view):

```
$(document).ready(function() {
$('p:eq(2)')
    .css('border', '1px solid #333')
    .click(function() {
```

```
    $(this).slideUp('slow')
      .next().slideDown('slow');
    });
  $('p:eq(3)').css('backgroundColor', '#ccc').hide();
});
```

A screenshot of these two effects in mid-slide confirms that they do, indeed, occur virtually simultaneously:

> The brave men, living and dead, who struggled here have consecrated it, far above our poor power to add or detract. The world will little note, nor long remember, what we say here, but it can never forget what they did here. It is for us the
>
> It is rather for us to be here dedicated to the great task remaining before us—that from these honored dead we take

The third paragraph, which started visible, is halfway through sliding up at the same time as the fourth paragraph, which started hidden, is halfway through sliding down.

Callbacks

In order to allow queuing effects on different elements, jQuery provides a **callback function** for each effect method. As we have seen with event handlers and with the .queue() method, callbacks are simply functions passed as method arguments. In the case of effects, they appear as the last argument of the method.

If we use a callback to queue the two slide effects, we can have the fourth paragraph slide down before the third paragraph slides up. Let's first look at how to set up the .slideDown() method with the callback:

```
$(document).ready(function() {
  $('p:eq(2)')
    .css('border', '1px solid #333')
    .click(function() {
      $(this).next().slideDown('slow',function() {
        // code here executes after 3rd paragraph's
        // slide down has ended
      });
    });
  $('p:eq(3)').css('backgroundColor', '#ccc').hide();
});
```

We do need to be careful here, however, about what is actually going to slide up. The context has changed for $(this) because the callback is inside the .slideDown() method. Here, $(this) is no longer the third paragraph, as it was at the point of the .click() method; rather, since the .slideDown() method is attached to $(this). next(), everything within that method now sees $(this) as the next sibling, or the fourth paragraph. Therefore, if we put $(this).slideUp('slow') inside the callback, we would end up hiding the same paragraph that we had just made visible.

A simple way to keep the reference of $(this) stable is to store it in a variable right away within the .click() method, like var $thirdPara = $(this).

Now $thirdPara will refer to the third paragraph, both outside and inside the callback. Here is what the code looks like using our new variable:

```
$(document).ready(function() {
  var $thirdPara = $('p:eq(2)');
  $thirdPara
    .css('border', '1px solid #333')
    .click(function() {
      $(this).next().slideDown('slow',function() {
        $thirdPara.slideUp('slow');
      });
    });
  $('p:eq(3)').css('backgroundColor', '#ccc').hide();
});
```

Using $thirdPara inside the .slideDown() callback relies on the properties of **closures**. We'll be discussing this important, yet difficult-to-master, topic in Appendix C.

This time, a snapshot halfway through the effects will reveal that both the third and the fourth paragraphs are visible; the fourth has finished sliding down and the third is about to begin sliding up:

The brave men, living and dead, who struggled here have consecrated it, far above our poor power to add or detract. The world will little note, nor long remember, what we say here, but it can never forget what they did here. It is for us the living, rather, to be dedicated here to the unfinished work which they who fought here have thus far so nobly advanced.

It is rather for us to be here dedicated to the great task remaining before us—that from these honored dead we take increased devotion to that cause for which they gave the last full measure of devotion—that we here highly resolve that these dead shall not have died in vain—that this nation, under God, shall have a new birth of freedom and that government of the people, by the people, for the people, shall not perish from the earth.

Now that we've discussed callbacks, we can return to the code from earlier in this chapter in which we queued a background-color change near the end of a series of effects. Instead of using the `.queue()` method, as we did earlier, we can simply use a callback function:

```
$(document).ready(function() {
  $('div.label').click(function() {
    var paraWidth = $('div.speech p').outerWidth();
    var $switcher = $(this).parent();
    var switcherWidth = $switcher.outerWidth();
    $switcher
      .fadeTo('slow',0.5)
      .animate({
        'left': paraWidth - switcherWidth
      }, 'slow')
      .fadeTo('slow',1.0)
      .slideUp('slow', function() {
        $switcher
          .css('backgroundColor', '#f00');
      })
      .slideDown('slow');
  });
});
```

Here again, the background color of `<div id="switcher">` changes to red after it slides up, and before it slides back down.

In a nutshell

With all the variations to consider when applying effects, it can become difficult to remember whether the effects will occur simultaneously or sequentially. A brief outline might help:

1. Effects on a single set of elements are:
   - *simultaneous* when applied as multiple properties in a single `.animate()` method
   - *queued* when applied in a chain of methods, unless the `queue` option is set to `false`
2. Effects on multiple sets of elements are:
   - *simultaneous* by default
   - *queued* when applied within the callback of another effect or within the callback of the `.queue()` method

Summary

By using effect methods that we have explored in this chapter, we should now be able to incrementally increase and decrease text size by using either the `.css()` or the `.animate()` method. We should also be able to apply various effects to gradually hide and show page elements in different ways and also to animate elements, simultaneously or sequentially, in a number of ways.

In the first four chapters of the book, all of our examples have involved manipulating elements that have been hard-coded into the page's HTML. In Chapter 5 we will explore ways in which we can use jQuery to create new elements and insert them into the DOM wherever we choose.

5
DOM Manipulation

Like a magician who appears to produce a bouquet of flowers out of thin air, jQuery can create elements, attributes, and text in a web page — as if by magic. But wait, there's more! With jQuery, we can also make any of these things vanish. And, we can take that bouquet of flowers and transform it into a `<div class="magic" id="flowerstodove">dove</div>`.

Manipulating attributes

Throughout the first four chapters of this book, we have been using the `.addClass()` and `.removeClass()` methods to demonstrate how we can change the appearance of elements on a page. Effectively, what these two methods are doing is manipulating the class attribute (or, in DOM scripting parlance, the `className` property). The `.addClass()` method creates or adds to the attribute, while `.removeClass()` deletes or shortens it. Add to these the `.toggleClass()` method, which alternates between adding and removing a class, and we have an efficient and robust way of handling classes.

Nevertheless, the `class` attribute is only one of several attributes that we may need to access or change: for example, `id` and `rel` and `href`. For manipulating these attributes, jQuery provides the `.attr()` and `.removeAttr()` methods. We could even use `.attr()` and `.removeAttr()` to modify the `class` attribute, but the specialized `.addClass()` and `.removeClass()` methods are better in this case because they correctly handle cases where multiple classes are applied to a single element, such as `<div class="first second">`.

Non-class attributes

Some attributes are not so easily manipulated without the help of jQuery. In addition, jQuery lets us modify more than one attribute at a time, similar to the way we worked with multiple CSS properties using the `.css()` method in Chapter 4.

For example, we can easily set the `id`, `rel`, and `title` attributes for links, all at once. Let's start with some sample HTML:

```html
<h1 id="f-title">Flatland: A Romance of Many Dimensions</h1>
<div id="f-author">by Edwin A. Abbott</div>
<h2>Part 1, Section 3</h2>
<h3 id="f-subtitle">
  Concerning the Inhabitants of Flatland
</h3>
<div id="excerpt">an excerpt</div>

<div class="chapter">

  <p class="square">Our Professional Men and Gentlemen are
    Squares (to which class I myself belong) and Five-Sided
    Figures or <a
    href="http://en.wikipedia.org/wiki/Pentagon">Pentagons
    </a>.
  </p>
  <p class="nobility hexagon">Next above these come the
    Nobility, of whom there are several degrees, beginning at
    Six-Sided Figures, or <a
    href="http://en.wikipedia.org/wiki/Hexagon">Hexagons</a>,
    and from thence rising in the number of their sides till
    they receive the honourable title of <a
    href="http://en.wikipedia.org/wiki/Polygon">Polygonal</a>,
    or many-Sided. Finally when the number of the sides
    becomes so numerous, and the sides themselves so small,
    that the figure cannot be distinguished from a <a
    href="http://en.wikipedia.org/wiki/Circle">circle</a>, he
    is included in the Circular or Priestly order; and this is
    the highest class of all.
  </p>

  <p><span class="pull-quote">It is a <span class="drop">Law
    of Nature</span> with us that a male child shall have
    <strong>one more side</strong> than his father</span>, so
    that each generation shall rise (as a rule) one step in
    the scale of development and nobility. Thus the son of a
    Square is a Pentagon; the son of a Pentagon, a Hexagon;
    and so on.
  </p>
<!-- . . . code continues . . . -->
</div>
```

Now we can iterate through each of the links inside `<div class="chapter">` and apply attributes to them one by one. If we only needed to set a common attribute value for all of the links, we could do so with a single line of code within our `$(document).ready()` handler:

```
$(document).ready(function() {
  $('div.chapter a').attr({'rel': 'external'});
});
```

This technique works because we want the new `rel` attribute to have the same value for each link. Often, though, the attributes we add or change must have different values for each element. One example of this is that for any given document, each `id` must be unique if we want our JavaScript code to behave predictably. To set a unique `id` for each link, we abandon the single-line solution in favor of jQuery's `.each()` method.

```
$(document).ready(function() {
  $('div.chapter a').each(function(index) {
    $(this).attr({
      'rel': 'external',
      'id': 'wikilink-' + index
    });
  });
});
```

The `.each()` method, which acts as an **explicit iterator**, is actually a more convenient form of the `for` loop. It can be employed when the code we want to use on each item in the selector's set of matched elements is too complex for the **implicit iteration** syntax. In our situation, the `.each()` method's anonymous function is passed an index that we can append to each `id`. This index argument acts as a counter, starting at `0` for the first link and incrementing by `1` with each successive link. Thus, setting the id to `'wikilink-' + index` gives the first link an `id` of `wikilink-0`, the second an `id` of `wikilink-1`, and so on.

In fact, we could have stuck with implicit iteration here, because the `.attr()` method can take a function as its second argument, similar to the way the `.filter()` method can do so with its single argument as we saw in Chapter 2 (see `http://docs.jquery.com/Attributes/attr#keyfn` for details). However, using `.each()` seems more convenient for our needs.

We'll use the `title` attribute to invite people to learn more about the linked term at Wikipedia. In the HTML example, all of the links point to Wikipedia. However, it's probably a good idea to make the selector expression a little more specific, selecting only links that contain `wikipedia` in the `href`, just in case we decide to add a non-Wikipedia link to the HTML at a later time:

```
$(document).ready(function() {
  $('div.chapter a[href*=wikipedia]').each(function(index) {
    var $thisLink = $(this);
    $thisLink.attr({
      'rel': 'external',
      'id': 'wikilink-' + index,
      'title': 'learn more about ' + $thisLink.text() +
                                      ' at Wikipedia'
    });
  });
});
```

One thing worth noting here is that we're now storing `$(this)` in a variable called `$thisLink`, simply because we end up using it more than once.

With all three attributes set, the HTML of the first link, for example, now looks like this:

```
<a href="http://en.wikipedia.org/wiki/Pentagon" rel="external"
   id="wikilink-0" title="learn more about Pentagons at
   Wikipedia">Pentagons</a>
```

The $() factory function revisited

From the start of this book, we've been using the `$()` function to access elements in a document. In a sense, this function lies at the very heart of the jQuery library, as it is used every time we attach an effect, event, or property to a matched set of elements.

What's more, the `$()` function has yet another trick within its parentheses—a feature so powerful that it can change not only the visual appearance but also the actual contents of a page. Simply by inserting a snippet of HTML code inside the parentheses, we can create an entirely new DOM structure from thin air.

Accessibility reminder

We should keep in mind, once again, the inherent danger in making certain functionality, visual appeal, or textual information available only to those with web browsers capable of (and enabled for) using JavaScript. Important information should be accessible to all, not just people who happen to be using the right software.

A feature commonly seen on FAQ pages is the **back to top** link that appears after each question-and-answer pair. It could be argued that these links serve no semantic purpose and therefore can be included via JavaScript legitimately as an enhancement for a subset of the visitors to a page. For our example, we'll add a **back to top** link after each paragraph, as well as the anchor to which the **back to top** links will take us. To begin, we simply create the new elements:

```
$(document).ready(function() {
  $('<a href="#top">back to top</a>');
  $('<a id="top"></a>');
});
```

Here is what the page looks like at this point:

Flatland: A Romance of Many Dimensions
by Edwin A. Abbott

Part 1, Section 3

Concerning the Inhabitants of Flatland
an excerpt

Our Professional Men and Gentlemen are Squares (to which class I myself belong) and Five-Sided Figures or Pentagons.

Next above these come the Nobility, of whom there are several degrees, beginning at Six-Sided Figures, or Hexagons, and from thence rising in the number of their sides till they receive the honourable title of Polygonal, or many-Sided. Finally when the number of the sides becomes so numerous, and the sides themselves so small, that the figure cannot be distinguished from a circle, he is included in the Circular or Priestly order; and this is the highest class of all.

It is a Law of Nature with us that a male child shall have **one more side** than his father, so that each generation shall rise (as a rule) one step in the scale of development and nobility. Thus the son of a Square is a Pentagon; the son of a Pentagon, a Hexagon; and so on.

But this rule applies not always to the Tradesman, and still less often to the Soldiers, and to the Workmen; who indeed can hardly be said to deserve the name of human Figures, since they have not all their sides equal. With them therefore the Law of Nature does not hold; and the son of an Isosceles (i.e. a Triangle with two sides equal) remains Isosceles still. Nevertheless, all hope is not such out, even from the Isosceles, that his posterity may ultimately rise above his degraded condition....

Rarely—in proportion to the vast numbers of Isosceles births—is a genuine and certifiable Equal-Sided Triangle produced from Isosceles parents. *"What need of a certificate?" a Spaceland critic may ask: "Is not the procreation of a Square Son a certificate from Nature herself, proving the Equal-sidedness of the Father?" I reply that no Lady of any position will marry an uncertified Triangle. Square offspring has sometimes resulted from a slightly Irregular*

But where are the **back to top** links and the anchor? Shouldn't they appear on the page? The answer is no. While the two lines do create the elements, they don't yet add the elements to the page. To do that, we can use one of the many jQuery **insertion methods**.

Inserting new elements

jQuery has two methods for inserting elements before other elements:
`.insertBefore()` and `.before()`. These two methods have the same function; their difference lies only in how they are **chained** to other methods. Another two methods, `.insertAfter()` and `.after()`, bear the same relationship with each other, but as their names suggest, they insert elements after other elements. For the **back to top** links we'll use the `.insertAfter()` method:

```
$(document).ready(function() {
  $('<a href="#top">back to top</a>')
    .insertAfter('div.chapter p');
  $('<a id="top"></a>');
});
```

The `.after()` method would accomplish the same thing as `.insertAfter()`, but with the selector expression preceding the method rather than following it. Using `.after()`, the first line inside `$(document).ready()` would look like this:

```
$('div.chapter p').after('<a href="#top">back to top</a>');
```

With `.insertAfter()`, we can continue acting on the created `<a>` element by chaining additional methods. With `.after()`, additional methods would act on the elements matched by the `$('div.chapter p')` selector instead.

So, now that we've actually inserted the links into the page (and into the DOM) after each paragraph that appears within `<div class="chapter">`, the **back to top** links will appear:

Flatland: A Romance of Many Dimensions
by Edwin A. Abbott

Part 1, Section 3

Concerning the Inhabitants of Flatland
an excerpt

Our Professional Men and Gentlemen are Squares (to which class I myself belong) and Five-Sided Figures or Pentagons.

back to top

Next above these come the Nobility, of whom there are several degrees, beginning at Six-Sided Figures, or Hexagons, and from thence rising in the number of their sides till they receive the honourable title of Polygonal, or many-Sided. Finally when the number of the sides becomes so numerous, and the sides themselves so small, that the figure cannot be distinguished from a circle, he is included in the Circular or Priestly order; and this is the highest class of all.

back to top

It is a Law of Nature with us that a male child shall have **one more side** than his father, so that each generation shall rise (as a rule) one step in the scale of development and nobility. Thus the son of a Square is a Pentagon; the son of a Pentagon, a Hexagon; and so on.

back to top

But this rule applies not always to the Tradesman, and still less often to the Soldiers, and to the Workmen; who indeed can hardly be said to deserve the name of human Figures, since they have not all their sides equal. With them therefore the Law of Nature does not hold; and the son of an Isosceles (i.e. a Triangle with two sides equal) remains Isosceles still. Nevertheless, all hope is not such out, even from the Isosceles, that his posterity may ultimately rise above his degraded condition....

back to top

Rarely—in proportion to the vast numbers of Isosceles births—is a genuine and

Unfortunately, the links won't work yet. We still need to insert the anchor with `id="top"`. For this, we can use one of the methods that insert elements inside of other elements.

```
$(document).ready(function() {
  $('<a href="#top">back to top</a>')
    .insertAfter('div.chapter p');
  $('<a id="top" name="top"></a>')
    .prependTo('body');
});
```

This additional code inserts the anchor right at the beginning of the `<body>`; in other words, at the top of the page. Now, with the `.insertAfter()` method for the links and the `.prependTo()` method for the anchor, we have a fully functioning set of **back to top** links for the page.

With **back to top** links, it doesn't make much sense to have them appear when the top of the page is still visible. A quick improvement to the script would start the links only after, say, the fourth paragraph. This is easy to accomplish with a little change to the selector expression: `.insertAfter('div.chapter p:gt(2)')`. Why the 2 here? Remember that JavaScript indexing starts at 0; therefore, the first paragraph is indexed as 0, the second is 1, the third is 2, and the fourth paragraph is 3. Our selector expression begins inserting the links after each paragraph when the index reaches 3, because that is the first one greater than 2.

The effect of this selector-expression change is now evident:

Flatland: A Romance of Many Dimensions
by Edwin A. Abbott

Part 1, Section 3

Concerning the Inhabitants of Flatland
an excerpt

Our Professional Men and Gentlemen are Squares (to which class I myself belong) and Five-Sided Figures or Pentagons.

Next above these come the Nobility, of whom there are several degrees, beginning at Six-Sided Figures, or Hexagons, and from thence rising in the number of their sides till they receive the honourable title of Polygonal, or many-Sided. Finally when the number of the sides becomes so numerous, and the sides themselves so small, that the figure cannot be distinguished from a circle, he is included in the Circular or Priestly order; and this is the highest class of all.

It is a Law of Nature with us that a male child shall have **one more side** than his father, so that each generation shall rise (as a rule) one step in the scale of development and nobility. Thus the son of a Square is a Pentagon; the son of a Pentagon, a Hexagon; and so on.

But this rule applies not always to the Tradesman, and still less often to the Soldiers, and to the Workmen; who indeed can hardly be said to deserve the name of human Figures, since they have not all their sides equal. With them therefore the Law of Nature does not hold; and the son of an Isosceles (i.e. a Triangle with two sides equal) remains Isosceles still. Nevertheless, all hope is not such out, even from the Isosceles, that his posterity may ultimately rise above his degraded condition....

back to top

Rarely—in proportion to the vast numbers of Isosceles births—is a genuine and certifiable Equal-Sided Triangle produced from Isosceles parents. *"What need of a*

Moving elements

With the **back to top** links, we created new elements and inserted them on the page. It's also possible to take elements from one place on the page and insert them into another place. A practical application of this type of insertion is the dynamic placement and formatting of footnotes. One footnote already appears in the original *Flatland* text that we are using for this example, but we'll also designate a couple of other portions of the text as footnotes for the purpose of this demonstration:

```
<p>Rarely&mdash;in proportion to the vast numbers of Isosceles
    births&mdash;is a genuine and certifiable Equal-Sided
    Triangle produced from Isosceles parents. <span
    class="footnote">"What need of a certificate?" a Spaceland
    critic may ask: "Is not the procreation of a Square Son a
    certificate from Nature herself, proving the Equalsidedness
    of the Father?" I reply that no Lady of any position will
    marry an uncertified Triangle. Square offspring has
    sometimes resulted from a slightly Irregular Triangle;
    but in almost every such case the Irregularity of the
    first generation is visited on the third; which either
    fails to attain the Pentagonal rank, or relapses to the
    Triangular.</span> Such a birth requires, as its
    antecedents, not only a series of carefully arranged
    intermarriages, but also a long-continued exercise of
    frugality and self-control on the part of the would-be
    ancestors of the coming Equilateral, and a patient,
    systematic, and continuous development of the Isosceles
    intellect through many generations.
</p>
<p>The birth of a True Equilateral Triangle from Isosceles
    parents is the subject of rejoicing in our country for many
    furlongs round. After a strict examination conducted by the
    Sanitary and Social Board, the infant, if certified as
    Regular, is with solemn ceremonial admitted into the class
    of Equilaterals. He is then immediately taken from his
    proud yet sorrowing parents and adopted by some childless
    Equilateral. <span class="footnote">The Equilateral is
    bound by oath never to permit the child henceforth to enter
    his former home or so much as to look upon his relations
    again, for fear lest the freshly developed organism may, by
    force of unconscious imitation, fall back again into his
    hereditary level.</span>
</p>
<p>How admirable is the Law of Compensation! <span
```

```
class="footnote">And how perfect a proof of the natural
fitness and, I may almost say, the divine origin of the
aristocratic constitution of the States of Flatland!</span>
By a judicious use of this Law of Nature, the Polygons and
Circles are almost always able to stifle sedition in its
very cradle, taking advantage of the irrepressible and
boundless hopefulness of the human mind.&hellip;
</p>
```

Each of these three paragraphs has a single footnote wrapped inside `<span class="footnote"></span>`. By marking up the HTML in this way, we can preserve the context of the footnote. With a CSS rule applied in the stylesheet to italicize the footnotes, the three paragraphs look like this:

Rarely—in proportion to the vast numbers of Isosceles births—is a genuine and certifiable Equal-Sided Triangle produced from Isosceles parents. *"What need of a certificate?" a Spaceland critic may ask: "Is not the procreation of a Square Son a certificate from Nature herself, proving the Equal-sidedness of the Father?" I reply that no Lady of any position will marry an uncertified Triangle. Square offspring has sometimes resulted from a slightly Irregular Triangle; but in almost every such case the Irregularity of the first generation is visited on the third; which either fails to attain the Pentagonal rank, or relapses to the Triangular.* Such a birth requires, as its antecedents, not only a series of carefully arranged intermarriages, but also a long-continued exercise of frugality and self-control on the part of the would-be ancestors of the coming Equilateral, and a patient, systematic, and continuous development of the Isosceles intellect through many generations.

back to top

The birth of a True Equilateral Triangle from Isosceles parents is the subject of rejoicing in our country for many furlongs round. After a strict examination conducted by the Sanitary and Social Board, the infant, if certified as Regular, is with solemn ceremonial admitted into the class of Equilaterals. He is then immediately taken from his proud yet sorrowing parents and adopted by some childless Equilateral. *The Equilateral is bound by oath never to permit the child henceforth to enter his former home or so much as to look upon his relations again, for fear lest the freshly developed organism may, by force of unconscious imitation, fall back again into his hereditary level.*

back to top

How admirable is the Law of Compensation! *And how perfect a proof of the natural fitness and, I may almost say, the divine origin of the aristocratic constitution of the States of Flatland!* By a judicious use of this Law of Nature, the Polygons and Circles are almost always able to stifle sedition in its very cradle, taking advantage of the irrepressible and boundless hopefulness of the human mind....

Now we can grab the footnotes and insert them in between `<div class="chapter">` and `<div id="footer">`. Keep in mind that even in cases of implicit iteration, the order of insertion is predefined, starting at the top of the DOM tree and working its way down. Since it's important to maintain the correct order of the footnotes in their new place on the page, we should use `.insertBefore('#footer')`.

This will place each footnote directly before the `<div id="footer">` so that footnote 1 is placed between `<div class="chapter">` and `<div id="footer">`, footnote 2 is placed between footnote 1 and `<div id="footer">`, and so on. Using `.insertAfter('div.chapter')`, on the other hand, would have the footnotes appear in reverse order. So far, our code looks like this:

```
$(document).ready(function() {
  $('span.footnote').insertBefore('#footer');
});
```

Unfortunately, though, we've run into a big problem. The footnotes are in `<span>` tags, which means they display `inline` by default, one right after the other with no separation:

> *"What need of a certificate?" a Spaceland critic may ask: "Is not the procreation of a Square Son a certificate from Nature herself, proving the Equal-sidedness of the Father?" I reply that no Lady of any position will marry an uncertified Triangle. Square offspring has sometimes resulted from a slightly Irregular Triangle; but in almost every such case the Irregularity of the first generation is visited on the third; which either fails to attain the Pentagonal rank, or relapses to the Triangular. The Equilateral is bound by oath never to permit the child henceforth to enter his former home or so much as to look upon his relations again, for fear lest the freshly developed organism may, by force of unconscious imitation, fall back again into his hereditary level. And how perfect a proof of the natural fitness and, I may almost say, the divine origin of the aristocratic constitution of the States of Flatland!*

One solution to this problem is to modify the CSS, making the `<span>` elements display as blocks, but only if they are not inside `<div class="chapter">`:

```
span.footnote {
  font-style: italic;
  font-family: "Times New Roman", Times, serif;
  display: block;
  margin: 1em 0;
}
.chapter span.footnote {
  display: inline;
}
```

The footnotes are now beginning to take shape:

> *"What need of a certificate?" a Spaceland critic may ask: "Is not the procreation of a Square Son a certificate from Nature herself, proving the Equal-sidedness of the Father?" I reply that no Lady of any position will marry an uncertified Triangle. Square offspring has sometimes resulted from a slightly Irregular Triangle; but in almost every such case the Irregularity of the first generation is visited on the third; which either fails to attain the Pentagonal rank, or relapses to the Triangular.*
>
> *The Equilateral is bound by oath never to permit the child henceforth to enter his former home or so much as to look upon his relations again, for fear lest the freshly developed organism may, by force of unconscious imitation, fall back again into his hereditary level.*
>
> *And how perfect a proof of the natural fitness and, I may almost say, the divine origin of the aristocratic constitution of the States of Flatland!*

At least they are distinct footnotes now; yet there is still a lot of work that can be done to them. A more robust footnote solution should:

1. Mark the location in the text from which each footnote is pulled.
2. Number each location, and provide a matching number for the footnote itself.
3. Create a link from the text location to its matching footnote, and from the footnote back to the text location.

These steps can be accomplished from within an `.each()` method; but first we'll set up a container element for the notes at the bottom of the page:

```
$(document).ready(function() {
  $('<ol id="notes"></ol>').insertAfter('div.chapter');
});
```

It seems reasonable enough to use an ordered list `<ol id="notes"></ol>` for the footnotes; after all, we want them to be numbered. Why not use an element that numbers them for us automatically? We've given the list an ID of `notes` and have inserted it after `<div class="chapter">`.

Marking, numbering, and linking the context

Now we're ready to mark and number the place from which we're pulling the footnote:

```
$(document).ready(function() {
  $('<ol id="notes"></ol>').insertAfter('div.chapter');
  $('span.footnote').each(function(index) {
    $(this)
      .before(
        ['<a href="#foot-note-',
          index+1,
          '" id="context-',
          index+1,
          '" class="context">',
          '<sup>' + (index+1) + '</sup>',
          '</a>'
        ].join('')
      )
  });
});
```

Here we start with the same selector as we used with the simpler footnote example, but we chain the `.each()` method to it.

Inside the `.each()` we begin with `$(this)`, which represents each footnote in succession, and we chain the `.before()` method to it.

The result of the **joined array** within the `.before()` method's parentheses is a superscripted link, that will be inserted before each footnote `<span>`. The first one, for example, will look like this when it's inserted in the DOM:

```
<a href="#foot-note-1" id="context-1"
                        class="context"><sup>1</sup></a>
```

The syntax may be unfamiliar at first glance, so let's take a moment to investigate what is going on. Inside the parentheses of the `.before()` method, we start with a pair of square brackets — `[ ]` — which represents an **array literal**. Each element within the array is followed by a comma (except, importantly, the final element). We've placed each element on its own line for the sake of readability. Then, once the array is built, we convert it back into a string by using the JavaScript `.join()` method. This method gets an empty string as its argument, represented by a pair of single quotation marks, because we don't want anything to appear between each array item when it is output as HTML.

Note the use of `index+1` throughout. Since counting begins at 0, we add 1 to start the `href` attributes at `#footnote-1`, the `id` attributes at `#context-1` and the actual link text at **1**. The `href` is particularly important because it must exactly match the footnote's `id` attribute (not including the # of course).

To be sure, the same result can be accomplished with a long concatenated string rather than a joined array:

```
.before('<a href="#foot-note-' + (index+1) +
            '" id="context-' + (index+1) +
               '" class="context"><sup>' +
            (index+1) + '</sup></a>');
```

Yet in this case, the array technique seems more manageable.

Much has been written on the web about the performance differences between joined arrays and concatenated strings. For the ultra-curious, the following article discusses a number of benchmark tests using the two techniques: http://www.sitepen.com/blog/2008/05/09/string-performance-an-analysis/

In most situations, however, these differences are imperceptible. If a script's performance is an issue, there are a number of other areas that have far greater impact (such as "caching" selectors, which we've already discussed).

Our three linked footnote markers now look like this:

Rarely—in proportion to the vast numbers of Isosceles births—is a genuine and certifiable Equal-Sided Triangle produced from Isosceles parents. [1] Such a birth requires, as its antecedents, not only a series of carefully arranged intermarriages, but also a long-continued exercise of frugality and self-control on the part of the would-be ancestors of the coming Equilateral, and a patient, systematic, and continuous development of the Isosceles intellect through many generations.

back to top

The birth of a True Equilateral Triangle from Isosceles parents is the subject of rejoicing in our country for many furlongs round. After a strict examination conducted by the Sanitary and Social Board, the infant, if certified as Regular, is with solemn ceremonial admitted into the class of Equilaterals. He is then immediately taken from his proud yet sorrowing parents and adopted by some childless Equilateral. [2]

back to top

How admirable is the Law of Compensation! [3] By a judicious use of this Law of Nature, the Polygons and Circles are almost always able to stifle sedition in its very cradle, taking advantage of the irrepressible and boundless hopefulness of the human mind....

three footnote markers

Appending footnotes

The next step is to move the `<span class="footnote">` elements, as we did with the simpler example. This time, however, we drop them into the newly created `<ol id="notes">`. We'll use `.appendTo()` here, again to maintain proper ordering, as each successive footnote will be inserted at the end of the element:

```
$(document).ready(function() {
    $('<ol id="notes"></ol>').insertAfter('div.chapter');
    $('span.footnote').each(function(index) {
      $(this)
        .before(
          ['<a href="#foot-note-',
            index+1,
            '" id="context-',
            index+1,
            '" class="context">',
            '<sup>' + (index+1) + '</sup>',
            '</a>'
          ].join('')
        )
        .appendTo('#notes')
    });
});
```

It's important to remember that `.appendTo()` is still being chained to `$(this)`, so that jQuery is saying, *Append the footnote span to the element with an ID of 'notes'*.

To each of the footnotes we just moved, we append another link—this one back to the number in the text:

```
$(document).ready(function() {
  $('<ol id="notes"></ol>').insertAfter('div.chapter');
  $('span.footnote').each(function(index) {
    $(this)
      .before(
        ['<a href="#foot-note-',
          index+1,
          '" id="context-',
          index+1,
          '" class="context">',
          '<sup>' + (index+1) + '</sup>',
          '</a>'
        ].join('')
      )
      .appendTo('#notes')
      .append( ' (<a href="#context-' + (index+1) +
                                  '">context</a>)' );
  });
});
```

Notice that the `href` points back to the `id` of the corresponding marker. Here you can see the footnotes again with a link appended to each:

The footnotes still lack their numbers, however. Even though they have been placed within an `<ol>`, each one must also be individually wrapped in its own `<li>`.

Wrapping elements

jQuery's primary method for wrapping elements around other elements is the appropriately named `.wrap()`. Because we want each `$(this)` to be wrapped in `<li></li>`, we can complete our footnote code like so:

```
$(document).ready(function() {
  $('<ol id="notes"></ol>').insertAfter('div.chapter');
  $('span.footnote').each(function(index) {
    $(this)
      .before(
        ['<a href="#foot-note-',
          index+1,
          '" id="context-',
          index+1,
          '" class="context">',
          '<sup>' + (index+1) + '</sup>',
          '</a>'
        ].join('')
      )
      .appendTo('#notes')
      .append( ' (<a href="#context-' + (index+1) +
                               '">context</a>)' )
      .wrap('<li id="foot-note-' + (index+1) +
                                '"></li>');
  });
});
```

Now each of the `<li>` elements comes complete with an `id` that matches the marker's `href`. At last, we have a set of numbered, linked footnotes:

1. *"What need of a certificate?" a Spaceland critic may ask: "Is not the procreation of a Square Son a certificate from Nature herself, proving the Equal-sidedness of the Father?" I reply that no Lady of any position will marry an uncertified Triangle. Square offspring has sometimes resulted from a slightly Irregular Triangle; but in almost every such case the Irregularity of the first generation is visited on the third; which either fails to attain the Pentagonal rank, or relapses to the Triangular. (context)*

2. *The Equilateral is bound by oath never to permit the child henceforth to enter his former home or so much as to look upon his relations again, for fear lest the freshly developed organism may, by force of unconscious imitation, fall back again into his hereditary level. (context)*

3. *And how perfect a proof of the natural fitness and, I may almost say, the divine origin of the aristocratic constitution of the States of Flatland! (context)*

Of course, the numbers could have been inserted before each footnote the same way they were in the paragraphs, but there is something deeply satisfying about having semantic markup dynamically generated by JavaScript.

The other jQuery methods for wrapping elements are `.wrapAll()` and `.wrapInner()`. See `http://docs.jquery.com/Manipulation/wrapAll` and `http://docs.jquery.com/Manipulation/wrapInner` for more information.

Copying elements

So far in this chapter we have inserted newly created elements, moved elements from one location in the document to another, and wrapped new elements around existing ones. Sometimes, though, we may want to copy elements. For example, a navigation menu that appears in the page's header could be copied and placed in the footer as well. In fact, whenever elements can be copied to enhance a page visually, it's a good opportunity to use a script. After all, why write something twice and double our chance of error when we can write it once and let jQuery do the heavy lifting?

For copying elements, jQuery's `.clone()` method is just what we need; it takes any set of matched elements and creates a copy of them for later use. As with the element creation process we explored earlier in this chapter, the copied elements will not appear in the document until we apply one of the insertion methods. For example, the following line creates a copy of the first paragraph inside `<div class="chapter">`:

```
$('div.chapter p:eq(0)').clone();
```

So far, the content on the page hasn't changed:

> **Concerning the Inhabitants of Flatland**
> *an excerpt*
>
> Our Professional Men and Gentlemen are Squares (to which class I myself belong) and Five-Sided Figures or Pentagons.
>
> Next above these come the Nobility, of whom there are several degrees, beginning at Six-Sided Figures, or Hexagons, and from thence rising in the number of their sides till they receive the honourable title of Polygonal, or many-Sided. Finally when the number of the sides becomes so numerous, and the sides themselves so small, that the figure cannot be distinguished from a circle, he is included in the Circular or Priestly order; and this is the highest class of all.
>
> It is a Law of Nature with us that a male child shall have **one more side** than his father, so that each generation shall rise (as a rule) one step in the scale of development and nobility. Thus the son of a Square is a Pentagon; the son of a

To continue the example, we can make the cloned paragraph appear before `<div class="chapter">`:

```
$('div.chapter p:eq(0)').clone().insertBefore('div.chapter');
```

Now the first paragraph appears twice, and because the first instance of it is no longer inside `<div class="chapter">`, it does not retain the styles associated with the div (most noticeably, the width):

Concerning the Inhabitants of Flatland
an excerpt

Our Professional Men and Gentlemen are Squares (to which class I myself belong) and Five-Sided Figures or <u>Pentagons</u>.

Our Professional Men and Gentlemen are Squares (to which class I myself belong) and Five-Sided Figures or <u>Pentagons</u>.

Next above these come the Nobility, of whom there are several degrees, beginning at Six-Sided Figures, or <u>Hexagons</u>, and from thence rising in the number of their sides till they receive the honourable title of <u>Polygonal</u>, or many-Sided. Finally when the number of the sides becomes so numerous, and the sides themselves so small, that the figure cannot be distinguished from a <u>circle</u>, he is included in the Circular or Priestly order; and this is the highest class of all.

It is a Law of Nature with us that a male child shall have **one more side** than his father, so that each generation shall rise (as a rule) one step in the scale of development and nobility. Thus the son of a Square is a Pentagon; the son of a

So, using an analogy that most people should be familiar with, `.clone()` is to the insertion methods as copy is to paste.

Clone with events

The `.clone()` method by default does not copy any **events** that are bound to the matching element or any of its descendants. However, it can take a single Boolean parameter that, when set to `true`, clones events as well: `.clone(true)`. This convenient event cloning allows us to avoid having to deal with manually rebinding events, as was discussed in Chapter 3.

Cloning for pull quotes

Many websites, like their print counterparts, use **pull quotes** to emphasize small portions of text and attract the reader's eye. We can easily accomplish this embellishment with the `.clone()` method. First, let's take another look at the third paragraph of our example text:

```
<p>
  <span class="pull-quote">It is a Law of Nature
  <span class="drop">with us</span> that a male child shall
  have <strong>one more side</strong> than his father</span>,
```

```
    so that each generation shall rise (as a rule) one step in
    the scale of development and nobility. Thus the son of a
    Square is a Pentagon; the son of a Pentagon, a Hexagon; and
    so on.
</p>
```

Notice that the paragraph begins with `<span class="pull-quote">`. This is the class we will be targeting for cloning. Once the copied text inside that `<span>` is pasted into another place, we need to modify its style properties to set it apart from the rest of the text.

A CSS diversion

To accomplish this type of styling, we'll add a `pulled` class to the copied `<span>` and give the class the following style rule in the stylesheet:

```
.pulled {
  background: #e5e5e5;
  position: absolute;
  width: 145px;
  top: -20px;
  right: -180px;
  padding: 12px 5px 12px 10px;
  font: italic 1.4em "Times New Roman", Times, serif;
}
```

The pull quote now gets a light gray background, some padding, and a different font. Most important, it's absolutely positioned, 20 pixels above and 20 pixels to the right of the nearest (`absolute` or `relative`) positioned ancestor in the DOM. If no ancestor has positioning (other than `static`) applied, the pull quote will be positioned relative to the document `<body>`. Because of this, we need to make sure in the jQuery code that the cloned pull quote's parent element has `position: relative` set.

While the top positioning is fairly intuitive, it may not be clear at first how the pull quote box will be located 20 pixels to the left of its positioned parent. We derive the number first from the total width of the pull-quote box, which is the value of the width property plus the left and right padding, or 145 px + 5 px + 10 px, or 160 px. We then set the `right` property of the pull quote. A value of 0 would align the pull quote's right side with that of its parent. Therefore, to place its left side 20 px to the right of the parent, we need to move it in a negative direction 20 pixels more than its total width, or -180 px.

Back to the code

Now we can get into the jQuery. Let's start with a selector expression for all of the `<span class="pull-quote">` elements, and attach an `.each()` method so that we can perform multiple actions as we iterate through them:

```
$(document).ready(function() {
  $('span.pull-quote').each(function(index) {
    //...
  });
});
```

Next, we find the parent paragraph of each pull quote and apply the CSS `position` property:

```
$(document).ready(function() {
  $('span.pull-quote').each(function(index) {
    var $parentParagraph = $(this).parent('p');
    $parentParagraph.css('position', 'relative');
  });
});
```

Once again, we store any selector that we'll be using more than once in a variable to improve performance and readability.

We can be sure now that the CSS is all set and ready for the pull quote. At this point we can clone each `<span>`, add the `pulled` class to the copy, and insert it into the beginning of the paragraph:

```
$(document).ready(function() {
  $('span.pull-quote').each(function(index) {
    var $parentParagraph = $(this).parent('p');
    $parentParagraph.css('position', 'relative');
    $(this).clone()
      .addClass('pulled')
      .prependTo($parentParagraph);
  });
});
```

Because we're using absolute positioning for the pull quote, the placement of it within the paragraph is irrelevant. As long as it remains inside the paragraph, it will be positioned in relation to the top and right of the paragraph, based on our CSS rules. If, however, we wanted to apply a `float` to the pull quote instead, its placement within the paragraph would affect its vertical position.

The paragraph, together with its pull quote, now looks like this:

> Circular or Priestly order; and this is the highest class of all.
>
> It is a Law of Nature with us that a male child shall have **one more side** than his father, so that each generation shall rise (as a rule) one step in the scale of development and nobility. Thus the son of a Square is a Pentagon; the son of a Pentagon, a Hexagon; and so on.
>
> But this rule applies not always to the Tradesman, and still less often to the Soldiers, and to the Workmen; who indeed can hardly be said to deserve the name of human Figures, since they have not all their sides equal. With them therefore the Law of Nature does not hold; and the son of an Isosceles (i.e. a Triangle with
>
> > *It is a Law of Nature with us that a male child shall have **one more side** than his father*

This is a good start, but pull quotes typically do not retain font formatting as this one does with the bold **one more side** text. What we want is the text of `<span class="pull-quote">`, stripped of any `<strong>`, `<em>`, `<a href>` or other inline tags. Additionally, it would be nice to be able to modify the pull quote a bit, dropping some words and replacing them with ellipses. For this, we have wrapped a few words of text in the example in a `<span>` tag: `<span class="drop">with us</span>`.

We'll apply the ellipsis first, and then replace all of the pull-quote HTML with a stripped, text-only version:

```
$(document).ready(function() {
  $('span.pull-quote').each(function(index) {
    var $parentParagraph = $(this).parent('p');
    $parentParagraph.css('position', 'relative');
    var $clonedCopy = $(this).clone();
    $clonedCopy
      .addClass('pulled')
      .find('span.drop')
        .html('&hellip;')
      .end()
      .prependTo($parentParagraph);
    var clonedText = $clonedCopy.text();
    $clonedCopy.html(clonedText);
  });
});
```

So, we start the cloning process this time by storing the clone in a variable. The variable is necessary this time because we can't work on it completely within the same chain. Notice, too, that after we find `<span class="drop">` and replace its HTML with an ellipsis (`&hellip;`), we use `.end()` to back out of the last query, `.find('span.drop')`. This way, we're inserting the whole copy, not just the ellipsis, at the beginning of the paragraph.

At the end, we set one more variable, `clonedText`, to the text-only contents of the copy; then we use these text-only contents as a replacement for the HTML of the copy. Now, the pull quote looks like this:

Circular or Priestly order; and this is the highest class of all.

It is a Law of Nature with us that a male child shall have **one more side** than his father, so that each generation shall rise (as a rule) one step in the scale of development and nobility. Thus the son of a Square is a Pentagon; the son of a Pentagon, a Hexagon; and so on.

But this rule applies not always to the Tradesman, and still less often to the Soldiers, and to the Workmen; who indeed can hardly be said to deserve the name of human Figures, since they have not all their sides equal. With them therefore the Law of Nature does not hold; and the son of an Isosceles (i.e. a Triangle with two sides equal) remains Isosceles still. Nevertheless, all hope is not such out, even from the Isosceles, that his posterity may ultimately rise above his degraded condition....

back to top

Rarely—in proportion to the vast numbers of Isosceles births—is a genuine and certifiable Equal-Sided Triangle produced from Isosceles parents. [1] Such a birth requires, as its antecedents, not only a series of carefully arranged intermarriages, but also a long-continued exercise of frugality and self-control on the part of the would-be ancestors of the coming Equilateral, and a patient, systematic, and continuous development of the Isosceles intellect through many generations.

back to top

The birth of a True Equilateral Triangle from Isosceles parents is the subject of rejoicing in our country for many furlongs round. After a strict examination conducted by the Sanitary and Social Board, the infant, if certified as Regular, is with solemn ceremonial admitted into the class of Equilaterals. He is then immediately taken from his proud yet sorrowing parents and adopted by some childless Equilateral. [2]

back to top

It is a Law of Nature ... that a male child shall have one more side than his father

The birth of a True Equilateral Triangle from Isosceles parents is the subject of rejoicing in our country ....

Evidently, another `<span class="pull-quote">` has been added to a later paragraph to ensure that the code works for multiple elements.

Prettifying the pull quotes

The pull quotes are now working as expected, with child elements stripped and ellipses added where text should be dropped.

Since one of the goals is to add visual appeal, though, we would do well to give the pull quotes rounded corners with drop shadows. However, the variable height of the pull-quote boxes is problematic because we'll need to apply two background images to a single element, which is impossible for every browser at the moment except the most recent builds of Safari.

To overcome this limitation, we can wrap another `<div>` around the pull quotes:

```
$(document).ready(function() {
  $('span.pull-quote').each(function(index) {
    var $parentParagraph = $(this).parent('p');
    $parentParagraph.css('position', 'relative');
    var $clonedCopy = $(this).clone();
    $clonedCopy
      .addClass('pulled')
      .find('span.drop')
        .html('&hellip;')
      .end()
      .prependTo($parentParagraph)
      .wrap('<div class="pulled-wrapper"></div>');
    var clonedText = $clonedCopy.text();
    $clonedCopy.html(clonedText);
  });
});
```

We also need to modify the CSS, of course, to account for the new `<div>` and the two background images:

```
.pulled-wrapper {
  background: url(pq-top.jpg) no-repeat left top;
  position: absolute;
  width: 160px;
  right: -180px;
  padding-top: 18px;
}
.pulled {
  background: url(pq-bottom.jpg) no-repeat left bottom;
  position: relative;
  display: block;
  width: 140px;
  padding: 0 10px 24px 10px;
  font: italic 1.4em "Times New Roman", Times, serif;
}
```

Here, some of the rules formerly applied to `<span class="pulled">` are applied to `<div class="pulled-wrapper">` instead. A couple of width and padding adjustments take into account the design of the background image borders, and the `.pulled` rule has its `position` and `display` properties modified in order to appear correctly for all browsers.

Here is one final look at the newly primped pull quotes in their native habitat:

It is a Law of Nature with us that a male child shall have **one more side** than his father, so that each generation shall rise (as a rule) one step in the scale of development and nobility. Thus the son of a Square is a Pentagon; the son of a Pentagon, a Hexagon; and so on.

But this rule applies not always to the Tradesman, and still less often to the Soldiers, and to the Workmen; who indeed can hardly be said to deserve the name of human Figures, since they have not all their sides equal. With them therefore the Law of Nature does not hold; and the son of an Isosceles (i.e. a Triangle with two sides equal) remains Isosceles still. Nevertheless, all hope is not such out, even from the Isosceles, that his posterity may ultimately rise above his degraded condition....

back to top

It is a Law of Nature ... that a male child shall have one more side than his father

Rarely—in proportion to the vast numbers of Isosceles births—is a genuine and certifiable Equal-Sided Triangle produced from Isosceles parents. [1] Such a birth requires, as its antecedents, not only a series of carefully arranged intermarriages, but also a long-continued exercise of frugality and self-control on the part of the would-be ancestors of the coming Equilateral, and a patient, systematic, and continuous development of the Isosceles intellect through many generations.

back to top

The birth of a True Equilateral Triangle from Isosceles parents is the subject of rejoicing in our country for many furlongs round. After a strict examination conducted by the Sanitary and Social Board, the infant, if certified as Regular, is with solemn ceremonial admitted into the class of Equilaterals. He is then immediately taken from his proud yet sorrowing parents and adopted by some childless Equilateral. [2]

back to top

The birth of a True Equilateral Triangle from Isosceles parents is the subject of rejoicing in our country ....

How admirable is the Law of Compensation! [3] By a judicious use of this Law of

DOM manipulation methods in a nutshell

The extensive DOM manipulation methods that jQuery provides vary according to their task and their location. The following outline can serve as a reminder of which methods we can use to accomplish any of these tasks, just about anywhere.

1. To **create** new elements from HTML, user the $() factory function.
2. To **insert** new element(s) **inside** every matched element, use:
   - `.append()`
   - `.appendTo()`
   - `.prepend()`
   - `.prependTo()`

3. To **insert** new element(s) **adjacent** to every matched element, use:
   - `.after()`
   - `.insertAfter()`
   - `.before()`
   - `.insertBefore()`

4. To **insert** new element(s) **around** every matched element, use:
   - `.wrap()`
   - `.wrapAll()`
   - `.wrapInner()`

5. To **replace** every matched element with new element(s) or text, use:
   - `.html()`
   - `.text()`
   - `.replaceAll()`
   - `.replaceWith()`

6. To **remove** element(s) **inside** every matched element, use:
   - `.empty()`

7. To **remove** every matched element and descendants from the document without actually deleting them, use:
   - `.remove()`

Summary

In this chapter we have created, copied, reassembled, and embellished content using jQuery's DOM modification methods. We've applied these methods to a single web page, transforming a handful of generic paragraphs to a footnoted, pull quoted, linked, and stylized literary excerpt.

The tutorial section of the book is nearly over, but before we move on to examine more complex, expanded examples, let's take a round-trip journey to the server via jQuery's AJAX methods.

AJAX

In recent years, it has become common to judge sites based on their use of specific technologies. One of the most prominent buzzwords used to describe new web applications is **AJAX-powered**. This label has been used to mean many different things, as the term encompasses a group of related capabilities and techniques.

Technically, **AJAX** is an acronym standing for **Asynchronous JavaScript and XML**. The technologies involved in an AJAX solution include:

- *JavaScript*, to capture interactions with the user or other browser-related events
- The **XMLHttpRequest** object, which allows requests to be made to the server without interrupting other browser tasks
- *XML* files on the server, or often other similar data formats such as HTML or JSON
- More *JavaScript*, to interpret the data from the server and present it on the page

AJAX technology has been hailed as the savior of the web landscape, transforming static web pages into interactive web applications. Many frameworks have sprung up to assist developers in taming it, because of the inconsistencies in the browsers' implementations of the XMLHttpRequest object; jQuery is no exception.

Let us see if AJAX can truly perform miracles.

Loading data on demand

Underneath all the hype and trappings, AJAX is just a means of loading data from the **server** to the web browser, or **client**, without a visible page refresh. This data can take many forms, and we have many options for what to do with it when it arrives. We'll see this by performing the same basic task in many ways.

We are going to build a page that displays entries from a dictionary, grouped by the starting letter of the dictionary entry. The HTML defining the content area of the page will look like this:

```
<div id="dictionary">
</div>
```

Yes, really! Our page will have no content to begin with. We are going to use jQuery's various AJAX methods to populate this `<div>` with dictionary entries.

We're going to need a way to trigger the loading process, so we'll add some links for our **event handlers** to latch onto:

```
<div class="letters">
  <div class="letter" id="letter-a">
    <h3><a href="#">A</a></h3>
  </div>
  <div class="letter" id="letter-b">
    <h3><a href="#">B</a></h3>
  </div>
  <div class="letter" id="letter-c">
    <h3><a href="#">C</a></h3>
  </div>
  <div class="letter" id="letter-d">
    <h3><a href="#">D</a></h3>
  </div>
</div>
```

As always, a real-world implementation should use **progressive enhancement** to make the page function without requiring JavaScript. Here, to simplify our example, the links do nothing until we add behaviors to them with jQuery.

Adding a few CSS rules, we get a page that looks like this:

The Devil's Dictionary

by Ambrose Bierce

A

B

C

D

Now we can focus on getting content onto the page.

Appending HTML

AJAX applications are often no more than a request for a chunk of HTML. This technique, sometimes referred to as **AHAH (Asynchronous HTTP and HTML)**, is almost trivial to implement with jQuery. First we need some HTML to insert, which we'll place in a file called a.html alongside our main document. This secondary HTML file begins:

```
<div class="entry">
  <h3 class="term">ABDICATION</h3>
  <div class="part">n.</div>
  <div class="definition">
    An act whereby a sovereign attests his sense of the high
    temperature of the throne.
    <div class="quote">
      <div class="quote-line">Poor Isabella's Dead, whose
          abdication</div>
      <div class="quote-line">Set all tongues wagging in the
          Spanish nation.</div>
      <div class="quote-line">For that performance 'twere
          unfair to scold her:</div>
      <div class="quote-line">She wisely left a throne too
          hot to hold her.</div>
      <div class="quote-line">To History she'll be no royal
          riddle &mdash;</div>
      <div class="quote-line">Merely a plain parched pea that
          jumped the griddle.</div>
      <div class="quote-author">G.J.</div>
    </div>
  </div>
</div>

<div class="entry">
  <h3 class="term">ABSOLUTE</h3>
  <div class="part">adj.</div>
  <div class="definition">
    Independent, irresponsible.  An absolute monarchy is one
    in which the sovereign does as he pleases so long as he
    pleases the assassins.  Not many absolute monarchies are
    left, most of them having been replaced by limited
    monarchies, where the sovereign's power for evil (and for
    good) is greatly curtailed, and by republics, which are
    governed by chance.
  </div>
</div>
```

The page continues with more entries in this HTML structure. Rendered on its own, this page is quite plain:

ABDICATION

n.

An act whereby a sovereign attests his sense of the high temperature of the throne.
Poor Isabella's Dead, whose abdication
Set all tongues wagging in the Spanish nation.
For that performance 'twere unfair to scold her:
She wisely left a throne too hot to hold her.
To History she'll be no royal riddle —
Merely a plain parched pea that jumped the griddle.
G.J.

ABSOLUTE

adj.

Independent, irresponsible. An absolute monarchy is one in which the sovereign does as he pleases so long as he pleases the assassins. Not many absolute monarchies are left, most of them having been replaced by limited monarchies, where the sovereign's power for evil (and for good) is greatly curtailed, and by republics, which are governed by chance.

ACKNOWLEDGE

v.t.

To confess. Acknowledgement of one another's faults is the highest duty imposed by our love of truth.

Note that `a.html` is not a true HTML document; it contains no `<html>`, `<head>`, or `<body>`, all of which are normally required. We usually call such a file a **snippet** or **fragment**; its only purpose is to be inserted into another HTML document, which we'll accomplish now:

```
$(document).ready(function() {
  $('#letter-a a').click(function() {
    $('#dictionary').load('a.html');
    return false;
  });
});
```

The `.load()` method does all our heavy lifting for us! We specify the target location for the HTML snippet by using a normal jQuery selector, and then pass the URL of the file to be loaded as a parameter to the method. Now, when the first link is clicked, the file is loaded and placed inside `<div id="dictionary">`. The browser will render the new HTML as soon as it is inserted:

The Devil's Dictionary

by Ambrose Bierce

A

B

C

D

ABDICATION   *n.*

An act whereby a sovereign attests his sense of the high temperature of the throne.

> Poor Isabella's Dead, whose abdication
> Set all tongues wagging in the Spanish nation.
> For that performance 'twere unfair to scold her:
> She wisely left a throne too hot to hold her.
> To History she'll be no royal riddle —
> Merely a plain parched pea that jumped the griddle.
>   G.J.

ABSOLUTE   *adj.*

Independent, irresponsible. An absolute monarchy is one in which the sovereign does as he pleases so long as he pleases the assassins. Not many absolute monarchies are left, most of them having been replaced by limited monarchies, where the sovereign's power for evil (and for good) is greatly curtailed, and by republics, which are governed by chance.

ACKNOWLEDGE   *v.t.*

To confess. Acknowledgement of one another's faults is the highest duty imposed by our love of truth.

AFFIANCED   *pp.*

Fitted with an ankle-ring for the ball-and-chain.

Note that the HTML is now styled, whereas before it was plain. This is due to the CSS rules in the main document; as soon as the new HTML snippet is inserted, the rules apply to its tags as well.

When testing this example, the dictionary definitions will probably appear instantaneously when the button is clicked. This is a hazard of working on our applications locally; it is hard to account for delays in transferring documents across the network. Suppose we added an alert box to display after the definitions are loaded:

```
$(document).ready(function() {
  $('#letter-a a').click(function() {
    $('#dictionary').load('a.html');
    alert('Loaded!');
    return false;
  });
});
```

We might assume from the structure of this code that the alert can only be displayed after the load has been performed. JavaScript execution is usually **synchronous**, working on one task after another in strict sequence.

However, when this particular code is tested on a production web server, the alert will quite possibly have come and gone before the load has completed, due to network lag. This happens because all AJAX calls are by default **asynchronous**. Otherwise, we'd have to call it SJAX, which hardly has the same ring to it! Asynchronous loading means that once the HTTP request to retrieve the HTML snippet is issued, script execution immediately resumes without waiting. Some time later, the browser receives the response from the server and handles it. This is generally desired behavior; it is unfriendly to lock up the whole web browser while waiting for data to be retrieved.

If actions must be delayed until the load has been completed, jQuery provides a **callback** for this. An example will be provided below.

Working with JavaScript objects

Pulling in fully-formed HTML on demand is very convenient, but there are times when we want our script to be able to do some processing of the data before it is displayed. In this case, we need to retrieve the data in a structure that we can traverse with JavaScript.

With jQuery's selectors, we could traverse the HTML we get back and manipulate it, but it must first be inserted into the document. A more native JavaScript data format can mean even less code.

Retrieving a JavaScript object

As we have often seen, **JavaScript objects** are just sets of **key-value pairs**, and can be defined succinctly using curly braces ({ }). JavaScript **arrays**, on the other hand, are defined on the fly with square brackets ([]). Combining these two concepts, we can easily express some very complex and rich data structures.

The term **JavaScript Object Notation (JSON)** was coined by Douglas Crockford to capitalize on this simple syntax. This notation can offer a concise alternative to the sometimes-bulky XML format:

```
{
  "key": "value",
  "key 2": [
    "array",
    "of",
    "items"
  ]
}
```

For information on some of the potential advantages of JSON, as well as implementations in many programming languages, visit `http://json.org/`.

We can encode our data using this format in many ways. We'll place some dictionary entries in a JSON file we'll call b.json, which begins as follows:

```
[
  {
    "term": "BACCHUS",
    "part": "n.",
    "definition": "A convenient deity invented by the...",
    "quote": [
      "Is public worship, then, a sin,",
      "That for devotions paid to Bacchus",
      "The lictors dare to run us in,",
      "And resolutely thump and whack us?"
    ],
    "author": "Jorace"
  },
  {
    "term": "BACKBITE",
    "part": "v.t.",
    "definition": "To speak of a man as you find him when..."
  },
  {
    "term": "BEARD",
    "part": "n.",
    "definition": "The hair that is commonly cut off by..."
  },
```

To retrieve this data, we'll use the $.getJSON() method, which fetches the file and processes it, providing the calling code with the resulting JavaScript object.

Global jQuery functions

To this point, all jQuery methods that we've used have been attached to a jQuery object that we've built with the $() factory function. The selectors have allowed us to specify a set of DOM nodes to work with, and the methods have operated on them in some way. This $.getJSON() function, however, is different. There is no logical DOM element to which it could apply; the resulting object has to be provided to the script, not injected into the page. For this reason, getJSON() is defined as a method of the **global jQuery object** (a single object called jQuery or $ defined once by the jQuery library), rather than of an individual **jQuery object instance** (the objects we create with the $() function).

If JavaScript had classes like other object-oriented languages, we'd call $.getJSON() a **class method**. For our purposes, we'll refer to this type of method as a **global function**; in effect, they are functions that use the jQuery **namespace** so as not to conflict with other function names.

To use this function, we pass it the file name as before:

```
$(document).ready(function() {
  $('#letter-b a').click(function() {
    $.getJSON('b.json');
    return false;
  });
});
```

This code has no apparent effect when we click the link. The function call loads the file, but we have not told JavaScript what to do with the resulting data. For this, we need to use a **callback function**.

The $.getJSON() function takes a second argument, which is a function to be called when the load is complete. As mentioned before, AJAX calls are **asynchronous**, and the callback provides a way to wait for the data to be transmitted rather than executing code right away. The callback function also takes an argument, which is filled with the resulting data. So, we can write:

```
$(document).ready(function() {
  $('#letter-b a').click(function() {
    $.getJSON('b.json', function(data) {
    });
    return false;
  });
});
```

Here we are using an **anonymous function** as our callback, as has been common in our jQuery code for brevity. A named function could equally be provided as the callback.

Inside this function, we can use the data variable to traverse the data structure as necessary. We'll need to iterate over the top-level array, building the HTML for each item. We could do this with a standard for loop, but instead we'll introduce another of jQuery's useful global functions, $.each(). We saw its counterpart, the .each() method, in Chapter 5. Instead of operating on a jQuery object, this function takes an array or map as its first parameter and a callback function as its second. Each time through the loop, the current **iteration index** and the current item in the array or map are passed as two parameters to the callback function.

```
$(document).ready(function() {
  $('#letter-b a').click(function() {
    $.getJSON('b.json', function(data) {
      $('#dictionary').empty();
      $.each(data, function(entryIndex, entry) {
        var html = '<div class="entry">';
        html += '<h3 class="term">' + entry['term'] + '</h3>';
        html += '<div class="part">' + entry['part'] + '</div>';
        html += '<div class="definition">';
        html += entry['definition'];
        html += '</div>';
        html += '</div>';
        $('#dictionary').append(html);
      });
    });
    return false;
  });
});
```

Before the loop, we empty out `<div id="dictionary">` so that we can fill it with our newly-constructed HTML. Then we use `$.each()` to examine each item in turn, building an HTML structure using the contents of the entry map. Finally, we turn this HTML into a DOM tree by appending it to the `<div>`.

 This approach presumes that the data is safe for HTML consumption; it should not contain any stray < characters, for example.

All that's left is to handle the entries with quotations, which takes another `$.each()` loop:

```
$(document).ready(function() {
  $('#letter-b a').click(function() {
    $.getJSON('b.json', function(data) {
      $('#dictionary').empty();
      $.each(data, function(entryIndex, entry) {
        var html = '<div class="entry">';
        html += '<h3 class="term">' + entry['term'] + '</h3>';
        html += '<div class="part">' + entry['part'] + '</div>';
        html += '<div class="definition">';
        html += entry['definition'];
        if (entry['quote']) {
          html += '<div class="quote">';
          $.each(entry['quote'], function(lineIndex, line) {
            html += '<div class="quote-line">' + line + '</div>';
```

```
        });
        if (entry['author']) {
            html += '<div class="quote-author">' + entry['author'] +
'</div>';
        }
        html += '</div>';
    }
    html += '</div>';
    html += '</div>';
    $('#dictionary').append(html);
    });
    });
    return false;
});
});
```

With this code in place, we can click the **B** link and confirm our results:

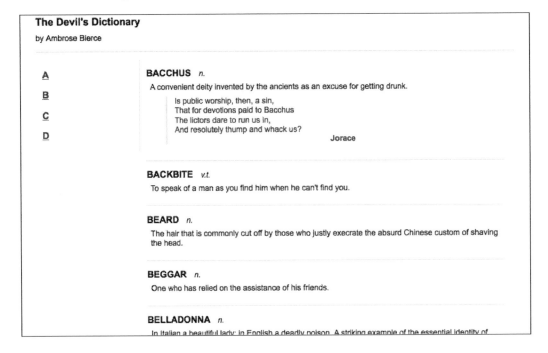

 The JSON format is concise, but not forgiving. Every bracket, brace, quote, and comma must be present and accounted for, or the file will not load. In most browsers, we won't even get an error message; the script will just silently fail.

Executing a script

Occasionally we don't want to retrieve all the JavaScript we will need when the page is first loaded. We might not know what scripts will be necessary until some user interaction occurs. We could introduce `<script>` tags on the fly when they are needed, but a more elegant way to inject additional code is to have jQuery load the `.js` file directly.

Pulling in a script is about as simple as loading an HTML fragment. In this case, we use the global function `$.getScript()`, which, like its siblings, accepts a URL locating the script file:

```
$(document).ready(function() {
  $('#letter-c a').click(function() {
    $.getScript('c.js');
    return false;
  });
});
```

In our last example, we then needed to process the result data so that we could do something useful with the loaded file. With a script file, though, the processing is automatic; the script is simply run.

Scripts fetched in this way are run in the **global context** of the current page. This means they have access to all globally-defined functions and variables, notably including jQuery itself. We can therefore mimic the JSON example to prepare and insert HTML on the page when the script is executed, and place this code in `c.js`:

```
var entries = [
  {
    "term": "CALAMITY",
    "part": "n.",
    "definition": "A more than commonly plain and..."
  },
  {
    "term": "CANNIBAL",
    "part": "n.",
    "definition": "A gastronome of the old school who..."
  },
  {
    "term": "CHILDHOOD",
    "part": "n.",
    "definition": "The period of human life intermediate..."
  },
  {
    "term": "CLARIONET",
    "part": "n.",
    "definition": "An instrument of torture operated by..."
```

```
    },
    {
      "term": "COMFORT",
      "part": "n.",
      "definition": "A state of mind produced by..."
    },
    {
      "term": "CORSAIR",
      "part": "n.",
      "definition": "A politician of the seas."
    }
  ];

  var html = '';

  $.each(entries, function() {
    html += '<div class="entry">';
    html += '<h3 class="term">' + this['term'] + '</h3>';
    html += '<div class="part">' + this['part'] + '</div>';
    html += '<div class="definition">' + this['definition'] + '</div>';
    html += '</div>';
  });

  $('#dictionary').html(html);
```

Now clicking on the **C** link has the expected result:

The Devil's Dictionary

by Ambrose Bierce

A

B

C

D

CALAMITY *n.*

A more than commonly plain and unmistakable reminder that the affairs of this life are not of our own ordering. Calamities are of two kinds: misfortune to ourselves, and good fortune to others.

CANNIBAL *n.*

A gastronome of the old school who preserves the simple tastes and adheres to the natural diet of the pre-pork period.

CHILDHOOD *n.*

The period of human life intermediate between the idiocy of infancy and the folly of youth — two removes from the sin of manhood and three from the remorse of age.

CLARIONET *n.*

An instrument of torture operated by a person with cotton in his ears. There are two instruments that are worse than a clarionet — two clarionets.

COMFORT *n.*

A state of mind produced by contemplation of a neighbor's uneasiness.

Loading an XML document

XML is part of the acronym AJAX, but we haven't actually loaded any XML yet. Doing so is straightforward, and mirrors the JSON technique fairly closely. First we'll need an XML file d.xml containing some data we wish to display:

```xml
<?xml version="1.0" encoding="UTF-8"?>
<entries>
  <entry term="DEFAME" part="v.t.">
    <definition>
      To lie about another.  To tell the truth about another.
    </definition>
  </entry>
  <entry term="DEFENCELESS" part="adj.">
    <definition>
      Unable to attack.
    </definition>
  </entry>
    <entry term="DELUSION" part="n.">
    <definition>
      The father of a most respectable family, comprising
      Enthusiasm, Affection, Self-denial, Faith, Hope,
      Charity and many other goodly sons and daughters.
    </definition>
    <quote author="Mumfrey Mappel">
      <line>All hail, Delusion!  Were it not for thee</line>
      <line>The world turned topsy-turvy we should see;
        </line>
      <line>For Vice, respectable with cleanly fancies,
        </line>
      <line>Would fly abandoned Virtue's gross advances.
        </line>
    </quote>
  </entry>
  <entry term="DIE" part="n.">
    <definition>
      The singular of "dice."  We seldom hear the word,
      because there is a prohibitory proverb, "Never say
      die."  At long intervals, however, some one says:  "The
      die is cast," which is not true, for it is cut.  The
      word is found in an immortal couplet by that eminent
      poet and domestic economist, Senator Depew:
    </definition>
    <quote>
      <line>A cube of cheese no larger than a die</line>
      <line>May bait the trap to catch a nibbling mie.</line>
    </quote>
  </entry>
</entries>
```

This data could be expressed in many ways, of course, and some would more closely mimic the structure we established for the HTML or JSON used earlier. Here, however, we're illustrating some of the features of XML designed to make it more readable to humans, such as the use of **attributes** for term and part rather than **tags**.

We'll start off our function in a familiar manner:

```
$(document).ready(function() {
  $('#letter-d a').click(function() {
    $.get('d.xml', function(data) {

    });
    return false;
  });
});
```

This time it's the $.get() function that does our work. In general, this function simply fetches the file at the supplied URL and provides the plain text to the callback. However, if the response is known to be XML because of its server-supplied **MIME type**, the callback will be handed the XML DOM tree.

Fortunately, as we have already seen, jQuery has substantial DOM traversing capabilities. We can use the normal .find(), .filter() and other traversal methods on the XML document just as we would on HTML:

```
$(document).ready(function() {
  $('#letter-d a').click(function() {
    $.get('d.xml', function(data) {
      $('#dictionary').empty();
      $(data).find('entry').each(function() {
        var $entry = $(this);
        var html = '<div class="entry">';
        html += '<h3 class="term">' + $entry.attr('term')
          + '</h3>';
        html += '<div class="part">' + $entry.attr('part')
          + '</div>';
        html += '<div class="definition">';
        html += $entry.find('definition').text();
        var $quote = $entry.find('quote');
        if ($quote.length) {
          html += '<div class="quote">';
          $quote.find('line').each(function() {
            html += '<div class="quote-line">'
              + $(this).text() + '</div>';
          });
          if ($quote.attr('author')) {
```

```
        html += '<div class="quote-author">'
            + $quote.attr('author') + '</div>';
      }
      html += '</div>';
    }
    html += '</div>';
    html += '</div>';
    $('#dictionary').append($(html));
  });
});
return false;
});
});
```

This has the expected effect when the **D** link is clicked:

The Devil's Dictionary

by Ambrose Bierce

A

B

C

D

DANCE *v.i.*

To leap about to the sound of tittering music, preferably with arms about your neighbor's wife or daughter. There are many kinds of dances, but all those requiring the participation of the two sexes have two characteristics in common: they are conspicuously innocent, and warmly loved by the vicious.

DAY *n.*

A period of twenty-four hours, mostly misspent. This period is divided into two parts, the day proper and the night, or day improper the former devoted to sins of business, the latter consecrated to the other sort. These two kinds of social activity overlap.

DEBT *n.*

An ingenious substitute for the chain and whip of the slave-driver.

As, pent in an aquarium, the troutlet
Swims round and round his tank to find an outlet,
Pressing his nose against the glass that holds him,
Nor ever sees the prison that enfolds him;
So the poor debtor, seeing naught around him,
Yet feels the narrow limits that impound him,
Grieves at his debt and studies to evade it,
And finds at last he might as well have paid it.

Barlow S. Vode

This is a new use for the DOM traversal methods we already know, shedding some light on the flexibility of jQuery's CSS selector support. CSS syntax is typically used to help beautify HTML pages, and thus selectors in standard .css files use HTML tag names such as div and body to locate content. However, jQuery can use arbitrary XML tag names, such as entry and definition here, just as readily as the standard HTML ones.

The advanced selector engine inside jQuery facilitates finding parts of the XML document in much more complicated situations, as well. For example, suppose we wanted to limit the displayed entries to those that have quotes that in turn have attributed authors. To do this, we can limit the entries to those with nested `<quote>` elements by changing `entry` to `entry:has(quote)`. Then we can further restrict the entries to those with `author` attributes on the `<quote>` elements by writing `entry:has(quote[author])`. The line with the initial selector now reads:

```
$(data).find('entry:has(quote[author])').each(function() {
```

This new selector expression restricts the returned entries correspondingly:

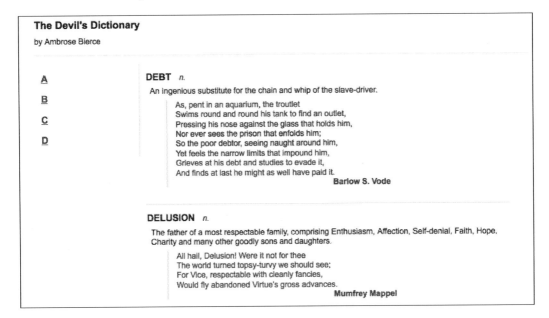

Choosing a data format

We have looked at four formats for our external data, each of which is handled natively by jQuery's AJAX functions. We have also verified that all four can handle the task at hand, loading information onto an existing page when the user requests it and not before. How, then, do we decide which one to use in our applications?

HTML snippets require very little work to implement. The external data can be loaded and inserted into the page with one simple method, which does not even require a callback function. No traversal of the data is necessary for the straightforward task of adding the new HTML into the existing page. On the other hand, the data is not necessarily structured in a way that makes it reusable for other applications. The external file is tightly coupled with its intended container.

JSON files are structured for simple reuse. They are compact, and easy to read. The data structure must be traversed to pull out the information and present it on the page, but this can be done with standard JavaScript techniques. Since the files can be parsed with a single call to JavaScript's `eval()`, reading in a JSON file is extremely fast. Any use of `eval()` does carry inherent risks, however. Errors in the JSON file can cause silent failure or even side effects on the page, so the data must be crafted carefully by a trusted party.

JavaScript files offer the ultimate in flexibility, but are not really a data storage mechanism. Since the files are language-specific, they cannot be used to provide the same information to disparate systems. Instead, the ability to load a JavaScript file means that behaviors that are rarely needed can be factored out into external files, reducing code size unless and until it is needed.

XML documents are the kings of portability. Because XML has become the *lingua franca* of the web service world, providing data in this format makes it very likely the data can be reused elsewhere. For example, Flickr (`http://flickr.com/`), del.icio.us (`http://del.icio.us/`) and Upcoming (`http://upcoming.org/`) all export XML representations of their data, which has allowed many interesting **mashups** of their data to arise. The XML format is somewhat bulky, though, and can be a bit slower to parse and manipulate than other options.

With these characteristics in mind, it is typically easiest to provide external data as HTML snippets, as long as the data is not needed in other applications as well. In cases where the data will be reused but the other applications can also be influenced, JSON is often a good choice due to its performance and size. When the remote application is not known, XML provides the greatest assurance that interoperability will be possible.

More than any other consideration, we should determine if the data is already available. If it is, chances are it's in one of these formats to begin with, so our decision may be made for us.

Passing data to the server

Our examples to this point have focused on the task of retrieving **static** data files from the web server. However, the AJAX technique really comes into its own only when the server can **dynamically** shape the data based on input from the browser. We're helped along by jQuery in this task as well; all of the methods we've covered so far can be modified so that data transfer becomes a two-way street.

Since demonstrating these techniques requires interaction with the web server, we'll need to use server-side code for the first time here. The examples given will use the **PHP** scripting language, which is very widely used as well as freely available. We will not cover how to set up a web server with PHP here; help on this can be found on the websites of Apache (http://apache.org/) or PHP (http://php.net/), or from your site's hosting company.

Performing a GET request

To illustrate the communication between client and server, we'll write a script that only sends one dictionary entry to the browser on each request. The entry chosen will depend on a parameter sent from the browser. Our script will pull its data from an internal data structure like this:

```php
<?php
$entries = array(
  'EAVESDROP' => array(
    'part' => 'v.i.',
    'definition' => 'Secretly to overhear a catalogue of the
      crimes and vices of another or yourself.',
    'quote' => array(
      'A lady with one of her ears applied',
      'To an open keyhole heard, inside,',
      'Two female gossips in converse free &mdash;',
      'The subject engaging them was she.',
      '"I think," said one, "and my husband thinks',
      'That she\'s a prying, inquisitive minx!"',
      'As soon as no more of it she could hear',
      'The lady, indignant, removed her ear.',
      '"I will not stay," she said, with a pout,',
      '"To hear my character lied about!"',
    ),
    'author' => 'Gopete Sherany',
  ),
  'EDIBLE' => array(
    'part' => 'adj.',
    'definition' => 'Good to eat, and wholesome to digest, as
      a worm to a toad, a toad to a snake, a snake to a pig,
      a pig to a man, and a man to a worm.',
  ),
  'EDUCATION' => array(
    'part' => 'n.',
```

```
        'definition' => 'That which discloses to the wise and
          disguises from the foolish their lack of
          understanding.',
    ),
);
?>
```

In a production version of this example, the data would probably be stored in a database and loaded on demand. Since the data is a part of the script here, the code to retrieve it is quite straightforward. We examine the data that has been posted and craft the HTML snippet to display:

```php
<?php
$term = strtoupper($_REQUEST['term']);
if (isset($entries[$term])) {
  $entry = $entries[$term];

  $html = '<div class="entry">';
  $html .= '<h3 class="term">';
  $html .= $term;
  $html .= '</h3>';
  $html .= '<div class="part">';
  $html .= $entry['part'];
  $html .= '</div>';
  $html .= '<div class="definition">';
  $html .= $entry['definition'];
  if (isset($entry['quote'])) {
    $html .= '<div class="quote">';
    foreach ($entry['quote'] as $line) {
      $html .= '<div class="quote-line">'. $line .'</div>';
    }
    if (isset($entry['author'])) {
      $html .= '<div class="quote-author">'. $entry['author']
        .'</div>';
    }
    $html .= '</div>';
  }
  $html .= '</div>';

  $html .= '</div>';

  print($html);
}
?>
```

Now requests to this script, which we'll call `e.php`, will return the HTML snippet corresponding to the term that was sent in the **GET** parameters. For example, when accessing the script with `e.php?term=eavesdrop`, we get back:

EAVESDROP

v.i.
Secretly to overhear a catalogue of the crimes and vices of another or yourself.
A lady with one of her ears applied
To an open keyhole heard, inside,
Two female gossips in converse free —
The subject engaging them was she.
"I think," said one, "and my husband thinks
That she's a prying, inquisitive minx!"
As soon as no more of it she could hear
The lady, indignant, removed her ear.
"I will not stay," she said, with a pout,
"To hear my character lied about!"
Gopete Sherany

Once again, we note the lack of formatting we saw with earlier HTML snippets, because CSS rules have not been applied.

Since we're showing how data is passed to the server, we will use a different method to request entries than the solitary buttons we've been relying on so far. Instead, we'll present a list of links for each term, and cause a click on any of them to load the corresponding definition. The HTML we'll add for this looks like:

```
<div class="letter" id="letter-e">
  <h3>E</h3>
  <ul>
    <li><a href="e.php?term=Eavesdrop">Eavesdrop</a></li>
    <li><a href="e.php?term=Edible">Edible</a></li>
    <li><a href="e.php?term=Education">Education</a></li>
    <li><a href="e.php?term=Eloquence">Eloquence</a></li>
    <li><a href="e.php?term=Elysium">Elysium</a></li>
    <li><a href="e.php?term=Emancipation">Emancipation</a>
      </li>
    <li><a href="e.php?term=Emotion">Emotion</a></li>
    <li><a href="e.php?term=Envelope">Envelope</a></li>
    <li><a href="e.php?term=Envy">Envy</a></li>
    <li><a href="e.php?term=Epitaph">Epitaph</a></li>
    <li><a href="e.php?term=Evangelist">Evangelist</a></li>
  </ul>
</div>
```

Now we need to get our JavaScript code to call the PHP script with the right parameters. We could do this with the normal `.load()` mechanism, appending the query string right to the URL and fetching data with addresses like `e.php?term=eavesdrop` directly. Instead, though, we can have jQuery construct the query string based on a map we provide to the `$.get()` function:

```
$(document).ready(function() {
  $('#letter-e a').click(function() {
    $.get('e.php', {'term': $(this).text()}, function(data) {
      $('#dictionary').html(data);
    });
    return false;
  });
});
```

Now that we have seen other AJAX interfaces that jQuery provides, the operation of this function seems familiar. The only difference is the second parameter, which allows us to supply a map of keys and values that become part of the query string. In this case, the key is always `term` but the value is taken from the text of each link. Now, clicking on the first link in the list causes its definition to appear:

The Devil's Dictionary

by Ambrose Bierce

A

B

C

D

E

Eavesdrop
Edible
Education
Eloquence
Elysium
Emancipation
Emotion
Envelope
Envy
Epitaph
Evangelist

EAVESDROP *v.i.*

Secretly to overhear a catalogue of the crimes and vices of another or yourself.

A lady with one of her ears applied
To an open keyhole heard, inside,
Two female gossips in converse free —
The subject engaging them was she.
"I think," said one, "and my husband thinks
That she's a prying, inquisitive minx!"
As soon as no more of it she could hear
The lady, indignant, removed her ear.
"I will not stay," she said, with a pout,
"To hear my character lied about!"

Gopete Sherany

All the links here have addresses given, even though we are not using them in the code. This provides an alternative method of navigating the information for users who have JavaScript turned off or unavailable (a form of **progressive enhancement**). To prevent the links from being followed normally when clicked, the event handler has to return `false`.

Performing a POST request

HTTP requests using the **POST** method are almost identical to those using GET. One of the most visible differences is that GET places its arguments in the query string portion of the URL, whereas POST requests do not. However, in AJAX calls, even this distinction is invisible to the average user. Generally, the only reason to choose one method over the other is to conform to the norms of the server-side code, or to provide for large amounts of transmitted data; GET has a more stringent limit. We have coded our PHP example to cope equally well with either method, so we can change from GET to POST simply by changing the jQuery function we call:

```
$(document).ready(function() {
  $('#letter-e a').click(function() {
    $.post('e.php', {'term': $(this).text()}, function(data) {
      $('#dictionary').html(data);
    });
    return false;
  });
});
```

The arguments are the same, and the request will now be made via POST. We can further simplify the code by using the `.load()` method, which uses POST by default when it is supplied with a map of arguments:

```
$(document).ready(function() {
  $('#letter-e a').click(function() {
    $('#dictionary').load('e.php', {'term': $(this).text()});
    return false;
  });
});
```

This cut-down version functions the same way when a link is clicked:

The Devil's Dictionary

by Ambrose Bierce

A

B

C

D

E

Eavesdrop
Edible
Education
Eloquence
Elysium
Emancipation
Emotion
Envelope
Envy
Epitaph
Evangelist

EMANCIPATION   *n.*

A bondman's change from the tyranny of another to the despotism of himself.

He was a slave: at word he went and came;
His iron collar cut him to the bone.
Then Liberty erased his owner's name,
Tightened the rivets and inscribed his own.

G.J.

Serializing a form

Sending data to the server often involves the user filling out **forms**. Rather than relying on the normal form submission mechanism, which will load the response in the entire browser window, we can use jQuery's AJAX toolkit to submit the form asynchronously and place the response inside the current page.

To try this out, we'll need to construct a simple form:

```
<div class="letter" id="letter-f">
  <h3>F</h3>
  <form>
    <input type="text" name="term" value="" id="term" />
    <input type="submit" name="search" value="search"
      id="search" />
  </form>
</div>
```

This time we'll return a set of entries from the PHP script by searching for the supplied search term as a substring of a dictionary term. The data structure will be of the same format as before, but the logic will be a bit different:

```
foreach ($entries as $term => $entry) {
  if (strpos($term, strtoupper($_REQUEST['term']))
        !== FALSE) {
    $html = '<div class="entry">';

    $html .= '<h3 class="term">';
    $html .= $term;
    $html .= '</h3>';

    $html .= '<div class="part">';
    $html .= $entry['part'];
    $html .= '</div>';

    $html .= '<div class="definition">';
    $html .= $entry['definition'];
    if (isset($entry['quote'])) {
      foreach ($entry['quote'] as $line) {
        $html .= '<div class="quote-line">'. $line .'</div>';
      }
      if (isset($entry['author'])) {
        $html .= '<div class="quote-author">'.
          $entry['author'] .'</div>';
      }
    }
```

```
        $html .= '</div>';

        $html .= '</div>';

        print($html);
    }
}
```

The call to `strpos()` scans the word for the supplied search string. Now we can react to a form submission and craft the proper query parameters by traversing the DOM tree:

```
$(document).ready(function() {
  $('#letter-f form').submit(function() {
    $('#dictionary').load('f.php',
      {'term': $('input[name="term"]').val()});
    return false;
  });
});
```

This code has the intended effect, but searching for input fields by name and appending them to a map one by one is cumbersome. In particular, this approach does not scale well as the form becomes more complex. Fortunately, jQuery offers a shortcut for this often-used idiom. The `.serialize()` method acts on a jQuery object and translates the matched DOM elements into a query string that can be passed along with an AJAX request. We can generalize our submission handler as follows:

```
$(document).ready(function() {
  $('#letter-f form').submit(function() {
    $.get('f.php', $(this).serialize(), function(data) {
      $('#dictionary').html(data);
    });
    return false;
  });
});
```

Now the same script will work to submit the form, even as the number of fields increases. When we perform a search, the matched entries are displayed:

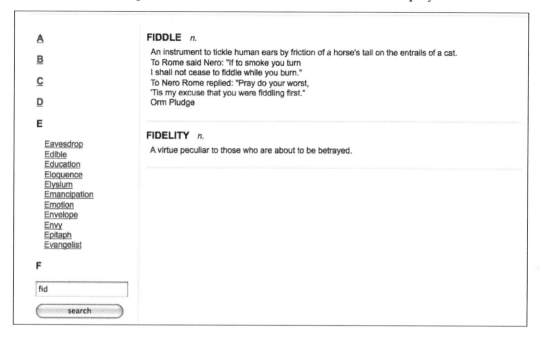

Keeping an eye on the request

So far, it has been sufficient for us to make a call to an AJAX method and patiently await the response. At times, though, it is handy to know a bit more about the HTTP request as it progresses. If such a need arises, jQuery offers a suite of functions that can be used to register **callbacks** when various AJAX-related events occur.

The `.ajaxStart()` and `.ajaxStop()` methods are two examples of these observer functions, and can be attached to any jQuery object. When an AJAX call begins with no other transfer in progress, the `.ajaxStart()` callback is fired. Conversely, when the last active request ends, the callback attached with `.ajaxStop()` will be executed. All of the observers are **global**, in that they are called when any AJAX communication occurs, regardless of what code initiates it.

We can use these methods to provide some feedback to the user in the case of a slow network connection. The HTML for the page can have a suitable loading message appended:

```
<div id="loading">
  Loading...
</div>
```

This message is just a piece of arbitrary HTML; it could include an animated GIF image to provide a **throbber**, for instance. In this case, we'll add a few simple styles to the CSS file, so that when the message is displayed, the page looks like:

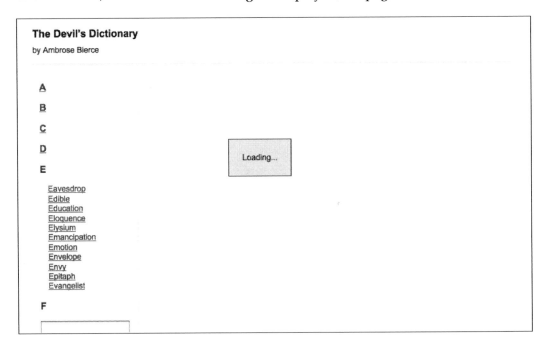

In keeping with the spirit of **progressive enhancement**, however, we won't put this HTML markup directly on the page. It's only relevant for us when JavaScript is available, so we will insert it using jQuery:

```
$(document).ready(function() {
  $('<div id="loading">Loading...</div>')
    .insertBefore('#dictionary')
});
```

Our CSS file will give this <div> a display: none; style rule so that the message is initially hidden. To display it at the right time, we just register it as an observer with .ajaxStart():

```
$(document).ready(function() {
  $('<div id="loading">Loading...</div>')
    .insertBefore('#dictionary')
    .ajaxStart(function() {
      $(this).show();
    });
});
```

We can **chain** the hiding behavior right onto this:

```
$(document).ready(function() {
  $('<div id="loading">Loading...</div>')
    .insertBefore('#dictionary')
    .ajaxStart(function() {
      $(this).show();
    }).ajaxStop(function() {
      $(this).hide();
    });
});
```

Voilà! We have our loading feedback.

Once again, note that these methods have no association with the particular ways in which the AJAX communications begin. The .load() attached to the **A** link and the .getJSON() attached to the **B** link both cause these actions to occur.

In this case, this global behavior is desirable. If we need to get more specific, though, we have a few options at our disposal. Some of the observer methods, like .ajaxError(), send their callback a reference to the XMLHttpRequest object. This can be used to differentiate one request from another, and provide different behaviors. Other more specific handling can be achieved by using the low-level $.ajax() function, which we'll discuss a bit later.

The most common way of interacting with the request, though, is the success callback, which we have already covered. We have used this in several of our examples to interpret the data coming back from the server and to populate the page with the results. It can be used for other feedback too, of course. Consider once again our .load() example:

```
$(document).ready(function() {
  $('#letter-a a').click(function() {
    $('#dictionary').load('a.html');
    return false;
  });
});
```

We can create a small enhancement here by making the loaded content fade into view rather than appear suddenly. The .load() can take a callback to be fired on completion:

```
$(document).ready(function() {
  $('#letter-a a').click(function() {
    $('#dictionary').hide().load('a.html', function() {
      $(this).fadeIn();
```

```
    });
    return false;
  });
});
```

First, we hide the target element, and then initiate the load. When the load is complete, we use the callback to show the newly-populated element by fading it in.

AJAX and events

Suppose we wanted to allow each dictionary term name to control the display of the definition that follows; clicking on the term name would show or hide the associated definition. With the techniques we have seen so far, this should be pretty straightforward:

```
$(document).ready(function() {
  $('.term').click(function() {
    $(this).siblings('.definition').slideToggle();
  });
});
```

When a term is clicked, this code finds siblings of the element that have a class of definition, and slides them up or down as appropriate.

All seems in order, but a click does nothing with this code. Unfortunately, the terms have not yet been added to the document when we attach the click handlers. Even if we managed to attach click handlers to these items, once we clicked on a different letter the handlers would no longer be attached.

This is a common problem with areas of a page populated by AJAX. A popular solution is to **rebind** handlers each time the page area is refreshed. This can be cumbersome, however, as the event binding code needs to be called each time anything causes the DOM structure of the page to change.

An often superior alternative was introduced in Chapter 3: We can implement **event delegation**, actually binding the event to an ancestor element that never changes. In this case, we'll attach the click handler to the document using .live() and catch our clicks that way:

```
$(document).ready(function() {
  $('.term').live('click', function() {
    $(this).siblings('.definition').slideToggle();
  });
});
```

The `.live()` method tells the browser to observe all clicks anywhere on the page. If (and only if) the clicked element matches the `.term` selector, then the handler is executed. Now the toggling behavior will take place on any term, even if it is added by a later AJAX transaction.

Security limitations

For all its utility in crafting dynamic web applications, `XMLHttpRequest` (the underlying browser technology behind jQuery's AJAX implementation) is subject to strict boundaries. To prevent various **cross-site scripting** attacks, it is not generally possible to request a document from a server other than the one that hosts the original page.

This is generally a positive situation. For example, some cite the implementation of JSON parsing by using `eval()` as insecure. If malicious code is present in the data file, it could be run by the `eval()` call. However, since the data file must reside on the same server as the web page itself, the ability to inject code in the data file is largely equivalent to the ability to inject code in the page directly. This means that, for the case of loading *trusted* JSON files, `eval()` is not a significant security concern.

There are many cases, though, in which it would be beneficial to load data from a third-party source. There are several ways to work around the security limitations and allow this to happen.

One method is to rely on the server to load the remote data, and then provide it when requested by the client. This is a very powerful approach as the server can perform pre-processing on the data as needed. For example, we could load XML files containing RSS news feeds from several sources, aggregate them into a single feed on the server, and publish this new file for the client when it is requested.

To load data from a remote location *without* server involvement, we have to get a bit sneakier. A popular approach for the case of loading foreign JavaScript files is injecting `<script>` tags on demand. Since jQuery can help us insert new DOM elements, it is simple to do this:

```
$(document.createElement('script'))
  .attr('src', 'http://example.com/example.js')
  .appendTo('head');
```

In fact, the `$.getScript()` method will automatically adapt to this technique if it detects a remote host in its URL argument, so even this is handled for us.

The browser will execute the loaded script, but there is no mechanism to retrieve results from the script. For this reason, the technique requires cooperation from the remote host. The loaded script must take some action, such as setting a global variable that has an effect on the local environment. Services that publish scripts that are executable in this way will also provide an API with which to interact with the remote script.

Another option is to use the `<iframe>` HTML tag to load remote data. This element allows any URL to be used as the source for its data fetching, even if it does not match the host page's server. The data can be loaded and easily displayed on the current page. Manipulating the data, however, typically requires the same cooperation needed for the `<script>` tag approach; scripts inside the `<iframe>` need to explicitly provide the data to objects in the parent document.

Using JSONP for remote data

The idea of using `<script>` tags to fetch JavaScript files from a remote source can be adapted to pull in JSON files from another server as well. To do this, we need to slightly modify the JSON file on the server, however. There are several mechanisms for doing this, one of which is directly supported by jQuery: **JSON with Padding**, or **JSONP**.

The JSONP file format consists of a standard JSON file that has been wrapped in parentheses and prepended with an arbitrary text string. This string, the "padding", is determined by the client requesting the data. Because of the parentheses, the client can either cause a function to be called or a variable to be set depending on what is sent as the padding string.

A PHP implementation of the JSONP technique is quite simple:

```php
<?php
  print($_GET['callback'] .'('. $data .')');
?>
```

Here, `$data` is a variable containing a string representation of a JSON file. When this script is called, the `callback` query string parameter is prepended to the resulting file that gets returned to the client.

To demonstrate this technique, we need only slightly modify our earlier JSON example to call this remote data source instead. The $.getJSON() function makes use of a special placeholder character, ?, to achieve this.

```javascript
$(document).ready(function() {
  var url = 'http://examples.learningjquery.com/jsonp/g.php';
  $('#letter-g a').click(function() {
```

```
$.getJSON(url + '?callback=?', function(data) {
  $('#dictionary').empty();
  $.each(data, function(entryIndex, entry) {
    var html = '<div class="entry">';
    html += '<h3 class="term">' + entry['term']
      + '</h3>';
    html += '<div class="part">' + entry['part']
      + '</div>';
    html += '<div class="definition">';
    html += entry['definition'];
    if (entry['quote']) {
      html += '<div class="quote">';
      $.each(entry['quote'], function(lineIndex, line) {
        html += '<div class="quote-line">' + line
          + '</div>';
      });
      if (entry['author']) {
        html += '<div class="quote-author">'
          + entry['author'] + '</div>';
      }
      html += '</div>';
    }
    html += '</div>';
    html += '</div>';
    $('#dictionary').append(html);
  });
});
return false;
});
});
```

We normally would not be allowed to fetch JSON from a remote server (examples. learningjquery.com in this case). However, since this file is set up to provide its data in the JSONP format, we can obtain the data by appending a query string to our URL, using ? as a placeholder for the value of the callback argument. When the request is made, jQuery replaces the ? for us, parses the result, and passes it to the success function as data just as if this were a local JSON request.

Note that the same security cautions hold here as before; whatever the server decides to return to the browser will execute on the user's computer. The JSONP technique should only be used with data coming from a *trusted* source.

Additional options

The AJAX toolbox provided by jQuery is well-stocked. We've covered several of the available options, but we've just scratched the surface. While there are too many variants to cover here, we will give an overview of some of the more prominent ways to customize AJAX communications.

The low-level AJAX method

We have seen several methods that all initiate AJAX transactions. Internally, jQuery maps each of these methods onto variants of the `$.ajax()` global function. Rather than presuming one particular type of AJAX activity, this function takes a map of options that can be used to customize its behavior.

Our first example loaded an HTML snippet using `$('#dictionary').load('a.html')`. This action could instead be accomplished with `$.ajax()` as follows:

```
$.ajax({
  url: 'a.html',
  type: 'GET',
  dataType: 'html',
  success: function(data) {
    $('#dictionary').html(data);
  }
});
```

We need to explicitly specify the request method, the data type that will be returned, and what to do with the resulting data. Clearly, this is less efficient use of programmer effort; however, with this extra work comes a great deal of flexibility. A few of the special capabilities that come with using a low-level `$.ajax()` call include:

- Preventing the browser from caching responses from the server. This can be useful if the server produces its data dynamically.

- Registering separate callback functions for when the request completes successfully, with an error, or in all cases.

- Suppressing the global handlers (such as ones registered with `$.ajaxStart()`) that are normally triggered by all AJAX interactions.

- Providing a user name and password for authentication with the remote host.

For details on using these and other options, consult *jQuery Reference Guide or* see the API reference online (`http://docs.jquery.com/Ajax/jQuery.ajax`).

Modifying default options

The `$.ajaxSetup()` function allows us to specify default values for each of the options used when AJAX methods are called. It takes a map of options identical to the ones available to `$.ajax()` itself, and causes these values to be used on all subsequent AJAX requests unless overridden.

```
$.ajaxSetup({
  url: 'a.html',
  type: 'POST',
  dataType: 'html'
});
$.ajax({
  type: 'GET',
  success: function(data) {
    $('#dictionary').html(data);
  }
});
```

This sequence of operations behaves the same as our preceding `$.ajax()` example. Note that the URL of the request is specified as a default value by the `$.ajaxSetup()` call, so it does not have to be provided when `$.ajax()` is invoked. In contrast, the `type` parameter is given a default value of POST, but this can still be overridden in the `$.ajax()` call to GET.

Loading parts of an HTML page

The first and simplest AJAX technique we discussed was fetching an HTML snippet and placing it on a page. Sometimes, though, the server already provides the HTML we need, but it is surrounded by an HTML page we do not want. When it is inconvenient to make the server provide the data in the format we desire, jQuery can help us on the client end.

Consider a case like our first example, but in which the document containing the dictionary definitions is a complete HTML page like this:

```
<html xmlns="http://www.w3.org/1999/xhtml" xml:lang="en"
    lang="en">
  <head>
    <meta http-equiv="Content-Type"
      content="text/html; charset=utf-8"/>
    <title>The Devil's Dictionary: H</title>
    <link rel="stylesheet" href="dictionary.css"
      type="text/css" media="screen" />
  </head>
```

```
<body>
  <div id="container">
    <div id="header">
      <h2>The Devil's Dictionary: H</h2>
      <div class="author">by Ambrose Bierce</div>
    </div>

    <div id="dictionary">
      <div class="entry">
        <h3 class="term">HABEAS CORPUS</h3>
        <div class="part">n.</div>
        <div class="definition">
          A writ by which a man may be taken out of jail
          when confined for the wrong crime.
        </div>
      </div>

      <div class="entry">
        <h3 class="term">HABIT</h3>
        <div class="part">n.</div>
        <div class="definition">
          A shackle for the free.
        </div>
      </div>
    </div>

  </div>
</body>
</html>
```

We can load the whole document into our page using the code we wrote earlier:

```
$(document).ready(function() {
  $('#letter-h a').click(function() {
    $('#dictionary').load('h.html');
    return false;
  });
});
```

This produces a strange effect, though, due to the pieces of the HTML page we don't want to include:

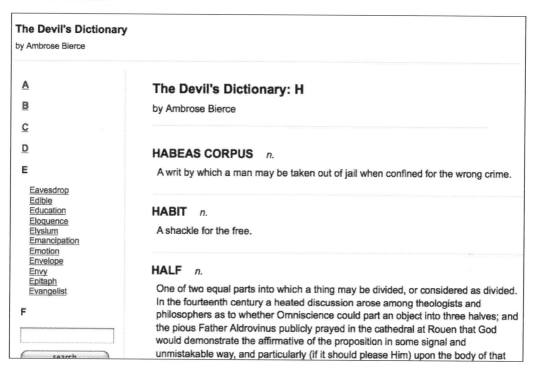

To remove these extraneous bits, we can use a new feature of the `.load()` method. When specifying the URL of the document to load, we can also provide a jQuery selector expression. If present, this expression is used to locate a portion of the loaded document. Only the matched part of the document is inserted into the page. In this case, we can use this technique to pull only the dictionary entries from the document and insert them:

```
$(document).ready(function() {
  $('#letter-h a').click(function() {
    $('#dictionary').load('h.html .entry');
    return false;
  });
});
```

Now the irrelevant portions of the document are excluded from the page:

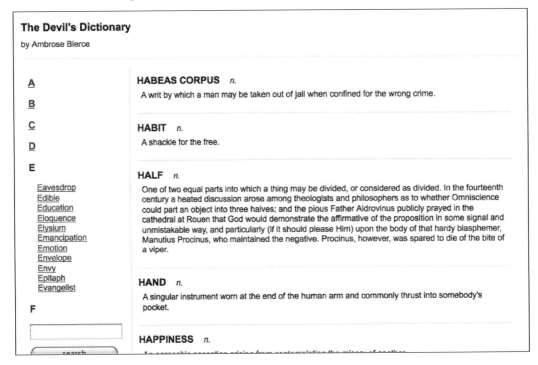

Summary

We have learned that AJAX methods provided by jQuery can help us to load data in several different formats from the server without a page refresh. We can execute scripts from the server on demand, and send data back to the server.

We've also learned how to deal with common challenges of asynchronous loading techniques, such as keeping handlers bound after a load has occurred and loading data from a third-party server.

This concludes the tutorial portion of the book. We are armed with the main tools offered by jQuery: selectors, events, effects, DOM manipulation, and asynchronous server requests. These are not the only ways jQuery can help us; we'll cover a few of the many abilities conferred by jQuery plugins in later chapters. But first, we'll examine a few combinations of these techniques that enhance our web pages in new and interesting ways.

7
Table Manipulation

In the first six chapters, we explored the jQuery library in a series of tutorials that focused on each jQuery component and used examples as a way to see those components in action. In Chapters 7 through 9 we invert the process; we'll begin with examples of real-world problems, and see how we can use jQuery methods to solve them.

Here, we will use an online bookstore as our model website, but the techniques we cook up can be applied to a wide variety of other sites as well, from weblogs to portfolios, from market-facing business sites to corporate intranets. Chapters 7 and 8 focus on two common elements of most sites — **tables** and **forms** — while Chapter 9 examines a couple of ways to visually enhance sets of information using animated **shufflers** and **rotators**.

As the web standards movement has become more pervasive in the last few years, table-based layout has increasingly been abandoned in favor of CSS-based designs. Although tables were often employed as a somewhat necessary stopgap measure in the 1990s to create multi-column and other complex layouts, they were never intended to be used in that way. On the other hand, CSS is a technology expressly created for these presentation tasks.

But this is not the place for an extended discussion on the proper role of tables. Suffice it to say that in this chapter we will use jQuery to apply techniques for increasing the readability, usability, and visual appeal of semantically marked up containers of **tabular data**. For a closer look at applying semantic, accessible HTML to tables, a good place to begin is Roger Johansson's blog entry, "Bring on the Tables" at `http://www.456bereastreet.com/archive/200410/bring_on_the_tables/`.

Some of the techniques we apply to tables in this chapter can be found in plugins such as Christian Bach's Table Sorter. For more information, visit the jQuery Plugin Repository at `http://plugins.jquery.com/`.

In this chapter, we cover:

- Sorting
- Pagination
- Row highlighting
- Tooltips
- Collapsing and expanding rows, and
- Filtering

Sorting and paging

Two of the most common tasks performed with tabular data are **sorting** and **paging**. In a large table, being able to rearrange the information that we're looking for is invaluable. Unfortunately, these helpful operations can be some of the trickiest to put into action.

First, we'll look at what it takes to perform table sorting, reordering data into a sequence that is most helpful to the user.

Server-side sorting

A common solution for data sorting is to perform it on the server side. Data in tables often comes from a **database**, which means that the code that pulls it out of the database can request it in a given sort order (using, for example, the **SQL** language's ORDER BY clause). If we have server-side code at our disposal, it is straightforward to begin with a reasonable default sort order.

Sorting is most useful, though, when the user can determine the sort order. A common method is to make the table headers (`<th>`) of sortable columns into links. These links can go to the current page, but with a **query string** appended indicating the column to sort by:

```
<table id="my-data">
  <thead>
    <tr>
      <th class="name">
        <a href="index.php?sort=name">Name</a>
      </th>
      <th class="date">
        <a href="index.php?sort=date">Date</a>
      </th>
    </tr>
```

```
    </thead>
    <tbody>
      . . .
    </tbody>
  </table>
```

The server can react to the query string parameter by returning the database contents in a different order.

Preventing page refreshes

This setup is simple, but requires a page refresh for each sort operation. As we have seen, jQuery allows us to eliminate such page refreshes by using AJAX methods. If we have the column headers set up as links as before, we can add jQuery code to change those links into AJAX requests:

```
$(document).ready(function() {
  $('#my-data th a').click(function() {
    $('#my-data tbody').load($(this).attr('href'));
    return false;
  });
});
```

Now when the anchors are clicked, jQuery sends an AJAX request to the server for the same page. When jQuery is used to make a page request using AJAX, it sets the X-Requested-With HTTP header to XMLHttpRequest so that the server can determine that an AJAX request is being made. The server code can be written to send back only the content of the <tbody> element itself, and not the surrounding page, when this parameter is present. This way we can take the response and insert it in place of the existing <tbody> element.

This is an example of progressive enhancement. The page works perfectly well without any JavaScript at all, as the links for server-side sorting are still present. When JavaScript is available, however, the AJAX hijacks the page request and allows the sort to occur without a full page load.

JavaScript sorting

There are times, though, when we either don't want to wait for server responses when sorting, or don't have a server-side scripting language available to us. A viable alternative in this case is to perform the sorting entirely on the browser using JavaScript client-side scripting.

For example, suppose we have a table listing books, the author names, release dates, and prices:

```
<table class="sortable">
  <thead>
    <tr>
      <th></th>
      <th>Title</th>
      <th>Author(s)</th>
      <th>Publish Date</th>
      <th>Price</th>
    </tr>
  </thead>
  <tbody>
    <tr>
      <td><img src="../images/covers/small/1847192386.png"
        width="49" height="61" alt="Building Websites with
        Joomla! 1.5 Beta 1" />
      </td>
      <td>Building Websites with Joomla! 1.5 Beta 1</td>
      <td>Hagen Graf</td>
      <td>Feb 2007</td>
      <td>$40.49</td>
    </tr>
    <tr>
      <td><img src="../images/covers/small/1904811620.png"
        width="49" height="61" alt="Learning Mambo: A
        Step-by-Step Tutorial to Building Your Website" />
      </td>
      <td>Learning Mambo: A Step-by-Step Tutorial to Building
        Your Website
      </td>
      <td>Douglas Paterson</td>
      <td>Dec 2006</td>
      <td>$40.49</td>
    </tr>
  </tbody>
</table>
```

	Title	Author(s)	Publish Date	Price
	Building Websites with Joomla! 1.5 Beta 1	Hagen Graf	Feb 2007	$40.49
	Learning Mambo: A Step-by-Step Tutorial to Building Your Website	Douglas Paterson	Dec 2006	$40.49
	Moodle E-Learning Course Development	William Rice	May 2006	$35.99
	AJAX and PHP: Building Responsive Web Applications	Cristian Darie, Mihai Bucica, Filip Chereches-Toşa, Bogdan Brinzarea	Mar 2006	$31.49
	OpenVPN: Building and Integrating Virtual Private Networks	Markus Feilner	May 2006	$53.99

We'd like to turn the table headers into buttons that sort the data by their respective columns. Let's explore some ways of doing this.

Row grouping tags

Note our use of the `<thead>` and `<tbody>` tags to segment the data into **row groupings**. Many HTML authors omit these implied tags, but they can prove useful in supplying us with more convenient CSS selectors to use. For example, suppose we wish to apply typical even/odd row striping to this table, but only to the body of the table:

```
$(document).ready(function() {
  $('table.sortable tbody tr:odd').addClass('odd');
  $('table.sortable tbody tr:even').addClass('even');
});
```

This will add alternating colors to the table, but leave the header untouched:

	Title	Author(s)	Publish Date	Price
	Building Websites with Joomla! 1.5 Beta 1	Hagen Graf	Feb 2007	$40.49
	Learning Mambo: A Step-by-Step Tutorial to Building Your Website	Douglas Paterson	Dec 2006	$40.49
	Moodle E-Learning Course Development	William Rice	May 2006	$35.99
	AJAX and PHP: Building Responsive Web Applications	Cristian Darie, Mihai Bucica, Filip Chereches-Toşa, Bogdan Brinzarea	Mar 2006	$31.49
	OpenVPN: Building and Integrating Virtual Private Networks	Markus Feilner	May 2006	$53.99

Using these row grouping tags, we will be able to easily select and manipulate the data rows without affecting the header.

Basic alphabetical sorting

Now let's perform a sort on the **Title** column of the table. We'll need a class on the table header cell so that we can select it properly:

```
<thead>
  <tr>
    <th></th>
    <th class="sort-alpha">Title</th>
    <th>Author(s)</th>
    <th>Publish Date</th>
    <th>Price</th>
  </tr>
</thead>
```

Using JavaScript to sort arrays

To perform the actual sort, we can use JavaScript's built in .sort() method. It does an in-place sort on an array, and can take a **comparator function** as an argument. This function compares two items in the array and should return a positive or negative number depending on which item should come first in the sorted array.

For example, take a simple array of numbers:

```
var arr = [52, 97, 3, 62, 10, 63, 64, 1, 9, 3, 4];
```

We can sort this array by calling arr.sort(). After this, the items are in the order:

```
[1, 10, 3, 3, 4, 52, 62, 63, 64, 9, 97]
```

By default, as we see here, the items are sorted **lexicographically** (in alphabetical order). In this case it might make more sense to sort the items **numerically**. To do this, we can supply a comparator function to the .sort() method:

```
arr.sort(function(a,b) {
  if (a < b)
    return -1;
  if (a > b)
    return 1;
  return 0;
});
```

This function returns a negative number if a should come first in the sorted array, a positive number if b should come first, and zero if the order of the items does not matter. With this information in hand, the .sort() method can sequence the items appropriately:

```
[1, 3, 3, 4, 9, 10, 52, 62, 63, 64, 97]
```

Using a comparator to sort table rows

Our initial sort routine looks like this:

```
$(document).ready(function() {
  $('table.sortable').each(function() {
    var $table = $(this);
    $('th', $table).each(function(column) {
      var $header = $(this);
      if ($header.is('.sort-alpha')) {
        $header.addClass('clickable').hover(function() {
          $header.addClass('hover');
        }, function() {
          $header.removeClass('hover');
```

```
        }).click(function() {
          var rows = $table.find('tbody > tr').get();
          rows.sort(function(a, b) {
            var keyA = $(a).children('td').eq(column).text()
              .toUpperCase();
            var keyB = $(b).children('td').eq(column).text()
              .toUpperCase();
            if (keyA < keyB) return -1;
            if (keyA > keyB) return 1;
            return 0;
          });
          $.each(rows, function(index, row) {
            $table.children('tbody').append(row);
          });
        });
      }
    });
  });
});
```

The first thing to note is our use of the `.each()` method to make the iteration **explicit**. Even though we could bind a `click` handler to all headers that have the `sort-alpha` class just by calling `$('table.sortable th.sort-alpha').click()`, this wouldn't allow us to easily capture a crucial bit of information: the **column index** of the clicked header. Because `.each()` passes the iteration index into its callback function, we can use it to find the relevant cell in each row of the data later.

Once we have found the header cell, we retrieve an array of all of the data rows. This is a great example of how `.get()` is useful in transforming a jQuery object into an array of DOM nodes; even though jQuery objects act like arrays in many respects, they don't have any of the native array methods available, such as `.sort()`.

Now that we have an array of DOM nodes, we can sort them, but to do this we need to write an appropriate comparator function. We want to sort the rows according to the textual contents of the relevant table cells, so this will be the information the comparator function will examine. We know which cell to look at because we captured the column index in the enclosing `.each()` call. We convert the text to uppercase because string comparisons in JavaScript are **case-sensitive** and we wish our sort to be **case-insensitive**. We store the key values in variables to avoid redundant calculations, compare them, and return a positive or negative number as discussed above.

Finally, with the array sorted, we loop through the rows and reinsert them into the table. Since `.append()` does not clone nodes, this *moves* them rather than copying them. Our table is now sorted.

This is an example of progressive enhancement's counterpart, **graceful degradation**. Unlike the AJAX solution discussed earlier, this technique cannot function without JavaScript; we are assuming the server has no scripting language available to it for this example. Since JavaScript is required for the sort to work, we are adding the `clickable` class through code only, thereby making sure that the interface indicates that sorting is possible (with a background image) only if the script can run. The page **degrades** into one that is still functional, albeit without sorting available.

We have moved the actual rows around, hence our alternating row colors are now out of whack:

◆ Title	◆ Author(s)	◆ Publish Date	◆ Price
Advanced Microsoft Content Management Server Development	Angus Logan, Stefan Goßner, Lim Mei Ying, Andrew Connell	Nov 2005	$53.99
AJAX and PHP: Building Responsive Web Applications	Cristian Darie, Mihai Bucica, Filip Chereches-Toşa, Bogdan Brinzarea	Mar 2006	$31.49
Alfresco Enterprise Content Management Implementation	Munwar Shariff	Jan 2007	$53.99
BPEL Cookbook: Best Practices for SOA-based Integration and composite applications development	Jerry Thomas, Doug Todd, Harish Gaur, Lawrence Pravin, Arun Poduval, The Hoa Nguyen, Yves Coene, Jeremy Bolie, Stany Blanvalet, Markus Zirn, Matjaz Juric, Sean Carey, Michael Cardella, Kevin Geminiuc, Praveen Ramachandran	Jul 2006	$40.49

We need to reapply the row colors after the sort is performed. We can do this by pulling the coloring code out into a function that we call when needed:

```
$(document).ready(function() {
  var alternateRowColors = function($table) {
    $('tbody tr:odd', $table)
      .removeClass('even').addClass('odd');
    $('tbody tr:even', $table)
      .removeClass('odd').addClass('even');
  };
  $('table.sortable').each(function() {
    var $table = $(this);
    alternateRowColors($table);
    $('th', $table).each(function(column) {
      var $header = $(this);
      if ($header.is('.sort-alpha')) {
        $header.addClass('clickable').hover(function() {
```

```
          $header.addClass('hover');
        }, function() {
          $header.removeClass('hover');
        }).click(function() {
          var rows = $table.find('tbody > tr').get();
          rows.sort(function(a, b) {
            var keyA = $(a).children('td').eq(column).text()
              .toUpperCase();
            var keyB = $(b).children('td').eq(column).text()
              .toUpperCase();
            if (keyA < keyB) return -1;
            if (keyA > keyB) return 1;
            return 0;
          });
          $.each(rows, function(index, row) {
            $table.children('tbody').append(row);
          });
          alternateRowColors($table);
        });
      }
    });
  });
});
```

This corrects the row coloring after the fact, fixing our issue:

⬍ Title	⬍ Author(s)	⬍ Publish Date	⬍ Price
Advanced Microsoft Content Management Server Development	Angus Logan, Stefan Goßner, Lim Mei Ying, Andrew Connell	Nov 2005	$53.99
AJAX and PHP: Building Responsive Web Applications	Cristian Darie, Mihai Bucica, Filip Chereches-Toşa, Bogdan Brinzarea	Mar 2006	$31.49
Alfresco Enterprise Content Management Implementation	Munwar Shariff	Jan 2007	$53.99
BPEL Cookbook: Best Practices for SOA-based integration and composite applications development	Jerry Thomas, Doug Todd, Harish Gaur, Lawrence Pravin, Arun Poduval, The Hoa Nguyen, Yves Coene, Jeremy Bolie, Stany Blanvalet, Markus Zirn, Matjaz Juric, Sean Carey, Michael Cardella, Kevin Geminiuc, Praveen Ramachandran	Jul 2006	$40.49

The power of plugins

The `alternateRowColors()` function that we wrote is a perfect candidate to become a jQuery **plugin**. In fact, any operation that we wish to apply to a set of DOM elements can easily be expressed as a plugin. To accomplish this, we need to modify our existing function only a little bit:

```
jQuery.fn.alternateRowColors = function() {
  $('tbody tr:odd', this)
    .removeClass('even').addClass('odd');
  $('tbody tr:even', this)
    .removeClass('odd').addClass('even');
  return this;
};
```

We have made three important changes to the function.

- It is defined as a new property of `jQuery.fn` rather than as a standalone function. This registers the function as a plugin method.

- We use the keyword `this` as a replacement for our `$table` parameter. Within a plugin method, `this` refers to the jQuery object that is being acted upon.

- Finally, we return `this` at the end of the function. Supplying the jQuery object as the return value makes our new method **chainable**.

 More information on writing jQuery plugins can be found in Chapter 11. There, we will discuss making a plugin ready for public consumption, as opposed to the small example here that is only to be used by our own code.

With our new plugin defined, we can call `$table.alternateRowColors()`, a more natural jQuery statement, instead of `alternateRowColors($table)`.

Performance concerns

Our code works, but it is quite slow. The culprit is the comparator function, which is performing a fair amount of work. This comparator will be called many times during the course of a sort, which means that every extra moment it spends on processing will be magnified.

The actual **sort algorithm** used by JavaScript is not defined by the standard. It may be a simple sort like a **bubble sort** (worst case of $\Theta(n^2)$ in computational complexity terms) or a more sophisticated approach like **quick sort** (which is $\Theta(n \log n)$ on average). It is safe to say, though, that doubling the number of items in an array will more than double the number of times the comparator function is called.

The remedy for our slow comparator is to **pre-compute** the keys for the comparison. We begin with our current, slow sort function:

```
rows.sort(function(a, b) {
  var keyA = $(a).children('td').eq(column).text()
    .toUpperCase();
  var keyB = $(b).children('td').eq(column).text()
    .toUpperCase();
  if (keyA < keyB) return -1;
  if (keyA > keyB) return 1;
  return 0;
});
```

We can pull out the key computation and do that in a separate loop:

```
$.each(rows, function(index, row) {
  row.sortKey = $(row).children('td').eq(column)
    .text().toUpperCase();
});
rows.sort(function(a, b) {
  if (a.sortKey < b.sortKey) return -1;
  if (a.sortKey > b.sortKey) return 1;
  return 0;
});
$.each(rows, function(index, row) {
  $table.children('tbody').append(row);
  row.sortKey = null;
});
```

In the new loop, we are doing all of the expensive work and storing the result in a new `.sortKey` property. This kind of property, attached to a DOM element but not a normal DOM attribute, is called an **expando**. This is a convenient place to store the key, since we need one per table row element. Now, we can examine this attribute within the comparator function, and our sort is markedly faster.

 We set the expando property to `null` after we're done with it to clean up after ourselves. This is not strictly necessary in this case, but is a good habit to establish because expando properties left lying around can be the cause of **memory leaks**. For more information, see Appendix C.

Instead of using expando properties, jQuery provides an alternative data storage mechanism we could use. The `.data()` method sets or retrieves arbitrary information associated with page elements, and the `.removeData()` method gets rid of any such stored information:

```
$.each(rows, function(index, row) {
  $(row).data('sortKey', $(row).children('td')
    .eq(column).text().toUpperCase());
});
rows.sort(function(a, b) {
  if ($(a).data('sortKey') < $(b).data('sortKey'))
    return -1;
  if ($(a).data('sortKey') > $(b).data('sortKey'))
    return 1;
  return 0;
});
$.each(rows, function(index, row) {
  $table.children('tbody').append(row);
  $(row).removeData('sortKey');
});
```

Using `.data()` instead of expando properties can, at times, be more convenient, since we are often working with jQuery objects rather than directly with DOM nodes. It also avoids potential problems with Internet Explorer memory leaks. However, for the remainder of this example, we will stick with expando properties in order to practice switching between operations on DOM nodes and operations on jQuery objects.

Finessing the sort keys

Now, we want to apply the same kind of sorting behavior to the **Author(s)** column of our table. By adding the `sort-alpha` class to its table header cell, the **Author(s)** column can be sorted with our existing code. Ideally authors should be sorted by last name, not first. Since some books have multiple authors, and some authors have middle names or initials listed, we need outside guidance to determine what part of the text to use as our sort key. We can supply this guidance by wrapping the relevant part of the cell in a tag:

```
<tr>
  <td><img src="../images/covers/small/1847192386.png"
    width="49" height="61" alt="Building Websites with
    Joomla! 1.5 Beta 1" />
  </td>
  <td>Building Websites with Joomla! 1.5 Beta 1</td>
  <td>Hagen <span class="sort-key">Graf</span></td>
  <td>Feb 2007</td>
  <td>$40.49</td>
</tr>
<tr>
```

```
    <td><img src="../images/covers/small/1904811620.png"
      width="49" height="61" alt="Learning Mambo: A
      Step-by-Step Tutorial to Building Your Website" />
    </td>
    <td>Learning Mambo: A Step-by-Step Tutorial to Building
      Your Website
    </td>
    <td>Douglas <span class="sort-key">Paterson</span></td>
    <td>Dec 2006</td>
    <td>$40.49</td>
  </tr>
```

Now, we have to modify our sorting code to take this tag into account without disturbing the existing behavior for the **Title** column, which is already working well. By prepending the marked sort key to the key we have previously calculated, we can sort first on the last name if it is called out, but on the whole string as a fallback:

```
$.each(rows, function(index, row) {
  var $cell = $(row).children('td').eq(column);
  row.sortKey = $cell.find('.sort-key').text().toUpperCase()
    + ' ' + $cell.text().toUpperCase();
});
```

Sorting by the **Author(s)** column now uses the provided key, thereby sorting by last name:

⬍ Title	⬍ Author(s)	⬍ Publish Date	⬍ Price
Programming Windows Workflow Foundation: Practical WF Techniques and Examples using XAML and C#	K. Scott Allen	Dec 2006	$40.49
Building Websites with XOOPS : A step-by-step tutorial	Steve Atwal	Oct 2006	$26.99
Learn OpenOffice.org Spreadsheet Macro Programming: OOoBasic and Calc automation	Dr. Mark Alexander Bain	Dec 2006	$35.99
UML 2.0 in Action: A project-based tutorial	Philippe Baumann, Henriette Baumann, Patrick Grassle	Sep 2005	$31.49

If two last names are identical, the sort uses the entire string as a tiebreaker for positioning.

Sorting other types of data

Our user should be able to sort not just by the **Title** and **Author(s)** columns, but the **Publish Date** and **Price** columns as well. Since we streamlined our comparator function, it can handle all kinds of data, but first the computed keys will need to be adjusted for other data types. For example, in the case of prices we need to strip off the leading $ character and parse the rest so that we can compare them numerically:

```
var key = parseFloat($cell.text().replace(/^[^\d.]*/, ''));
row.sortKey = isNaN(key) ? 0 : key;
```

The regular expression used here removes any leading characters other than numbers and decimal points, passing the result on to `parseFloat()`. The result of `parseFloat()` then needs to be checked, because if no number can be extracted from the text, `NaN` (**not a number**) is returned. This can wreak havoc on `.sort()`.

For the date cells, we can use the JavaScript `Date` object:

```
row.sortKey = Date.parse('1 ' + $cell.text());
```

The dates in this table contain a month and year only; `Date.parse()` requires a fully-specified date, so we prepend the string with `1`. This provides a day to complement the month and year, and the combination is then converted into a **timestamp**, which can be sorted using our normal comparator.

We can apportion these expressions across separate functions, and call the appropriate one based on the class applied to the table header:

```
jQuery.fn.alternateRowColors = function() {
  $('tbody tr:odd', this)
    .removeClass('even').addClass('odd');
  $('tbody tr:even', this)
    .removeClass('odd').addClass('even');
  return this;
};
$(document).ready(function() {
  $('table.sortable').each(function() {
    var $table = $(this);
    $table.alternateRowColors();
    $('th', $table).each(function(column) {
      var $header = $(this);
      var findSortKey;
      if ($header.is('.sort-alpha')) {
        findSortKey = function($cell) {
          return $cell.find('.sort-key')
            .text().toUpperCase()
```

```
                       + ' ' + $cell.text().toUpperCase();
        };
      }
      else if ($header.is('.sort-numeric')) {
        findSortKey = function($cell) {
          var key = $cell.text().replace(/^[^\d.]*/, '');
          key = parseFloat(key);
          return isNaN(key) ? 0 : key;
        };
      }
      else if ($header.is('.sort-date')) {
        findSortKey = function($cell) {
          return Date.parse('1 ' + $cell.text());
        };
      }

      if (findSortKey) {
        $header.addClass('clickable').hover(function() {
          $header.addClass('hover');
        }, function() {
          $header.removeClass('hover');
        }).click(function() {
          var rows = $table.find('tbody > tr').get();
          $.each(rows, function(index, row) {
            var $cell = $(row).children('td').eq(column);
            row.sortKey = findSortKey($cell);
          });
          rows.sort(function(a, b) {
            if (a.sortKey < b.sortKey) return -1;
            if (a.sortKey > b.sortKey) return 1;
            return 0;
          });
          $.each(rows, function(index, row) {
            $table.children('tbody').append(row);
            row.sortKey = null;
          });
          $table.alternateRowColors();
        });
      }
    });
  });
});
```

The `findSortKey` variable doubles as the function to calculate the key, and a flag to indicate whether the column header is marked with a class making it sortable. We can now sort on date or price:

⬍ Title	⬍ Author(s)	⬍ Publish Date	⬍ Price
Building Websites with the ASP.NET Community Starter Kit	Cristian Darie, K. Scott Allen	May 2004	$40.49
Building Websites with Plone	Cameron Cooper	Nov 2004	$44.99
Windows Server 2003 Active Directory Design and Implementation: Creating, Migrating, and Merging Networks	John Savill	Jan 2005	$53.99
SSL VPN: Understanding, evaluating and planning secure, web-based remote access	Tim Speed, Joseph Steinberg	Mar 2005	$44.99

⬍ Title	⬍ Author(s)	⬍ Publish Date	⬍ Price
User Training for Busy Programmers	William Rice	Jun 2005	$11.69
Creating your MySQL Database: Practical Design Tips and Techniques	Marc Delisle	Nov 2006	$17.99
Pluggable Authentication Modules: The Definitive Guide to PAM for Linux SysAdmins and C Developers	Kenneth Geisshirt	Jan 2007	$17.99
Invision Power Board 2: A User Guide	David Mytton	Jul 2005	$22.49

Column highlighting

It can be a nice user interface enhancement to visually remind the user of what has been done in the past. By highlighting the column that was most recently used for sorting, we can focus the user's attention on the part of the table that is most likely to be relevant. Fortunately, since we've already determined how to select the table cells in the column, applying a class to those cells is simple:

```
$table.find('td').removeClass('sorted')
  .filter(':nth-child(' + (column + 1) + ')')
  .addClass('sorted');
```

This snippet first removes the `sorted` class from all cells, then adds it to cells that are in the same column we just used for our sort. Note that we have to add 1 to the column index we found earlier, since the `:nth-child()` selector is **one-based** rather than **zero-based**. With this code in place, we get a highlighted column after any sort operation:

	⬍ Title	⬍ Author(s)	⬍ Publish Date	⬍ Price
	Programming Windows Workflow Foundation: Practical WF Techniques and Examples using XAML and C#	K. Scott Allen	Dec 2006	$40.49
	Building Websites with XOOPS : A step-by-step tutorial	Steve Atwal	Oct 2006	$26.99
	Learn OpenOffice.org Spreadsheet Macro Programming: OOoBasic and Calc automation	Dr. Mark Alexander Bain	Dec 2006	$35.99
	UML 2.0 in Action: A project-based tutorial	Philippe Baumann, Henriette Baumann, Patrick Grassle	Sep 2005	$31.49

Alternating sort directions

Our final sorting enhancement is to allow for both **ascending** and **descending** sort orders. When the user clicks on a column that is already sorted, we want to reverse the current sort order.

To reverse a sort, all we have to do is to invert the values returned by our comparator. We can do this with a simple variable:

```
if (a.sortKey < b.sortKey) return -sortDirection;
if (a.sortKey > b.sortKey) return sortDirection;
```

If `sortDirection` equals 1, then the sort will be the same as before. If it equals -1, the sort will be reversed. We can use classes to keep track of the current sort order of a column:

```
jQuery.fn.alternateRowColors = function() {
  $('tbody tr:odd', this)
    .removeClass('even').addClass('odd');
  $('tbody tr:even', this)
    .removeClass('odd').addClass('even');
  return this;
};
$(document).ready(function() {
  $('table.sortable').each(function() {
    var $table = $(this);
    $table.alternateRowColors();
    $('th', $table).each(function(column) {
      var $header = $(this);
      var findSortKey;
      if ($header.is('.sort-alpha')) {
        findSortKey = function($cell) {
          return $cell.find('.sort-key').text().toUpperCase()
            + ' ' + $cell.text().toUpperCase();
        };
      }
      else if ($header.is('.sort-numeric')) {
        findSortKey = function($cell) {
          var key = $cell.text().replace(/^[^\d.]*/, '');
          key = parseFloat(key);
          return isNaN(key) ? 0 : key;
        };
      }
      else if ($header.is('.sort-date')) {
        findSortKey = function($cell) {
          return Date.parse('1 ' + $cell.text());
        };
      }
      if (findSortKey) {
        $header.addClass('clickable').hover(function() {
```

```
          $header.addClass('hover');
        }, function() {
          $header.removeClass('hover');
        }).click(function() {
          var sortDirection = 1;
          if ($header.is('.sorted-asc')) {
            sortDirection = -1;
          }
          var rows = $table.find('tbody > tr').get();
          $.each(rows, function(index, row) {
            var $cell = $(row).children('td').eq(column);
            row.sortKey = findSortKey($cell);
          });
          rows.sort(function(a, b) {
            if (a.sortKey < b.sortKey) return -sortDirection;
            if (a.sortKey > b.sortKey) return sortDirection;
            return 0;
          });
          $.each(rows, function(index, row) {
            $table.children('tbody').append(row);
            row.sortKey = null;
          });
          $table.find('th').removeClass('sorted-asc')
            .removeClass('sorted-desc');
          if (sortDirection == 1) {
            $header.addClass('sorted-asc');
          }
          else {
            $header.addClass('sorted-desc');
          }
          $table.find('td').removeClass('sorted')
            .filter(':nth-child(' + (column + 1) + ')')
            .addClass('sorted');
          $table.alternateRowColors();
        });
      }
    });
  });
});
```

As a side benefit, since we use classes to store the sort direction we can style the column headers to indicate the current order as well:

	‡ Title	‡ Author(s)	▼ Publish Date	‡ Price
	Microsoft AJAX C# Essentials: Building Responsive ASP.NET 2.0 Applications	Cristian Darie, Bogdan Brinzarea	Mar 2007	$31.99
	MediaWiki Administrators' Tutorial Guide	Mizanur Rahman	Mar 2007	$31.99
COMING SOON	CherryPy Essentials: Rapid Python Web Application Development	Sylvain Hellegouarch	Mar 2007	$31.99
	Visual SourceSafe 2005 Software Configuration Management in Practice	Alexandru Serban	Feb 2007	$44.99

Server-side pagination

Sorting is a great way to wade through a large amount of data to find information. We can also help the user focus on a portion of a large data set by **paginating** the data.

Much like sorting, pagination is often performed on the server. If the data to be displayed is stored in a database, it is easy to pull out one chunk of information at a time using MySQL's LIMIT clause, ROWNUM in Oracle, or equivalent methods in other database engines.

As with our initial sorting example, pagination can be triggered by sending information to the server in a query string, such as index.php?page=52. And again, as before, we can perform this task either with a full page load or by using AJAX to pull in just one chunk of the table. This strategy is browser-independent, and can handle large data sets very well.

Sorting and paging go together

Data that is long enough to benefit from sorting is likely long enough to be a candidate for paging. It is not unusual to wish to combine these two techniques for data presentation. Since they both affect the set of data that is present on a page, though, it is important to consider their interactions while implementing them.

Both sorting and pagination can be accomplished either on the server, or in the web browser. However, we must keep the strategies for the two tasks in sync; otherwise, we can end up with confusing behavior. Suppose, for example, we have a table with eight rows and two columns in it, sorted initially by the first column. If the data is re-sorted by the second column, many rows may change places:

A	4		E	1
B	5		C	2
C	2		G	3
D	7		A	4
E	1		B	5
F	8		H	6
G	3		D	7
H	6		F	8
Before			After	

Now let's consider what happens when pagination is added to the mix. Suppose only the first four rows are provided by the server and the browser attempts to sort the data. If paging is done by the server and sorting by the browser, the entire data set is not available for the sorting routine, making the results incorrect:

A	4		C	2
B	5		A	4
C	2		B	5
D	7		D	7
Before			After	

Only the data already present on the page can be manipulated by JavaScript. To prevent this from being a problem, we must either perform both tasks on the server (polling the server for the correct data set on every page or sort operation), or both in the browser (with all possible data available to JavaScript at all times), so that the first displayed results are indeed the first rows in the data set:

A	4		E	1
B	5		C	2
C	2		G	3
D	7		A	4
Before			After	

JavaScript pagination

So, let's examine how we would add JavaScript pagination to the table we have already made sortable in the browser. First, we'll focus on displaying a particular page of data, disregarding user interaction for now.

```
$(document).ready(function() {
  $('table.paginated').each(function() {
    var currentPage = 0;
    var numPerPage = 10;
    var $table = $(this);
    $table.find('tbody tr').hide()
      .slice(currentPage * numPerPage,
        (currentPage + 1) * numPerPage)
      .show();
  });
});
```

This code displays the first page—ten rows of data.

Once again we rely on the presence of a `<tbody>` element to separate data from headers; we don't want to have the headers or footers disappear when moving on to the second page. For selecting the rows containing data, we hide all the rows first, then select the rows on the current page, showing the selected rows. The `.slice()` method shown here works like the array method of the same name; it reduces the selection to the elements in between the two positions given.

The most error-prone task in writing this code is formulating the expressions to use in the `.slice()` filter. We need to find the indices of the rows at the beginning and end of the current page. For the beginning row, we just multiply the current page number by the number of rows on each page. Multiplying the number of rows by one more than the current page number gives us the beginning row of the next page; the `.slice()` method fetches the rows up to and not including this second parameter.

Displaying the pager

To add user interaction to the mix, we need to place a **pager** next to the table: a set of links for navigating to different pages of data. We could do this by simply inserting links for the pages in the HTML markup, but this would violate the **progressive enhancement** principle we've been espousing. Instead, we should add the links using JavaScript, so that users without scripting available are not misled by links that cannot work.

To display the links, we need to calculate the number of pages and create a corresponding number of DOM elements:

```
var numRows = $table.find('tbody tr').length;
var numPages = Math.ceil(numRows / numPerPage);

var $pager = $('<div class="pager"></div>');
for (var page = 0; page < numPages; page++) {
  $('<span class="page-number">' + (page + 1) + '</span>')
    .appendTo($pager).addClass('clickable');
}
$pager.insertBefore($table);
```

The number of pages can be found by dividing the number of data rows by the number of items we wish to display on each page. Since the division may not yield an integer, we must round the result up using `Math.ceil()` to ensure that the final partial page will be accessible. Then, with this number in hand, we create buttons for each page and position the new pager above the table:

Enabling the pager buttons

To make these new buttons actually work, we need to update the `currentPage` variable and then run our pagination routine. At first blush, it seems we should be able to do this by setting `currentPage` to `page`, which is the current value of the iterator that creates the buttons:

```
$(document).ready(function() {
  $('table.paginated').each(function() {
    var currentPage = 0;
    var numPerPage = 10;
    var $table = $(this);
    var repaginate = function() {
      $table.find('tbody tr').hide()
        .slice(currentPage * numPerPage,
          (currentPage + 1) * numPerPage)
        .show();
    };
    var numRows = $table.find('tbody tr').length;
```

```
        var numPages = Math.ceil(numRows / numPerPage);
        var $pager = $('<div class="pager"></div>');
        for (var page = 0; page < numPages; page++) {
          $('<span class="page-number"></span>').text(page + 1)
            .click(function() {
              currentPage = page;
              repaginate();
            }).appendTo($pager).addClass('clickable');
        }
        $pager.insertBefore($table);

    });
  });
```

This works, in that the new `repaginate()` function is called when the page loads and when any of the page links are clicked. All of the links present us with a table that has no data rows, though:

The problem is that in defining our `click` handler, we have created a **closure**. The `click` handler refers to the `page` variable, which is defined *outside* the function. When the variable changes the next time through the loop, this also affects the `click` handlers that we have already set up for the earlier buttons. The net effect is that, for a pager with 7 pages, each button directs us to page 8 (the final value of `page` when the loop is complete).

More information on how closures work can be found in Appendix C.

To correct this problem, we'll take advantage of one of the more advanced features of jQuery's event binding methods. We can add a set of **custom event data** to the handler when we bind it that will still be available when the handler is eventually called. With this capability in our bag of tricks, we can write:

```
    $('<span class="page-number"></span>').text(page + 1)
      .bind('click', {newPage: page}, function(event) {
        currentPage = event.data['newPage'];
        repaginate();
      }).appendTo($pager).addClass('clickable');
```

The new page number is passed into the handler by way of the event's `data` property. In this way the page number escapes the hazards of the closure, and is frozen in time at the value it contained when the handler was bound. Now our pager links can correctly take us to different pages:

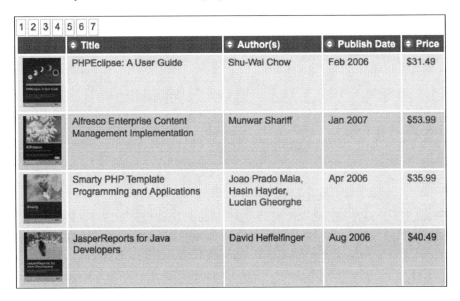

Marking the current page

Our pager can be made more user-friendly by highlighting the current page number. We just need to update the classes on the buttons every time one is clicked:

```
$(document).ready(function() {
  $('table.paginated').each(function() {
    var currentPage = 0;
    var numPerPage = 10;
    var $table = $(this);
    var repaginate = function() {
      $table.find('tbody tr').hide()
        .slice(currentPage * numPerPage,
          (currentPage + 1) * numPerPage)
        .show();
    };
    var numRows = $table.find('tbody tr').length;
    var numPages = Math.ceil(numRows / numPerPage);
    var $pager = $('<div class="pager"></div>');
    for (var page = 0; page < numPages; page++) {
      $('<span class="page-number"></span>').text(page + 1)
```

```
            .bind('click', {newPage: page}, function(event) {
              currentPage = event.data['newPage'];
              repaginate();
              $(this).addClass('active')
                .siblings().removeClass('active');
          }).appendTo($pager).addClass('clickable');
      }
      $pager.insertBefore($table)
        .find('span.page-number:first').addClass('active');
    });
  });
```

Now we have an indicator of the current status of the pager:

Paging with sorting

We began this discussion by noting that sorting and paging controls needed to be aware of one another to avoid confusing results. Now that we have a working pager, we need to make sort operations respect the current page selection.

Doing this is as simple as calling our `repaginate()` function whenever a sort is performed. The **scope** of the function, though, makes this problematic. We can't reach `repaginate()` from our sorting routine because it is contained inside a different `$(document).ready()` handler. We could just consolidate the two pieces of code, but instead let's be a bit sneakier. We can **decouple** the behaviors, so that a sort calls the `repaginate` behavior if it exists, but ignores it otherwise. To accomplish this, we'll use a handler for a **custom event**.

In our earlier event handling discussion, we limited ourselves to event names that were triggered by the web browser, such as `click` and `mouseup`. The `.bind()` and `.trigger()` methods are not limited to these events, though; we can use any string as an event name. Using this capability, we can define a new event called `repaginate` as a stand-in for the function we've been calling:

```
$table.bind('repaginate', function() {
  $table.find('tbody tr').hide()
    .slice(currentPage * numPerPage,
      (currentPage + 1) * numPerPage)
    .show();
});
```

Now in places where we were calling `repaginate()`, we can call:

```
$table.trigger('repaginate');
```

We can issue this call in our sort code as well. It will do nothing if the table does not have a pager, so we can mix and match the two capabilities as desired.

The finished code

The completed sorting and paging code in its entirety follows:

```
jQuery.fn.alternateRowColors = function() {
  $('tbody tr:odd', this)
    .removeClass('even').addClass('odd');
  $('tbody tr:even', this)
    .removeClass('odd').addClass('even');
  return this;
};
$(document).ready(function() {
  $('table.sortable').each(function() {
    var $table = $(this);
    $table.alternateRowColors();
    $('th', $table).each(function(column) {
      var $header = $(this);
      var findSortKey;
      if ($header.is('.sort-alpha')) {
        findSortKey = function($cell) {
          return $cell.find('.sort-key').text().toUpperCase()
            + ' ' + $cell.text().toUpperCase();
        };
      }
      else if ($header.is('.sort-numeric')) {
        findSortKey = function($cell) {
```

```
      var key = $cell.text().replace(/^[^\d.]*/, '');
      key = parseFloat(key);
      return isNaN(key) ? 0 : key;
    };
  }
  else if ($header.is('.sort-date')) {
    findSortKey = function($cell) {
      return Date.parse('1 ' + $cell.text());
    };
  }
  if (findSortKey) {
    $header.addClass('clickable').hover(function() {
      $header.addClass('hover');
    }, function() {
      $header.removeClass('hover');
    }).click(function() {
      var sortDirection = 1;
      if ($header.is('.sorted-asc')) {
        sortDirection = -1;
      }
      var rows = $table.find('tbody > tr').get();
      $.each(rows, function(index, row) {
        var $cell = $(row).children('td').eq(column);
        row.sortKey = findSortKey($cell);
      });
      rows.sort(function(a, b) {
        if (a.sortKey < b.sortKey) return -sortDirection;
        if (a.sortKey > b.sortKey) return sortDirection;
        return 0;
      });
      $.each(rows, function(index, row) {
        $table.children('tbody').append(row);
        row.sortKey = null;
      });
      $table.find('th').removeClass('sorted-asc')
        .removeClass('sorted-desc');
      if (sortDirection == 1) {
        $header.addClass('sorted-asc');
      }
      else {
        $header.addClass('sorted-desc');
      }
      $table.find('td').removeClass('sorted')
        .filter(':nth-child(' + (column + 1) + ')')
        .addClass('sorted');
      $table.alternateRowColors();
      $table.trigger('repaginate');
```

```
          });
        }
      });
    });
  });
  $(document).ready(function() {
    $('table.paginated').each(function() {
      var currentPage = 0;
      var numPerPage = 10;
      var $table = $(this);
      $table.bind('repaginate', function() {
        $table.find('tbody tr').hide()
          .slice(currentPage * numPerPage,
            (currentPage + 1) * numPerPage)
          .show();
      });
      var numRows = $table.find('tbody tr').length;
      var numPages = Math.ceil(numRows / numPerPage);
      var $pager = $('<div class="pager"></div>');
      for (var page = 0; page < numPages; page++) {
        $('<span class="page-number"></span>').text(page + 1)
          .bind('click', {newPage: page}, function(event) {
            currentPage = event.data['newPage'];
            $table.trigger('repaginate');
            $(this).addClass('active')
              .siblings().removeClass('active');
          }).appendTo($pager).addClass('clickable');
      }
      $pager.insertBefore($table)
        .find('span.page-number:first').addClass('active');
    });
  });
```

Modifying table appearance

We have now looked at some ways of ordering the rows of data in a table to provide
assistance to the user in finding the desired information. It is often the case, though,
that there is still a lot of data to sift through after any sorting or paging is performed.
We can assist the user by manipulating not just the order and quantity of displayed
rows, but the appearance of those that are shown.

Row highlighting

One practical way to guide the user's eye is to **highlight** rows to give a visual cue about what data is important. To examine some highlighting strategies, we need a table to work with. This time, we'll start with a table of news items. The table will be a little more complicated than the last; it will include some rows used as **subheadings**, in addition to a main heading row. The HTML structure is as follows:

```
<table>
  <thead>
    <tr>
      <th>Date</th>
      <th>Headline</th>
      <th>Author</th>
      <th>Topic</th>
    </tr>
  </thead>
  <tbody>
    <tr>
      <th colspan="4">2008</th>
    </tr>
    <tr>
      <td>Sep 28</td>
      <td>jQuery, Microsoft, and Nokia</td>
      <td>John Resig</td>
      <td>third-party</td>
    </tr>
        ...
    <tr>
      <td>Jan 15</td>
      <td>jQuery 1.2.2: 2nd Birthday Present</td>
      <td>John Resig</td>
      <td>release</td>
    </tr>
  </tbody>
  <tbody>
    <tr>
      <th colspan="4">2007</th>
    </tr>
    <tr>
      <td>Dec 8</td>
      <td>jQuery Plugins site updated</td>
      <td>Mike Hostetler</td>
      <td>announcement</td>
    </tr>
```

```
      . . .
    <tr>
      <td>Jan 11</td>
      <td>Selector Speeds</td>
      <td>John Resig</td>
      <td>source</td>
    </tr>
  </tbody>
    . . .
</table>
```

Note the use of multiple `<tbody>` sections. This is valid HTML markup for grouping sets of rows together. We have placed the section subheadings within these groupings, using `<th>` elements to set them off. With basic CSS added, this table renders as follows:

Date	Headline	Author	Topic
2008			
Sep 28	jQuery, Microsoft, and Nokia	John Resig	third-party
Aug 31	jQuery Conference 2008 Agenda	Rey Bango	conference
Aug 29	jQuery.com Site Redesign	John Resig	announcement
Aug 15	Registration Open for jQuery Conference 2008	Karl Swedberg	conference
Jul 14	jQuery UI 1.5.2	Paul Bakaus	release
Jun 26	jQuery UI 1.5.1	Paul Bakaus	release
Jun 26	jQuery Camp 2008 Announced	Rey Bango	conference
Jun 9	jQuery UI v1.5 Released, Focus on Consistent API and Effects	Paul Bakaus	release
Jun 4	jQuery 1.2.6: Events 100% faster	John Resig	release
Mar 7	jQuery UI Worldwide Sprint: March 14-15	Richard Worth	conference
Feb 8	jQuery 1.2.3: AIR, Namespacing, and UI Alpha	John Resig	release
Jan 23	jQuery UI and beyond: The jQuery-Liferay partnership	Paul Bakaus	announcement
Jan 15	jQuery 1.2.2: 2nd Birthday Present	John Resig	release
2007			
Dec 8	jQuery Plugins site updated	Mike Hostetler	announcement
Dec 6	Flot, a new plotting plugin for jQuery	Bradley Sepos	plug-in
Nov 2	Google Using jQuery	Rey Bango	third-party

Row striping

We have already seen one simple example of row highlighting earlier in this chapter, and before that in Chapter 2. **Striping** rows is a common way to guide the user's eye across multiple columns accurately.

As we have seen, row striping can be as simple as a couple of lines to add classes to odd and even rows:

```
$(document).ready(function() {
  $('table.striped tr:odd).addClass('odd');
  $('table.striped tr:even).addClass('even');
});
```

While this code works fine for simple table structures, if we introduce additional rows we do not want to be striped (such as the subheading rows we are using for the years in our table), the basic odd-even pattern no longer suffices. If, for example, the **2006** row would be classified as even, the rows before and after it would both be odd, which is likely not desirable.

Jan 13	jQuery wallpapers		Nate Cavanaugh	miscellaneous
Jan 11	Selector Speeds		John Resig	source
2006				
Dec 27	The Path to 1.1		John Resig	source
Dec 18	Meet The People Behind jQuery		John Resig	announcement
Dec 13	Helping you understand jQuery		John Resig	tutorial

We can ensure that our alternating-row pattern begins anew with each years' worth of news items by using the :nth-child() pseudo-class we learned about in Chapter 2:

```
$(document).ready(function() {
  $('table.striped tr:nth-child(odd)').addClass('odd');
  $('table.striped tr:nth-child(even)').addClass('even');
});
```

Jan 13	jQuery wallpapers		Nate Cavanaugh	miscellaneous
Jan 11	Selector Speeds		John Resig	source
2006				
Dec 27	The Path to 1.1		John Resig	source
Dec 18	Meet The People Behind jQuery		John Resig	announcement
Dec 13	Helping you understand jQuery		John Resig	tutorial

Each group of rows now begins with an odd row, but the subheading rows are included in this calculation. So instead, we could exclude the subheading rows from consideration with the :has() pseudo-class:

```
$(document).ready(function() {
  $('table.striped tr:not(:has(th)):odd').addClass('odd');
  $('table.striped tr:not(:has(th)):even').addClass('even');
});
```

Jan 13	jQuery wallpapers		Nate Cavanaugh	miscellaneous
Jan 11	Selector Speeds		John Resig	source
2006				
Dec 27	The Path to 1.1		John Resig	source
Dec 18	Meet The People Behind jQuery		John Resig	announcement
Dec 13	Helping you understand jQuery		John Resig	tutorial

Now the subheadings are excluded, but groupings will begin with an odd or even row depending on which classification applied to the previous data row. Reconciling these two behaviors can be a bit tricky; one straightforward option is introducing some **explicit iteration** using the .each() method.

```
$(document).ready(function() {
  $('table.striped tbody').each(function() {
    $(this).find('tr:not(:has(th)):odd').addClass('odd');
    $(this).find('tr:not(:has(th)):even').addClass('even');
  });
});
```

Now each grouping is striped independently, and subheading rows are excluded from the calculations.

Jan 14	jQuery Birthday: 1.1, New Site, New Docs		John Resig	announcement
Jan 13	jQuery wallpapers		Nate Cavanaugh	miscellaneous
Jan 11	Selector Speeds		John Resig	source
2006				
Dec 27	The Path to 1.1		John Resig	source
Dec 18	Meet The People Behind jQuery		John Resig	announcement
Dec 13	Helping you understand jQuery		John Resig	tutorial

Advanced row striping

These manipulations of odd and even rows have set us up for some more complicated techniques. In particularly dense tables, even alternating row colors can be confusing to the eye, and it can be beneficial to alternate colors at a larger interval. As an example, we will modify the striping of our news table to color its rows three-at-a-time.

In Chapter 2, we introduced the `.filter()` method for selecting page elements in a very flexible way. Recalling that `.filter()` can take not just a selector expression, but also a **filter function**, we can write:

```
$(document).ready(function() {
  $('table.striped tbody').each(function() {
    $(this).find('tr:not(:has(th))').filter(function(index) {
      return (index % 6) < 3;
    }).addClass('odd');
  });
});
```

This code accomplishes a lot in a small space, so let's break it down piece-by-piece.

First, we use the `.each()` method as before to segment our task neatly by row grouping. We want our three-row stripes to begin anew after each subheading, so this technique allows us to work one section at a time. Then, we use `.find()` as in our last example to locate all of the rows that do not have `<th>` elements (and thus are not subheadings).

Now, we need to select the first three elements of this set, skip three elements, and so forth. This is where `.filter()` comes into play. The filter function takes an argument containing the index of the item within the matched set—that is, the row number in the section of the table we're examining. If, and only if, our filter function returns `true`, the element will remain in the set.

The **modulo operator** (`%`) provides us with the information we need. The expression `index % 6` evaluates to the remainder of the row number when divided by 6; if this remainder is 0, 1, or 2, then we'll mark the row as `odd`; if it is 3, 4, or 5, the row will be `even`.

The code, as presented, only marks the `odd` sets of rows. To also apply the `even` class, we could write another filter that applied the opposite filter, or we can get a bit more creative:

```
$(document).ready(function() {
  $('table.striped tbody').each(function() {
    $(this).find('tr:not(:has(th))').addClass('even')
```

```
      .filter(function(index) {
        return (index % 6) < 3;
      }).removeClass('even').addClass('odd');
    });
  });
```

Here we apply the even class to all of the rows, and remove it if we add the odd class. Our table now has stylish alternating row groupings, which begin anew with each new section of the table.

Date	Headline	Author	Topic
2008			
Sep 28	jQuery, Microsoft, and Nokia	John Resig	third-party
Aug 31	jQuery Conference 2008 Agenda	Rey Bango	conference
Aug 29	jQuery.com Site Redesign	John Resig	announcement
Aug 15	Registration Open for jQuery Conference 2008	Karl Swedberg	conference
Jul 14	jQuery UI 1.5.2	Paul Bakaus	release
Jun 26	jQuery UI 1.5.1	Paul Bakaus	release
Jun 26	jQuery Camp 2008 Announced	Rey Bango	conference
Jun 9	jQuery UI v1.5 Released, Focus on Consistent API and Effects	Paul Bakaus	release
Jun 4	jQuery 1.2.6: Events 100% faster	John Resig	release
Mar 7	jQuery UI Worldwide Sprint: March 14-15	Richard Worth	conference
Feb 8	jQuery 1.2.3: AIR, Namespacing, and UI Alpha	John Resig	release
Jan 23	jQuery UI and beyond: The jQuery-Liferay partnership	Paul Bakaus	announcement
Jan 15	jQuery 1.2.2: 2nd Birthday Present	John Resig	release
2007			
Dec 8	jQuery Plugins site updated	Mike Hostetler	announcement
Dec 6	Flot, a new plotting plugin for jQuery	Bradley Sepos	plug-in
Nov 2	Google Using jQuery	Rey Bango	third-party
Sep 17	jQuery UI: Interactions and Widgets	John Resig	announcement
Sep 10	jQuery 1.2: jQuery.extend("Awesome")	John Resig	release
Sep 6	jQueryCamp '07 (Boston)	John Resig	conference
Aug 24	jQuery 1.1.4: Faster, More Tests, Ready for 1.2	John Resig	release
Jul 17	SF jQuery Meetup and Ajax Experience	John Resig	conference

Interactive row highlighting

Another visual enhancement that we can apply to our news article table is row highlighting based on user interaction. Here we'll respond to clicking on an author's name by highlighting all rows that have the same name in their **Author** cell. Just as we did with the row striping, we can modify the appearance of these highlighted rows by adding a class:

```
#content tr.highlight {
  background: #ff6;
}
```

It's important that we give this new `highlight` class adequate **specificity**, so that the background color will override that of the `even` and `odd` classes.

Now we need to select the appropriate cell and attach behavior to it using the `.click()` method:

```
$(document).ready(function() {
  var $authorCells = $('table.striped td:nth-child(3)');
  $authorCells.click(function() {
    // Perform our highlighting here.
  });
});
```

Notice that we use the `:nth-child(n)` pseudo-class as part of the selector expression that points to the third column where the author information is. In case the table structure were to later change, we would want this constant 3 to be in only one place in the code, so it could be easily updated. For this reason, and for efficiency, we store the result of our selector in the `$authorCells` variable rather than repeating the selector each time it is needed.

 Recall that unlike JavaScript indices, the CSS-based `:nth-child(n)` pseudo-class begins numbering at 1, not 0.

When the user clicks a cell in the third column, we want the cell's text to be compared to that of the same column's cell in every other row. If it matches, the `highlight` class will be toggled. In other words, the class will be added if it isn't already there and removed if it is. This way, we can click on an author cell to remove the row highlighting if that cell or one with the same author has already been clicked.

```
$(document).ready(function() {
  var $authorCells = $('table.striped td:nth-child(3)');
  $authorCells.click(function() {
    var authorName = $(this).text();
    $authorCells.each(function(index) {
      if (authorName == $(this).text()) {
        $(this).parent().toggleClass('highlight');
      }
    });
  });
});
```

The code is working well at this point, except when a user clicks on two authors' names in succession. Rather than switching the highlighted rows from one author to the next as we might expect, we end up with the highlight class on both groups of rows. To avoid this behavior, we can add an else statement to the code, removing the highlight class for any row that does not have the same author name as the one clicked:

```
$(document).ready(function() {
  var $authorCells = $('table.striped td:nth-child(3)');
  $authorCells.click(function() {
    var authorName = $(this).text();
    $authorCells.each(function(index) {
      if (authorName == $(this).text()) {
        $(this).parent().toggleClass('highlight');
      }
      else {
        $(this).parent().removeClass('highlight');
      }
    });
  });
});
```

Now when we click on **Rey Bango**, for example, we can see all of his articles much more easily:

Date	Headline	Author	Topic
2008			
Sep 28	jQuery, Microsoft, and Nokia	John Resig	third-party
Aug 31	jQuery Conference 2008 Agenda	Rey Bango	conference
Aug 29	jQuery.com Site Redesign	John Resig	announcement
Aug 15	Registration Open for jQuery Conference 2008	Karl Swedberg	conference
Jul 14	jQuery UI 1.5.2	Paul Bakaus	release
Jun 26	jQuery UI 1.5.1	Paul Bakaus	release
Jun 26	jQuery Camp 2008 Announced	Rey Bango	conference
Jun 9	jQuery UI v1.5 Released, Focus on Consistent API and Effects	Paul Bakaus	release
Jun 4	jQuery 1.2.6: Events 100% faster	John Resig	release
Mar 7	jQuery UI Worldwide Sprint: March 14-15	Richard Worth	conference
Feb 8	jQuery 1.2.3: AIR, Namespacing, and UI Alpha	John Resig	release
Jan 23	jQuery UI and beyond: The jQuery-Liferay partnership	Paul Bakaus	announcement
Jan 15	jQuery 1.2.2: 2nd Birthday Present	John Resig	release
2007			
Dec 8	jQuery Plugins site updated	Mike Hostetler	announcement
Dec 6	Flot, a new plotting plugin for jQuery	Bradley Sepos	plug-in
Nov 2	Google Using jQuery	Rey Bango	third-party
Sep 17	jQuery UI: Interactions and Widgets	John Resig	announcement

If we then click on **John Resig** in any one of the cells, the highlighting will be removed from Rey Bango's rows and added to John's.

Tooltips

Although the row highlighting might be a useful feature, so far it's not apparent to the user that the feature even exists. We can begin to remedy this situation by giving all author cells a `clickable` class, which we have styled to change the mouse cursor to a pointer when it is within the cell:

```
$(document).ready(function() {
  var $authorCells = $('table.striped td:nth-child(3)');
  $authorCells
    .addClass('clickable')
    .click(function() {
      var authorName = $(this).text();
      $authorCells.each(function(index) {
        if (authorName == $(this).text()) {
          $(this).parent().toggleClass('highlight');
        }
        else {
          $(this).parent().removeClass('highlight');
        }
      });
    });
});
```

The `clickable` class is a step in the right direction, for sure, but it still doesn't tell the user what will happen when the cell is clicked. As far as the user of the page knows, that click could just as easily trigger another behavior, such as sending the user to another page. Some further indication of what will happen upon clicking is in order.

Tooltips are a familiar feature of many software applications, including web browsers. We can address this usability challenge by displaying a tooltip when the mouse hovers over one of the **Author** cells. The text of the tooltip can describe to users the effect their action will have, with a message such as **Highlight all articles by Rey Bango**. This text will be contained in a <div>, which we can append to the <body>. The $tooltip variable will be used throughout the script to refer to this newly created element:

```
var $tooltip = $('<div id="tooltip"></div>').appendTo('body');
```

There are three basic operations we will have to perform repeatedly on our tooltip:

1. Showing the tooltip when the mouse is over the interactive element,
2. Hiding it when the mouse leaves the area,
3. Repositioning the tooltip when the mouse moves.

We'll write functions for each of these tasks first, then wire them up to browser events using jQuery.

Let's start with `positionTooltip`, which we'll reference when the mouse moves over any of the **Author** cells:

```
var positionTooltip = function(event) {
  var tPosX = event.pageX;
  var tPosY = event.pageY + 20;
  $tooltip.css({top: tPosY, left: tPosX});
};
```

Here we use the `pageX` and `pageY` properties of the `event` object to set the `top` and `left` positions of the tooltip. When this function is invoked in response to a mouse event, such as `mousemove`, `event.pageX` and `event.pageY` will give us the coordinates of the mouse cursor, so `tPosX` and `tPosY` will refer to a screen location 20 pixels below the mouse cursor.

Next we need to write our `showTooltip()` function, to place the tooltip on the screen.

```
var showTooltip = function(event) {
  var authorName = $(this).text();
  $tooltip
    .text('Highlight all articles by ' + authorName)
    .show();
  positionTooltip(event);
};
```

The `showTooltip()` function is rather straightforward. We populate the tooltip's contents using a string built from the cell contents (which will be the author's name), and show it.

We then place it in the proper location on the page with the `positionTooltip()` function. Since the tooltip has been appended to the body element, we'll need some CSS to make the it float above the page in the right location:

```
#tooltip {
  position: absolute;
  z-index: 2;
```

```
  background: #efd;
  border: 1px solid #ccc;
  padding: 3px;
}
```

Finally, we write a simple `hideTooltip()` function:

```
var hideTooltip = function() {
  $tooltip.hide();
};
```

And now that we have functions for showing, hiding, and positioning the tooltip, we can reference them at the appropriate places in our code:

```
$(document).ready(function() {
  var $authorCells = $('table.striped td:nth-child(3)');
  var $tooltip = $('<div id="tooltip"></div>').appendTo('body');

  var positionTooltip = function(event) {
    var tPosX = event.pageX;
    var tPosY = event.pageY + 20;
    $tooltip.css({top: tPosY, left: tPosX});
  };
  var showTooltip = function(event) {
    var authorName = $(this).text();
    $tooltip
      .text('Highlight all articles by ' + authorName)
      .show();
    positionTooltip(event);
  };
  var hideTooltip = function() {
    $tooltip.hide();
  };
  $authorCells
    .addClass('clickable')
    .hover(showTooltip, hideTooltip)
    .mousemove(positionTooltip)
    .click(function(event) {
      var authorName = $(this).text();
      $authorCells.each(function(index) {
        if (authorName == $(this).text()) {
          $(this).parent().toggleClass('highlight');
        }
        else {
          $(this).parent().removeClass('highlight');
        }
      });
    });
});
```

Note that the arguments to the `.hover()` and `.mousemove()` methods are **referencing** functions that are defined elsewhere. As such, we omit the parentheses that would follow calls to the functions. The tooltip now appears when we hover over an author cell, moves with the mouse movement, and disappears when we move the mouse cursor out of the cell.

Jun 26	jQuery Camp 2008 Announced	Key Bango	conference
Jun 9	jQuery UI v1.5 Released, Focus on Consistent API and Effects	Paul Bakaus	release
Jun 4	jQuery 1.2.6: Events 100% faster	John Resig	release
Mar 7	jQuery UI Worldwide Sprint: March 14-15	Richard Worth	conference
Feb 8	jQuery 1.2.3: AIR, Namespacing, and UI Alpha	John Resig	release

Highlight all articles by Paul Bakaus

A problem with our current implementation is that the tooltip continues to suggest clicking on a cell to highlight the articles even after those articles have been highlighted:

Jun 26	jQuery Camp 2008 Announced	Key Bango	conference
Jun 9	jQuery UI v1.5 Released, Focus on Consistent API and Effects	Paul Bakaus	release
Jun 4	jQuery 1.2.6: Events 100% faster	John Resig	release
Mar 7	jQuery UI Worldwide Sprint: March 14-15	Richard Worth	conference
Feb 8	jQuery 1.2.3: AIR, Namespacing, and UI Alpha	John Resig	release
Jan 23	jQuery UI and beyond: The jQuery-Liferay partnership	Paul Bakaus	announcement

Highlight all articles by John Resig

We need a way to change the tooltip's text if the row has the `highlight` class. We can accomplish this by placing a conditional test in the `showTooltip()` function to check for the presence of the class. If the current cell's parent `<tr>` has the `highlight` class, we want to use the word **Unhighlight** instead of **Highlight** when we create the tooltip:

```
var action = 'Highlight';
if ($(this).parent().is('.highlight')) {
  action = 'Unhighlight';
}
$tooltip
  .text(action + ' all articles by ' + authorName)
  .show();
```

This correctly chooses tooltip text when the mouse enters a cell, but we also need to recalculate the label at the time the mouse is clicked. For that, we need to call the `showTooltip()` function inside the `click` event handler:

```
$(document).ready(function() {
    var $authorCells = $('table.striped td:nth-child(3)');
    var $tooltip = $('<div id="tooltip"></div>').appendTo('body');
```

```
  var positionTooltip = function(event) {
    var tPosX = event.pageX;
    var tPosY = event.pageY + 20;
    $tooltip.css({top: tPosY, left: tPosX});
  };
  var showTooltip = function(event) {
    var authorName = $(this).text();
    var action = 'Highlight';
    if ($(this).parent().is('.highlight')) {
      action = 'Unhighlight';
    }
    $tooltip
      .text(action + ' all articles by ' + authorName)
      .show();
    positionTooltip(event);
  };
  var hideTooltip = function() {
    $tooltip.hide();
  };

  $authorCells
    .addClass('clickable')
    .hover(showTooltip, hideTooltip)
    .mousemove(positionTooltip)
    .click(function(event) {
      var authorName = $(this).text();
      $authorCells.each(function(index) {
        if (authorName == $(this).text()) {
          $(this).parent().toggleClass('highlight');
        }
        else {
          $(this).parent().removeClass('highlight');
        }
      });
      showTooltip.call(this, event);
    });
});
```

By using the JavaScript `call()` function, we can invoke `showTooltip()` as if it were running within the scope of the `click` handler of the cell with the author's name. We need to do this so that the `this` keyword refers to the correct object (this table cell) during the execution of `showTooltip()`.

Now the tooltip offers a more intelligent suggestion when the pointer hovers over a row that is already highlighted.

Collapsing and expanding sections

When a large set of data is divided into sections, it can be useful to hide information that we aren't interested in at the moment. In our table of news articles, rows are grouped by year; **collapsing**, or hiding, a year of articles can be a convenient way to get a broad view of all of the table's data without having to scroll so much.

To make the sections of the news article table collapsible, we first need to create a page element that will be used to trigger the behavior. One standard interface for collapsible items is a minus sign, with a corresponding plus sign for expandable items. We'll insert the icon with JavaScript, following standard **progressive enhancement** techniques.

```
$(document).ready(function() {
  var collapseIcon = '../images/bullet_toggle_minus.png';
  var collapseText = 'Collapse this section';
  var expandIcon = '../images/bullet_toggle_plus.png';
  var expandText = 'Expand this section';
  $('table.collapsible tbody').each(function() {
    var $section = $(this);
    $('<img />').attr('src', collapseIcon)
      .attr('alt', collapseText)
      .prependTo($section.find('th'));
  });
});
```

We have stored the locations of the icons, as well as their alternate textual representations, in variables at the beginning of the function. This allows us to refer to them easily, and provides a simple way to make changes if necessary. We've done the image injection in an .each() loop, which will prove convenient later as we will need to refer to the enclosing <tbody> element again; it will be available to us through the $section variable we've defined here.

Next, we'll need to make the icons trigger the collapsing and expanding of rows. The addition of a clickable class provides the necessary user feedback, and a class on the <tbody> element helps us keep track of whether the rows are currently visible or not.

```
$(document).ready(function() {
  var collapseIcon = '../images/bullet_toggle_minus.png';
  var collapseText = 'Collapse this section';
  var expandIcon = '../images/bullet_toggle_plus.png';
  var expandText = 'Expand this section';
  $('table.collapsible tbody').each(function() {
    var $section = $(this);
    $('<img />').attr('src', collapseIcon)
      .attr('alt', collapseText)
      .prependTo($section.find('th'))
      .addClass('clickable')
      .click(function() {
        if ($section.is('.collapsed')) {
          $section.removeClass('collapsed')
            .find('tr:not(:has(th))').fadeIn('fast');
          $(this).attr('src', collapseIcon)
            .attr('alt', collapseText);
        }
        else {
          $section.addClass('collapsed')
            .find('tr:not(:has(th))').fadeOut('fast');
          $(this).attr('src', expandIcon)
            .attr('alt', expandText);
        }
      });
  });
});
```

When a click occurs, we do the following:

1. Add or remove the `collapsed` class on the `<tbody>` element, to keep track of the current state of the table section.

2. Locate all rows in the section that do not contain headings, and show or hide them using a fading transition.

3. Toggle the current state of the icon, changing its `src` and `alt` attributes to reflect the action it will now trigger when clicked.

With this code in place, clicking on the **Collapse this section** icon next to **2007** makes the table look like this:

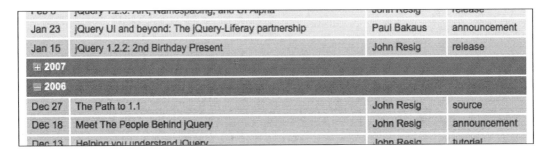

The 2007 news articles aren't removed; they are just hidden until we click the **Expand this section** icon that now appears in that row.

> Table rows present particular obstacles to animation, since browsers use different values (`table-row` and `block`) for their visible `display` property. The `.hide()` and `.show()` methods, without animation, are always safe to use with table rows. If animation is desired, `.fadeIn()` and `.fadeOut()` can be used as well.

Filtering

Earlier we examined sorting and paging as techniques for helping users focus on relevant portions of a table's data. We saw that both could be implemented either with server-side technology, or with JavaScript. **Filtering** completes this arsenal of data arrangement strategies. By displaying to the user only the table rows that match a given criterion, we can strip away needless distractions.

We have already seen how to perform one type of filter: **highlighting** a set of rows. Now we will extend this idea to actually **hiding** rows that don't match the filter.

We can begin by creating a place to put our filtering links. In a typical **progressive enhancement** strategy, we insert these controls using JavaScript so that people without scripting available do not see the options:

```
$(document).ready(function() {
  $('table.filterable').each(function() {
    var $table = $(this);

    $table.find('th').each(function(column) {
      if ($(this).is('.filter-column')) {
        var $filters = $('<div class="filters"></div>');
        $('<h3></h3>')
          .text('Filter by ' + $(this).text() + ':')
          .appendTo($filters);
        $filters.insertBefore($table);
      }
    });
  });
});
```

We get the label for the filter box from the column headers so that this code can be reused for other tables quite easily. Now we have a heading awaiting some buttons:

Date	Headline	Author	Topic	
2008				**Filter by Topic:**
Sep 28	jQuery, Microsoft, and Nokia	John Resig	third-party	
Aug 31	jQuery Conference 2008 Agenda	Rey Bango	conference	
Aug 29	jQuery.com Site Redesign	John Resig	announcement	
Aug 15	Registration Open for jQuery Conference 2008	Karl Swedberg	conference	
Jul 14	jQuery UI 1.5.2	Paul Bakaus	release	

Filter options

Now, we can move on to actually implementing a filter. To start with, we will add filters for a couple of known topics. The code for this is quite similar to the author highlighting example from before:

```
$(document).ready(function() {
  $('table.filterable').each(function() {
    var $table = $(this);

    $table.find('th').each(function(column) {
      if ($(this).is('.filter-column')) {
        var $filters = $('<div class="filters"></div>');
        $('<h3></h3>')
```

```
            .text('Filter by ' + $(this).text() + ':')
            .appendTo($filters);

        var keywords = ['conference', 'release'];
        $.each(keywords, function(index, keyword) {
          $('<div class="filter"></div>').text(keyword)
            .bind('click', {key: keyword}, function(event) {
              $('tr:not(:has(th))', $table).each(function() {
                var value = $('td', this).eq(column).text();
                if (value == event.data['key']) {
                  $(this).show();
                }
                else {
                  $(this).hide();
                }
              });
              $(this).addClass('active')
                .siblings().removeClass('active');
            }).addClass('clickable').appendTo($filters);
        });

        $filters.insertBefore($table);
      }
    });
  });
});
```

Starting with a static array of keywords to filter by, we loop through and create a filtering link for each. Just as in the paging example, we need to use the data parameter of .bind() to avoid accidental problems due to the properties of **closures**. Then, in the click handler, we compare each cell's contents against the keyword and hide the row if there is no match. Since our row selector excludes rows containing a <th> element, we don't need to worry about subheadings being hidden.

Both of the links now work as advertised:

Date	Headline	Author	Topic		Filter by Topic:
⊟ 2008					conference
Aug 31	jQuery Conference 2008 Agenda	Rey Bango	conference		release
Aug 15	Registration Open for jQuery Conference 2008	Karl Swedberg	conference		
Jun 26	jQuery Camp 2008 Announced	Rey Bango	conference		
Mar 7	jQuery UI Worldwide Sprint: March 14-15	Richard Worth	conference		
⊟ 2007					

Collecting filter options from content

Now we need to expand the filter options to cover the range of available topics in the table. Rather than hard-coding all of the topics, we can gather them from the text that has been entered in the table. We can change the definition of keywords to read:

```
var keywords = {};
$table.find('td:nth-child(' + (column + 1) + ')')
  .each(function() {
    keywords[$(this).text()] = $(this).text();
  });
```

This code relies on two tricks:

1. By using a **map** rather than an **array** to hold the keywords as they are found, we eliminate duplicates automatically; each key can have only one value, and keys are always unique.

2. jQuery's $.each() function lets us operate on arrays and maps identically, so no subsequent code has to change.

Now we have a full complement of filter options:

Date	Headline	Author	Topic	Filter by Topic:
2008				third-party
Sep 28	jQuery, Microsoft, and Nokia	John Resig	third-party	conference
2007				announcement
Nov 2	Google Using jQuery	Rey Bango	third-party	release
Feb 20	jQuery and Jack Slocum's Ext	John Resig	third-party	plug-in
2006				standards
Oct 25	Friends of Firefox - Mozilla Utilizes jQuery	Will Jessup	third-party	documentation
				tutorial
2005				miscellaneous
Dec 14	Google Homepage API	John Resig	third-party	source
Dec 12	Sparklines with Javascript and Canvas	John Resig	third-party	

Reversing the filters

For completeness, we need a way to get back to the full list after we have filtered it. Adding an option for all topics is pretty straightforward:

```
$('<div class="filter">all</div>').click(function() {
  $table.find('tbody tr').show();
  $(this).addClass('active')
    .siblings().removeClass('active');
}).addClass('clickable active').appendTo($filters);
```

This gives us an **all** link that simply shows all rows of the table. For good measure, this new link is marked `active` to begin with.

Interacting with other code

We learned with our sorting and paging code that we can't treat the various features we write as islands. The behaviors we build can interact in sometimes surprising ways; for this reason, it is worth revisiting our earlier efforts to examine how they coexist with the new filtering capabilities we have added.

Row striping

The advanced row striping we put in place earlier is confused by our new filters. Since the tables are not re-striped after a filter is performed, rows retain their coloring as if the filtered rows were still present.

To account for the filtered rows, the row-striping code needs to be able to find them. The jQuery pseudo-class `:visible` can assist us in collecting the correct set of rows to stripe. While we're making this change, we can prepare our row-striping code to be invoked from other places by creating a custom event type for it, as we did when making sorting and paging work together.

```
$(document).ready(function() {
  $('table.striped').bind('stripe', function() {
    $('tbody', this).each(function() {
      $(this).find('tr:visible:not(:has(th))')
        .removeClass('odd').addClass('even')
        .filter(function(index) {
          return (index % 6) < 3;
```

```
        }).removeClass('even').addClass('odd');
    });
  }).trigger('stripe');
});
```

In our filtering code, we can now call `$table.trigger('stripe')` each time a filtering operation occurs. With both the new event handler and its triggers in place, the filtering operation respects row striping:

Date	Headline	Author	Topic
⊞ 2008			
Jul 14	jQuery UI 1.5.2	Paul Bakaus	release
Jun 26	jQuery UI 1.5.1	Paul Bakaus	release
Jun 9	jQuery UI v1.5 Released, Focus on Consistent API and Effects	Paul Bakaus	release
Jun 4	jQuery 1.2.6: Events 100% faster	John Resig	release
Feb 8	jQuery 1.2.3: AIR, Namespacing, and UI Alpha	John Resig	release
Jan 15	jQuery 1.2.2: 2nd Birthday Present	John Resig	release
⊟ 2007			
Sep 10	jQuery 1.2: jQuery.extend("Awesome")	John Resig	release
Aug 24	jQuery 1.1.4: Faster, More Tests, Ready for	John	release

Filter by Topic:

all
third-party
conference
announcement
release
plug-in
standards
documentation
tutorial
miscellaneous
source

Expanding and collapsing

The expanding and collapsing behavior added earlier also conflicts with our filters. If a section is collapsed and a new filter is chosen, then the matching items are displayed, even if in the collapsed section. Conversely, if the table is filtered and a section is expanded, then all items in the expanded section are displayed regardless of whether they match the filter.

One way to address the latter situation is to change the way we show and hide rows. If we use a class to indicate a row should be hidden, we don't need to explicitly call `.hide()` and `.show()`. By replacing `.hide()` with `.addClass('filtered')` and `.show()` with `.removeClass('filtered')`, along with a CSS rule for the class, we can accomplish the hiding and showing but play more nicely with the collapsing code. If the class is removed and the row is collapsed, the row will not be inadvertently displayed.

Introducing this new `filtered` class also helps us with the converse issue. We can test for the presence of `filtered` when performing a section expansion, skipping these rows instead of showing them. Testing for this class is a simple matter of adding `:not(.filtered)` to the selector expression used during expansion.

Now our features play nicely, each able to hide and show the rows independently.

The finished code

Our second example page has demonstrated table row striping, highlighting, tooltips, collapsing/expanding, and filtering. Taken together, the JavaScript code for this page is:

```
$(document).ready(function() {
  $('table.striped').bind('stripe', function() {
    $('tbody', this).each(function() {
      $(this).find('tr:visible:not(:has(th))')
        .removeClass('odd').addClass('even')
        .filter(function(index) {
          return (index % 6) < 3;
        }).removeClass('even').addClass('odd');
    });
  }).trigger('stripe');
});

$(document).ready(function() {
  var $authorCells = $('table.striped td:nth-child(3)');
  var $tooltip = $('<div id="tooltip"></div>').appendTo('body');

  var positionTooltip = function(event) {
    var tPosX = event.pageX;
    var tPosY = event.pageY + 20;
    $tooltip.css({top: tPosY, left: tPosX});
  };
  var showTooltip = function(event) {
    var authorName = $(this).text();
    var action = 'Highlight';
    if ($(this).parent().is('.highlight')) {
      action = 'Unhighlight';
    }
    $tooltip
      .text(action + ' all articles by ' + authorName)
      .show();
    positionTooltip(event);
  };
```

```
    var hideTooltip = function() {
      $tooltip.hide();
    };

    $authorCells
      .addClass('clickable')
      .hover(showTooltip, hideTooltip)
      .mousemove(positionTooltip)
      .click(function(event) {
        var authorName = $(this).text();
        $authorCells.each(function(index) {
          if (authorName == $(this).text()) {
            $(this).parent().toggleClass('highlight');
          }
          else {
            $(this).parent().removeClass('highlight');
          }
        });
        showTooltip.call(this, event);
      });
  });

  $(document).ready(function() {
    var collapseIcon = '../images/bullet_toggle_minus.png';
    var collapseText = 'Collapse this section';
    var expandIcon = '../images/bullet_toggle_plus.png';
    var expandText = 'Expand this section';
    $('table.collapsible tbody').each(function() {
      var $section = $(this);
      $('<img />').attr('src', collapseIcon)
        .attr('alt', collapseText)
        .prependTo($section.find('th'))
        .addClass('clickable')
        .click(function() {
          if ($section.is('.collapsed')) {
            $section.removeClass('collapsed')
              .find('tr:not(:has(th)):not(.filtered)')
              .fadeIn('fast');
            $(this).attr('src', collapseIcon)
              .attr('alt', collapseText);
          }
          else {
            $section.addClass('collapsed')
              .find('tr:not(:has(th))')
              .fadeOut('fast', function() {
```

```
                   $(this).css('display', 'none');
                 });
               $(this).attr('src', expandIcon)
                 .attr('alt', expandText);
           }
           $section.parent().trigger('stripe');
         });
      });
    });

$(document).ready(function() {
   $('table.filterable').each(function() {
      var $table = $(this);

      $table.find('th').each(function(column) {
         if ($(this).is('.filter-column')) {
            var $filters = $('<div class="filters"></div>');
            $('<h3></h3>')
               .text('Filter by ' + $(this).text() + ':')
               .appendTo($filters);

            $('<div class="filter">all</div>').click(function() {
               $table.find('tbody tr').removeClass('filtered');
               $(this).addClass('active')
                  .siblings().removeClass('active');
               $table.trigger('stripe');
            }).addClass('clickable active').appendTo($filters);

            var keywords = {};
            $table.find('td:nth-child(' + (column + 1) + ')')
               .each(function() {
                  keywords[$(this).text()] = $(this).text();
               });

            $.each(keywords, function(index, keyword) {
               $('<div class="filter"></div>').text(keyword)
                  .bind('click', {key: keyword}, function(event) {
                     $('tr:not(:has(th))', $table).each(function() {
                        var value = $('td', this).eq(column).text();
                        if (value == event.data['key']) {
                           $(this).removeClass('filtered');
                        }
                        else {
                           $(this).addClass('filtered');
                        }
                     });
                     $(this).addClass('active')
```

```
            .siblings().removeClass('active');
          $table.trigger('stripe');
        }).addClass('clickable').appendTo($filters);
    });

    $filters.insertBefore($table);
  }
 });
 });
});
```

Summary

In this chapter, we have explored some of the ways to slice and dice the tables on our sites, reconfiguring them into beautiful and functional containers for our data. We have covered **sorting** data in tables, using different kinds of data (words, numbers, dates) as sort keys along with **paginating** tables into easily-viewed chunks. We have learned sophisticated **row striping** techniques and JavaScript-powered **tooltips**. We have also walked through **expanding** and **collapsing** content as well as **filtering** and **highlighting** of rows that match the given criteria.

We've even touched briefly on some quite advanced topics, such as sorting and paging with server-side code and AJAX techniques, dynamically calculating page coordinates for elements, and writing a jQuery plugin.

As we have seen, properly semantic HTML tables wrap a great deal of subtlety and complexity in a small package. Fortunately, jQuery can help us easily tame these creatures, allowing the full power of tabular data to come to the surface.

8
Forms with Function

Nearly every website that requires feedback from the user will employ a **form** in one capacity or another. Throughout the life of the Internet, forms have played the role of pack mule, carrying information from the end user back to the website's publisher—dependably, reliably, but with very little grace or style. Perhaps this lack of flair was caused by the repetitious, arduous journey to the server and back; or perhaps it had something to do with the uncompromising elements the form had to work with and their unwillingness to follow the latest fashion. Whatever the reason, it wasn't until recently, with the resurgence of client-side scripting, that forms found new vigor, purpose, and style. In this chapter, we will look at ways in which we can breathe new life into forms. We'll enhance their style, create validation routines for them, use them for calculations, and send their results to the server while nobody is watching.

Improving a basic form

As we apply jQuery to websites, we must always ask ourselves how pages will look and function when JavaScript is unavailable to our visitors (unless, of course, we know exactly who every visitor will be and how their browsers will be configured). This is not to say, however, that we can't create a more beautiful or feature-full site for visitors with JavaScript turned on. The principle of **progressive enhancement** is popular among JavaScript developers because it respects the needs of all users while providing something extra to most of them. To demonstrate progressive enhancement with respect to forms, we'll create a contact form that we can improve in both appearance and behavior using jQuery.

Progressively enhanced form styling

First, let's make some aesthetic tweaks to our form. Without JavaScript enabled, the form's first fieldset is rendered like this:

While it certainly appears functional, and contains plenty of information to guide the user through each field, it could definitely stand some improvement. We'll progressively enhance this group in three ways:

1. Modify the DOM to allow for flexible styling of the `<legend>`.

2. Change the required field message (**required**) to an asterisk (*) and the special field message (**required only when the corresponding checkbox is checked**) to a double asterisk (**). Bold the label for each required field and place a key at the top of the form explaining what the asterisk and double asterisk mean.

3. Hide each checkbox's corresponding text input on page load, and then toggle them, visible and hidden, when the user checks and unchecks the boxes.

We start with the `<fieldset>`'s HTML:

```
<fieldset>
  <legend>Personal Info</legend>
  <ol>
    <li>
      <label for="first-name">First Name</label>
      <input class="required" type="text" name="first-name"
                                          id="first-name" />
      <span>(required)</span>
    </li>
    <li>
      <label for="last-name">Last Name</label>
      <input class="required" type="text" name="last-name"
                                          id="last-name" />
      <span>(required)</span>
    </li>
```

```
        <li>How would you like to be contacted?
                            (choose at least one method)
        <ul>
          <li>
            <label for="by-email">
              <input type="checkbox" name="by-contact-type"
                          value="E-mail" id="by-email" />
              by E-Mail
            </label>
            <input class="conditional" type="text" name="email"
                                            id="email" />
            <span>(required when corresponding checkbox
            checked)</span>
          </li>
          <li>
            <label for="by-phone">
              <input type="checkbox" name="by-contact-type"
                          value="Phone" id="by-phone" />
              by Phone
            </label>
            <input class="conditional" type="text" name="phone"
                                            id="phone" />
            <span>(required when corresponding checkbox
              checked)</span>
          </li>
          <li>
            <label for="by-fax">
              <input type="checkbox" name="by-contact-type"
                value="Fax" id="by-fax" />
              by Fax
            </label>
            <input class="conditional" type="text" name="fax"
                                            id="fax" />
            <span>(required when corresponding checkbox
                                        checked)</span>
          </li>
        </ul>
      </li>
    </ol>
</fieldset>
```

One thing to note here is that each element or pair of elements is considered a
list item (`<li>`). All elements are placed within an **ordered list** (`<ol>`), and the
checkboxes (along with their text fields) are placed within a nested **unordered list**
(`<ul>`). Furthermore, we use the `<label>` element to indicate the name of each
field. For text fields, the `<label>` precedes the `<input>`; for checkboxes, it encloses
the `<input>`. While there is no "standard" element structure for elements within
a fieldset, the ordered list seems to come as close as anything to representing the
semantic meaning of the items in a contact form.

With our HTML in place, we're now ready to use jQuery for the progressive enhancement.

The legend

The form's **legend** is a notoriously difficult element to style with CSS. Browser inconsistencies and positioning limitations make working with it an exercise in frustration. Yet, if we're concerned about using meaningful, well-structured page elements, the legend is an attractive, if not visually appealing, choice for displaying a title in our form's `<fieldset>`.

Left with only HTML and CSS, we're forced to compromise either semantic markup or flexible design choices. However, we can change the HTML as the page loads, turning each `<legend>` into an `<h3>` for people viewing the page, while machines reading the page—and those without JavaScript available—still see the `<legend>`. This can be done straightforwardly using jQuery's `.replaceWith()` method:

```
$(document).ready(function() {
  $('legend').each(function(index) {
    $(this).replaceWith('<h3>' + $(this).text() + '</h3>');
  });
});
```

Notice here that we can't rely on jQuery's implicit iteration. With each element we replace, we need to insert that element's unique text contents. For this we rely on the `.each()` method, which allows us to target the particular text with `$(this)`.

Now, when we apply a blue background and white text color to the `<h3>` in the stylesheet, the form's first fieldset looks like this:

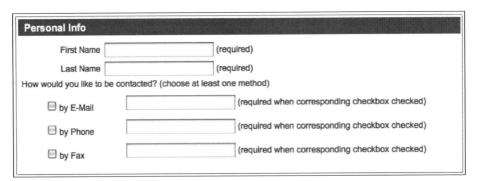

An alternative approach that keeps the `<legend>` elements intact involves wrapping their contents with a `<span>` tag:

```
$(document).ready(function() {
  $('legend').wrapInner('<span></span>');
});
```

Wrapping a `<span>` inside the `<legend>` has at least two advantages over replacing the `<legend>` with an `<h3>`: it retains the semantic meaning of the `<legend>` for screen readers with JavaScript support and it requires less work on the part of the script. The disadvantage is that it makes the heading style a little harder to achieve. At the very least, we have to set the `position` property of both the `<fieldset>` and the `<span>`, as well as the `padding-top` of the `<fieldset>` and the `width` of the `<span>`:

```
fieldset {
   position: relative;
   padding-top: 1.5em;
}

legend span {
   position: absolute;
   width: 100%;
}
```

Whether we choose to replace the form's `<legend>` elements or insert a `<span>` into them, they are now sufficiently styled for our purposes; it's time to clean up the required field messages.

Required field messages

In our contact form, required fields have `class="required"` to allow for styling as well as response to user input; the input fields for each type of contact have `class="conditional"` applied to them. We're going to use these classes to change the instructions printed within parentheses to the right of each input.

We start by setting variables for `requiredFlag` and `conditionalFlag`, and then we fill the `<span>` element next to each required and conditional field with the text stored in those variables:

```
$(document).ready(function() {
  var requiredFlag = ' * ';
  var conditionalFlag = ' ** ';

  $('form :input')
    .filter('.required')
```

```
            .next('span').text(requiredFlag).end()
        .end()
        .filter('.conditional')
            .next('span').text(conditionalFlag);
    });
```

Using `.end()` allows us to extend the chain of methods so that we continue to work with the same set of elements and keep object creation and DOM traversal to a minimum. Each `.end()` method takes the selection back one step, reverting the matched set of elements to what it was before the last traversal method. Here we use two in a row: the first `.end()` reverts the matched set to `.filter('.required')` and the second reverts it to `$('form :input')`. Thus, when `.filter('.conditional')` selects elements with `class="conditional"`, it applies to all inputs within the form.

Now, since a single asterisk (*) may not immediately capture the user's attention, we'll also add `class="req-label"` to the `<label>` for each required field and apply `font-weight:bold` to that class. To do so, we can extend the chain even further.

```
$(document).ready(function() {
var requiredFlag = ' * ';
  var conditionalFlag = ' ** ';

  $('form :input')
    .filter('.required')
      .next('span').text(requiredFlag).end()
      .prev('label').addClass('req-label').end()
    .end()
    .filter('.conditional')
      .next('span').text(conditionalFlag);
  });
```

Such a long chain of methods can be difficult to follow, so a consistent line-break and indentation pattern is essential.

The fieldset with the modified text and the added class now looks like this:

Not bad. Still, the required and conditional field messages really weren't so bad after all; they were just too repetitive. Let's take the first instance of each message and display it above the form next to the flag we're using to symbolize it.

Before we populate the `<span>` elements holding the messages with their respective flags, we need to store the initial messages in a couple of variables. Then we can strip out the parentheses by using a **regular expression**:

```
$(document).ready(function() {
  var requiredFlag = ' * ';
  var conditionalFlag = ' ** ';

  var requiredKey = $('input.required:first')
                            .next('span').text();
  var conditionalKey = $('input.conditional:first')
                            .next('span').text();

  requiredKey = requiredFlag +
            requiredKey.replace(/^\((.+)\)$/,'$1');
  conditionalKey = conditionalFlag +
          conditionalKey.replace(/^\((.+)\)$/,'$1');

// . . . code continues
});
```

The first two additional lines declare variables—`requiredKey` and `conditionalKey`—to store each field type's text. The second two lines modify the text in those variables, concatenating each flag, and its respective text, minus the parentheses. Perhaps the regular expression, along with its `.replace()` method, warrants further explanation.

A regular expression digression

The regular expression is contained within the two forward slashes, and looks like this: `/^\((.+)\)$/`. The first character, `^`, indicates that what follows needs to appear at the beginning of the string. It's followed by two characters, `\(`, which look for an opening parenthesis. The back-slash **escapes** the character that follows, telling the regular-expression parser to treat it literally. This is necessary because parentheses are among the characters that have special meaning in regular expressions, as we'll see next. The next four characters, `(.+)`, look for one or more (represented by `+`) characters of any kind within the same line (represented by `.`) and put them in a group by use of the parentheses. The final three characters, `\)$`, look for a closing parenthesis at the end of the string. So, all together the regular expression is selecting an opening parenthesis, followed by a group of characters, and ending with a closing parenthesis.

The `.replace()` method looks within a particular context for a string represented by a regular expression and replaces it with another string. The syntax looks like this:

```
'context'.replace(/regular-expression/, 'replacement')
```

The context strings of our two `.replace()` methods are the variables `requiredKey` and `conditionalKey`. We've already looked at the regular expression part of this, contained within the two slashes. A comma separates the regular expression and the replacement string, which in our two cases is `'$1'`. The `$1` placeholder represents the first **group** in the regular expression. Since, again, our regular expression has one group of one or more characters, with a parenthesis on either side, the replacement string will be everything inside, and not including, the parentheses.

Inserting the field-message legend

Now that we've retrieved the field messages without the parentheses, we can insert them, along with their corresponding flags, above the form:

```
$(document).ready(function() {
  var requiredFlag = ' * ';
  var conditionalFlag = ' ** ';

  var requiredKey = $('input.required:first')
                                .next('span').text();
  var conditionalKey = $('input.conditional:first')
                                .next('span').text();

  requiredKey = requiredFlag +
              requiredKey.replace(/^\(((.+)\)$/,'$1');
  conditionalKey = conditionalFlag +
            conditionalKey.replace(/^\(((.+)\)$/,'$1');

  $('<p></p>')
    .addClass('field-keys')
    .append(requiredKey + '<br />')
    .append(conditionalKey)
    .insertBefore('#contact');
});
```

The five new lines should look relatively familiar by now. Here is what they do:

1. Create a new paragraph element.

2. Give the paragraph a class of `field-keys`.

3. Append `requiredKey` and a line break to the paragraph.

4. Append `conditionalKey` to the paragraph.

5. Insert the paragraph and everything we've appended inside it before the contact form.

When using `.append()` with an HTML string, as we do here, we need to be careful that any special HTML characters are properly escaped. In this case, the `.text()` method we used when declaring the variables has done this for us.

When we define some styles for `.field-keys` in the stylesheet, the result looks like this:

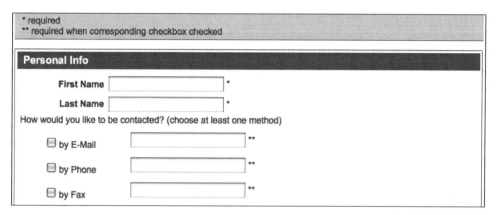

Our jQuery work for the first fieldset is almost complete.

Conditionally displayed fields

Let's further improve the group of fields that ask visitors how they would like to be contacted. Since the text inputs need to be entered only if their corresponding checkboxes are checked, we can hide them, along with their corresponding flags, when the document is initially loaded:

```
$(document).ready(function() {
  $('input.conditional').next('span').andSelf().hide();
});
```

The fieldset now has its streamlined interface:

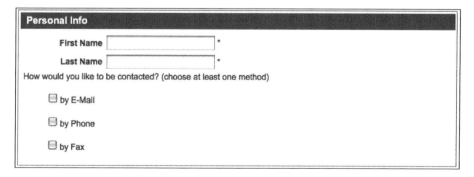

To make the text inputs and flags appear, we attach the `.click()` method to each checkbox. We'll do so within the context of each conditional text input so that we can set a couple of variables for reuse:

```
$(document).ready(function() {
  $('input.conditional').next('span').andSelf().hide()
  .end().end()
  .each(function() {
    var $thisInput = $(this);
    var $thisFlag = $thisInput.next('span');
    $thisInput.prev('label').find(':checkbox')
    .click(function() {
      // code continues . . .
    });
  });
});
```

Here again we make use of two `.end()` methods, this time so we can attach the `.each()` method to the original `$('input.conditional')` selector.

Now we have a variable for the current text input and the current flag. When the user clicks the checkbox, we see if it is checked; if it is, we show the text input, show the flag, and add the `req-label` class to the parent `<label>` element:

```
$(document).ready(function() {
  $('input.conditional').next('span').andSelf().hide()
  .end().end()
  .each(function() {
    var $thisInput = $(this);
    var $thisFlag = $thisInput.next('span');
    $thisInput.prev('label').find(':checkbox')
    .click(function() {
      if (this.checked) {
        $thisInput.show();
        $thisFlag.show();
        $(this).parent('label').addClass('req-label');
      }
    });
  });
});
```

For testing whether a box is checked here, `this.checked` is preferred because we have direct access to the DOM node via the `this` keyword. When the **DOM node** is not so accessible, we can use `$('selector').is(':checked')` instead, since `.is()` returns a **Boolean** (`true` or `false`).

We're left with two more things to do:

1. Ensure that the checkboxes are unchecked when the page initially loads, since some browsers will retain the state of form elements on page refresh.

2. Add an `else` condition that hides the conditional elements and removes the `req-label` class when the checkbox is not checked.

```
$(document).ready(function() {
  $('input.conditional').next('span').andSelf().hide()
  .end().end()
  .each(function() {
    var $thisInput = $(this);
    var $thisFlag = $thisInput.next('span');
    $thisInput.prev('label').find(':checkbox')
    .attr('checked', false)
    .click(function() {
      if (this.checked) {
        $thisInput.show();
        $thisFlag.show();
        $(this).parent('label').addClass('req-label');
      } else {
        $thisInput.hide();
        $thisFlag.hide();
        $(this).parent('label')
                        .removeClass('req-label');
      }
    });
  });
});
```

And that concludes the styling portion of this form makeover. Next, we'll add some client-side validation.

Form validation

Before we add validation to any form with jQuery, we need to remember one important rule: **client-side validation** is not a substitute for server-side validation. Again, we cannot rely on users to have JavaScript enabled. If we truly require certain fields to be entered, or to be entered in a particular format, JavaScript alone can't guarantee the result we demand. Some users prefer not to enable JavaScript, some devices simply don't support it, and a few users could intentionally submit malicious data by circumventing JavaScript restrictions.

Why then should we bother implementing validation with jQuery? Client-side form validation using jQuery can offer one advantage over server-side validation: **immediate feedback**. Server-side code, whether it's ASP, PHP, or any other fancy acronym, needs the page to be reloaded to take effect (unless it is accessed asynchronously, of course, which in any case requires JavaScript). With jQuery, we can capitalize on the prompt response of client-side code by applying validation to each required field when it loses focus (on `blur`), or when a key is pressed (on `keyup`).

Required fields

For our contact form, we'll check for the `required` class on each input when the user tabs or clicks out of it. Before we begin with this code, however, we should make a quick trip back to our conditional text fields. To simplify our validation routine, we can add the `required` class to the `<input>` when it is shown, and remove the class when the `<input>` is subsequently hidden. This portion of the code now looks like this:

```
$thisInput.prev('label').find(':checkbox')
  .attr('checked', false)
  .click(function() {
    if (this.checked) {
      $thisInput.show().addClass('required');
      $thisFlag.show();
      $(this).parent('label').addClass('req-label');
    } else {
      $thisInput.hide().removeClass('required');
      $thisFlag.hide();
      $(this).parent('label').removeClass('req-label');
    }
});
```

With all of the `required` classes in place, we're ready to respond when the user leaves one of these fields empty. A message will be placed after the required flag, and the field's `<li>` element will receive styles to alert the user through `class="warning"`:

```
$(document).ready(function() {
  $('form :input').blur(function() {
    if ($(this).hasClass('required')) {
      var $listItem = $(this).parents('li:first');
      if (this.value == '') {
        var errorMessage = 'This is a required field';
        $('<span></span>')
```

```
            .addClass('error-message')
            .text(errorMessage)
            .appendTo($listItem);
          $listItem.addClass('warning');
        }
      }
    });
  });
```

The code has two `if` statements for each form input on `blur`: the first checks for the `required` class, and the second checks for an empty string. If both conditions are met, we construct an error message, put it in `<span class="error-message">`, and append it all to the parent `<li>`.

We want to give a slightly different message if the field is one of the conditional text fields — **only required when its corresponding checkbox is checked**. We'll concatenate a qualifier message to the standard error message. To do so, we can nest one more `if` statement that checks for the `conditional` class only after the first two `if` conditions have been met:

```
$(document).ready(function() {
  $('form :input').blur(function() {
    if ($(this).hasClass('required')) {
      var $listItem = $(this).parents('li:first');
      if (this.value == '') {
        var errorMessage = 'This is a required field';
        if ($(this).hasClass('conditional')) {
          errorMessage += ', when its related ' +
                              'checkbox is checked';
}
        $('<span></span>')
          .addClass('error-message')
          .text(errorMessage)
          .appendTo($listItem);
        $listItem.addClass('warning');
      }
    }
  });
});
```

Our code works great the first time the user leaves a field blank; however, two problems with the code are evident when the user subsequently enters and leaves the field:

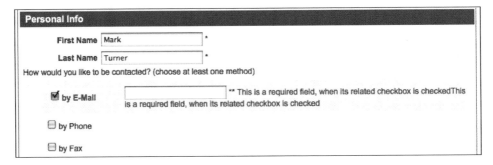

If the field remains blank, the error message is repeated as many times as the user leaves the field. If the field has text entered, the class="warning" is not removed. Obviously, we want only one message per field, and we want the message to be removed if the user fixes the error. We can fix both problems by removing class= "warning" from the current field's parent <li> and any <span class="error-message"> within the same <li> every time the field is blurred, before running through the validation checks:

```
$(document).ready(function() {
  $('form :input').blur(function() {
    $(this).parents('li:first').removeClass('warning')
    .find('span.error-message').remove();
    if ($(this).hasClass('required')) {
      var $listItem = $(this).parents('li:first');
      if (this.value == '') {
        var errorMessage = 'This is a required field';
        if ($(this).hasClass('conditional')) {
          errorMessage += ', when its related checkbox
                                          is checked';
        }
        $('<span></span>')
          .addClass('error-message')
          .text(errorMessage)
          .appendTo($listItem);
        $listItem.addClass('warning');
      }
    }
  });
});
```

Finally, we have a functioning validation script for required, and conditionally required, fields. Even after repeatedly entering and leaving required fields, our error messages now display correctly:

Personal Info

First Name | Mark | *
Last Name | Turner | *

How would you like to be contacted? (choose at least one method)

☑ **by E-Mail** [   ] ** This is a required field, when its related checkbox is checked

☑ **by Phone** [   ] ** This is a required field, when its related checkbox is checked

☐ by Fax

But wait! We want to remove the `<li>` element's warning class and its `<span class="error-message">` elements when the user unchecks a checkbox too! We can do that by visiting our previous checkbox code once more and getting it to trigger `blur` on the corresponding text field when its checkbox is unchecked:

```
if (this.checked) {
    $thisInput.show().addClass('required');
    $thisFlag.show();
    $(this).parent('label').addClass('req-label');
} else {
    $thisInput.hide().removeClass('required').blur();
    $thisFlag.hide();
    $(this).parent('label').removeClass('req-label');
}
```

Now when a checkbox is unchecked, the related warning styles, and error messages, will be out of sight and out of mind.

Required formats

There is one further type of validation to implement in our contact form—correct **input formats**. Sometimes it can be helpful to provide a warning if text is entered into a field incorrectly (rather than simply having it blank). Prime candidates for this type of warning are email, phone, and credit-card fields. For our demonstration, we will put in place a relatively simple regular-expression test for the email field. Let's take a look at the full code for the email validation before we dig into the regular expression in particular:

```
$(document).ready(function() {
//  . . . code continues . . .
    if (this.id == 'email') {
        var $listItem = $(this).parents('li:first');
```

```
        if ($(this).is(':hidden')) {
          this.value = '';
        }
        if (this.value != '' &&
        !/.+@.+\.[a-zA-Z]{2,4}$/.test(this.value)) {
          var errorMessage = 'Please use proper e-mail format'
                                  + ' (e.g. joe@example.com)';
          $('<span></span>')
            .addClass('error-message')
            .text(errorMessage)
            .appendTo($listItem);
          $listItem.addClass('warning');
        }
      }
    }
// . . . code continues . . .
});
```

The code performs the following tasks:

- Tests for the `id` of the email field; if the test is successful:
  - Sets a variable for the parent list item.
  - Tests for the hidden state of the email field. If it is hidden (which happens when its corresponding checkbox is unchecked), its value is set to an empty string. This allows our previous warning class and error message removal to work properly for email fields as well.
  - Tests that the field value is not an empty string and that the field value does not match the regular expression. If the two tests are successful, the script:
    - Creates an error message
    - Inserts the message in `<span class="error-message">`
    - Appends the `<span class="error-message">` element and its contents to the parent list item
    - Adds the `warning` class to the parent list item

Now let's take a look at the regular expression in isolation:

```
!/.+@.+\.[a-zA-Z]{2,4}$/.test(this.value)
```

Although this regular expression is similar to the one we created earlier in the chapter, it uses the `.test()` method rather than the `.replace()` method, since we only need it to return `true` or `false`. As before, the regular expression goes between the two forward slashes. It is then tested against a string that is placed inside the parentheses of `.test()`, in this case the value of the email field.

In this regular expression, we look for a group of one or more non-linefeed characters (`.+`), followed by an `@` symbol, and then followed by another group of one or more non-linefeed characters. So far, a string such as `lucia@example` would pass the test, as would millions of other permutations, even though it is not a valid email address.

We can make the test more precise by looking for a `.` character, followed by two through four letters between `a` and `z` at the end of the string. That is exactly what the remaining portion of the regular expression does. It first looks for a character between `a` and `z` or `A` and `Z` — `[a-zA-Z]`. It then says that a letter in that range can appear two through four times only — `{2,4}`. Finally, it insists that those two through four letters appear at the end of the string: `$`. Now a string such as `lucia@example.com` would return `true`, whereas `lucia@example` — or `lucia@example.2fn` or `lucia@example.example` or `lucia-example.com` — would return `false`.

But we want `true` returned (and the error message, etc., created) only if the proper email address format is *not* entered. That's why we precede the test expression with the exclamation mark (**not operator**):

```
!/.+@.+\.[a-zA-Z]{2,4}$/.test(this.value)
```

A final check

The validation code is now almost complete for the contact form. We can validate the form's fields one more time when the user attempts to submit it, this time all at once. Using the `.submit()` event handler on the form (not the **Send** button) we trigger `blur` on all of the required fields:

```
$(document).ready(function() {
    $('form').submit(function() {
        $('#submit-message').remove();
        $(':input.required').trigger('blur');
    });
});
```

Note here that we've sneaked in a line to remove an element that does not yet exist: `<div id="submit-message">`. We'll add this element in the next step. We're just preemptively removing it here because we already know that we'll need to do it based on the problems we encountered with creating multiple error messages earlier in the chapter.

After triggering `blur`, we get the total number of `warning` classes in the current form. If there are any at all, we'll create a new `<div id="submit-message">` and insert it before the **Send** button where the user is most likely to see it. We also stop the form from actually being submitted:

```
$(document).ready(function() {
  $('form').submit(function() {
    $('#submit-message').remove();
    $(':input.required').trigger('blur');
    var numWarnings = $('.warning', this).length;
    if (numWarnings) {
      $('<div></div>')
      .attr({
        'id': 'submit-message',
        'class': 'warning'
      })
      .append('Please correct errors with ' +
                         numWarnings + ' fields')
      .insertBefore('#send');
      return false;
    }
  });
});
```

In addition to providing a generic request to fix errors, the message indicates the number of fields that need to be fixed:

> Please correct errors with 3 fields
>
> Send

We can do better than that, however; rather than just showing the number of errors, we can list the names of the fields that contain errors:

```
$(document).ready(function() {
  $('form').submit(function() {
    $('#submit-message').remove();
    $(':input.required').trigger('blur');
    var numWarnings = $('.warning', this).length;
    if (numWarnings) {
      var list = [];
      $('.warning label').each(function() {
        list.push($(this).text());
      });
```

```
        $('<div></div>')
        .attr({
          'id': 'submit-message',
          'class': 'warning'
        })
        .append('Please correct errors with the following ' +
                            numWarnings + ' fields:<br />')
        .append('&bull; ' + list.join('<br />&bull; '))
        .insertBefore('#send');
        return false;
      };
    });
  });
```

The first change to the code is the `list` variable set to an empty array. Then, we get each label that is a descendant of an element with the `warning` class and push its text into the `list` array (with the native JavaScript `push` function). Now, the text of each of these labels constitutes a separate element in the `list` array.

We modify our first version of the `<div id="submit-message">` content a bit and append our `list` array to it. Using the native JavaScript `join()` function to convert the array into a string, we join each of the array's elements with a line break and a bullet:

Admittedly, the HTML for the field list is presentational rather than semantic. However, for an ephemeral list—one that is generated by JavaScript as a last step and meant to be discarded as soon as possible—we'll forgive this quick and dirty code for the sake of ease and brevity.

Checkbox manipulation

Our contact form also has a **Miscellaneous** section, which contains a list of checkboxes.

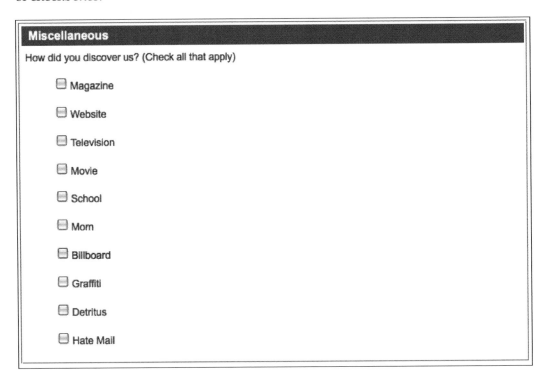

To round out our enhancements to the contact form, we'll help the user manage this list. A group of 10 checkboxes can be daunting, especially if the user wishes to click most or all of them. An option to check, or uncheck, all of the checkboxes comes in handy in this type of situation. So, let's create one.

To begin, we create a new `<li>` element, fill it with a `<label>`, inside which we place `<input type="checkbox" id="discover-all">` and some text, and prepend it all to the `<ul>` element inside `<li class="discover">`:

```
$(document).ready(function() {
  $('<li></li>')
  .html('<label><input type="checkbox" id="discover-all" />' +
                        ' <em>check all</em></label>')
  .prependTo('li.discover > ul');
});
```

Now we have a new checkbox with a label that reads **check all**. But it doesn't do anything yet. We need to attach the `.click()` method to it:

```
$(document).ready(function() {
  $('<li></li>')
  .html('<label><input type="checkbox" id="discover-all" />' +
                       ' <em>check all</em></label>')
  .prependTo('li.discover > ul');
  $('#discover-all').click(function() {
    var $checkboxes = $(this).parents('ul:first')
                                .find(':checkbox');
    if (this.checked) {
      $checkboxes.attr('checked', true);
    } else {
      $checkboxes.attr('checked', '');
    }
  });
});
```

Inside this event handler, we first set the `$checkboxes` variable, which consists of a jQuery object containing every checkbox within the current list. With the variable set, manipulating the checkboxes becomes a matter of checking them if the **check all** checkbox is checked, and unchecking them if the **check all** one is unchecked.

A finishing touch can be applied to this checkbox feature by adding a `checkall` class to the **check all** checkbox's label, and changing its text to **un-check all** after it has been checked by the user:

```
$(document).ready(function() {
$('<li></li>')
  .html('<label><input type="checkbox" id="discover-all" />' +
                       ' <em>check all</em></label>')
  .prependTo('li.discover > ul');
  $('#discover-all').click(function() {
    var $checkboxes = $(this) .parents('ul:first')
                                  .find(':checkbox');
    if (this.checked) {
      $(this).next().text(' un-check all');
      $checkboxes.attr('checked', true);
    } else {
      $(this).next().text(' check all');
      $checkboxes.attr('checked', '');
    };
  })
  .parent('label').addClass('checkall');
});
```

The group of checkboxes, along with the **check all** box, now looks like this:

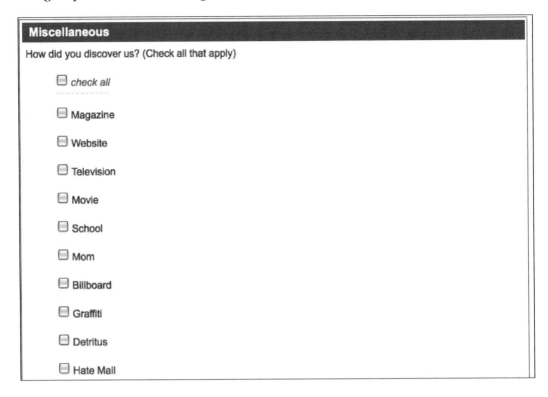

And with the **check all** box checked, the group looks like this:

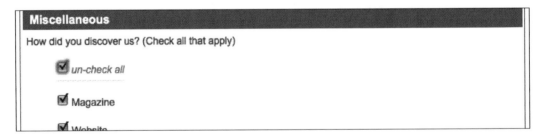

The finished code

Here it is, the finished code for the contact form:

```
$(document).ready(function() {

    // Enhance style of form elements.

    $('legend').each(function(index) {
```

```
        $(this).replaceWith('<h3>' + $(this).text() + '</h3>');
});

var requiredFlag = ' * ';
var conditionalFlag = ' ** ';
var requiredKey = $('input.required:first')
                            .next('span').text();
var conditionalKey = $('input.conditional:first')
                            .next('span').text();

requiredKey = requiredFlag +
            requiredKey.replace(/^\((.+)\)$/,'$1');
conditionalKey = conditionalFlag +
            conditionalKey.replace(/^\((.+)\)$/,'$1');

$('<p></p>')
  .addClass('field-keys')
  .append(requiredKey + '<br />')
  .append(conditionalKey)
  .insertBefore('#contact');

$('form :input')
  .filter('.required')
    .next('span').text(requiredFlag).end()
    .prev('label').addClass('req-label').end()
  .end()
  .filter('.conditional')
    .next('span').text(conditionalFlag);

// Checkbox toggle: conditional text inputs.

$('input.conditional').next('span').andSelf().hide()
.end().end()
.each(function() {
  var $thisInput = $(this);
  var $thisFlag = $thisInput.next('span');
  $thisInput.prev('label').find(':checkbox')
  .attr('checked', false)
  .click(function() {
    if (this.checked) {
      $thisInput.show().addClass('required');
      $thisFlag.show();
      $(this).parent('label').addClass('req-label');
    } else {
      $thisInput.hide().removeClass('required').blur();
      $thisFlag.hide();
      $(this).parent('label').removeClass('req-label');
```

```
      }
    });
  });

  // Validate fields on blur.

  $('form :input').blur(function() {
    $(this).parents('li:first').removeClass('warning')
    .find('span.error-message').remove();

    if ($(this).hasClass('required')) {
      var $listItem = $(this).parents('li:first');
      if (this.value == '') {
        var errorMessage = 'This is a required field';
        if ($(this).is('.conditional')) {
          errorMessage += ', when its related checkbox is
                                                  checked';
        }
        $('<span></span>')
          .addClass('error-message')
          .text(errorMessage)
          .appendTo($listItem);
        $listItem.addClass('warning');
      }
    }

    if (this.id == 'email') {
      var $listItem = $(this).parents('li:first');
      if ($(this).is(':hidden')) {
        this.value = '';
      }
      if (this.value != '' &&
      !/.+@.+\.[a-zA-Z]{2,4}$/.test(this.value)) {
        var errorMessage = 'Please use proper e-mail format'
                                  + ' (e.g. joe@example.com)';
        $('<span></span>')
          .addClass('error-message')
          .text(errorMessage)
          .appendTo($listItem);
        $listItem.addClass('warning');
      }
    }
  });

  // Validate form on submit.

  $('form').submit(function() {
```

```
    $('#submit-message').remove();
    $(':input.required').trigger('blur');
  var numWarnings = $('.warning', this).length;
    if (numWarnings) {
      var fieldList = [];
      $('.warning label').each(function() {
        fieldList.push($(this).text());
      });
      $('<div></div>')
      .attr({
        'id': 'submit-message',
        'class': 'warning'
      })
      .append('Please correct errors with the following ' +
                        numWarnings + ' fields:<br />')
      .append('&bull; ' + fieldList.join('<br />&bull; '))
      .insertBefore('#send');
    return false;
  };
});

// Checkboxes
$('form :checkbox').removeAttr('checked');

// Checkboxes with (un)check all.
$('<li></li>')
.html('<label><input type="checkbox" id="discover-all" />' +
                      ' <em>check all</em></label>')
.prependTo('li.discover > ul');
$('#discover-all').click(function() {
  var $checkboxes = $(this) .parents('ul:first')
                              .find(':checkbox');
  if (this.checked) {
    $(this).next().text(' un-check all');
    $checkboxes.attr('checked', true);
  } else {
    $(this).next().text(' check all');
    $checkboxes.attr('checked', '');
  };
})
.parent('label').addClass('checkall');

});
```

Although we've made significant improvements to the contact form, there is still much that could be done. Validation, for example, comes in a number of varieties. For a flexible validation plugin, visit `http://plugins.jquery.com/project/validate/`.

Compact forms

Some forms are much simpler than contact forms. In fact, many sites incorporate a single-field form on every single page: a **search function** for the site. The usual trappings of a form—field labels, submit buttons, and the text—are cumbersome for such a small, single-purpose part of the page. We can use jQuery to help slim down the form while retaining its functionalities, and even enhance its behavior to be much more usable than a full-page equivalent.

Placeholder text for fields

The `<label>` element for a form field is an essential component of accessible websites. Every field should be labeled so that screen readers and other assistive devices can identify which field is used, and for what purpose. Even in the HTML source, the label helps describe the field:

```
<form id="search" action="search/index.php" method="get">
  <label for="search-text">search the site</label>
  <input type="text" name="search-text" id="search-text" />
</form>
```

Without styling, we see the label right before the field:

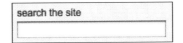

While this doesn't take up much room, in some site layouts even this single line of text might be too much. We could hide the text with CSS, but this then provides the user with no way to know what the field is for. Instead, we'll use CSS to position the label on top of the field, only if JavaScript is available, by adding a class to the search form:

```
$(document).ready(function() {
  var $search = $('#search').addClass('overlabel');
});
```

In a single line we're adding a class to the search form and storing the selector in a variable so that we can refer to it later. The stylesheet uses the `overlabel` class to style the label:

```css
.overlabel {
  position: relative;
}
.overlabel label {
  position: absolute;
  top: 6px;
  left: 3px;
  color: #999;
  cursor: text;
}
```

Not only does the added class position the label properly, but it also grays out the text to distinguish it as a placeholder:

This is a nice effect, but it has a couple problems:

1. The label text obscures any text that the user enters into the text field.
2. The input can only be accessed now by tabbing into it. Since the label is covering the input, the user is prevented from clicking into it.

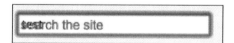

To avoid the first problem, we need to hide the label text when the field gets **focus**, and show it again when the focus is lost, as long as there is no user-entered text in the field.

 Discussion about keyboard focus can be found in Chapter 3.

Hiding the label text on focus is simple enough:

```
$(document).ready(function() {
  var $search = $('#search').addClass('overlabel');
  var $searchInput = $search.find('input');
  var $searchLabel = $search.find('label');

  $searchInput
  .focus(function() {
    $searchLabel.hide();
  })
  .blur(function() {
    if (this.value == '') {
      $searchLabel.show();
    }
  });
});
```

The label is now neatly hidden when the user types text into the field:

The second problem is now quite easy to solve as well. We can both hide the label text and give the user access to the input by letting a click on the label trigger the `focus` event for the input:

```
$(document).ready(function() {
  var $search = $('#search').addClass('overlabel');
  var $searchInput = $search.find('input');
  var $searchLabel = $search.find('label');

  $searchInput
  .focus(function() {
    $searchLabel.hide();
  })
  .blur(function() {
    if (this.value == '') {
      $searchLabel.show();
    }
  });

  $searchLabel.click(function() {
    $searchInput.trigger('focus');
  });
});
```

Finally, we need to handle the case in which text remains in the input when the page is refreshed—similar to what we had to do with the conditional inputs in the form validation section earlier in this chapter. If the input has a value, the label is hidden:

```
$(document).ready(function() {
  var $search = $('#search').addClass('overlabel');
  var $searchInput = $search.find('input');
  var $searchLabel = $search.find('label');

  if ($searchInput.val()) {
    $searchLabel.hide();
  }

  $searchInput
  .focus(function() {
    $searchLabel.hide();
  })
  .blur(function() {
    if (this.value == '') {
      $searchLabel.show();
    }
  });

  $searchLabel.click(function() {
    $searchInput.trigger('focus');
  });
});
```

One advantage of using the label rather than inserting a default value directly into the text input is that this technique can be adapted to any text field without having to worry about a potential conflict with a validation script.

AJAX auto-completion

We can further spruce up our search field by offering **auto-completion** of its contents. This feature will allow users to type the beginning of a search term and be presented with all of the possible terms that begin with the typed string. Since the list of terms can be drawn from a database that is driving the site, the user can know that search results are forthcoming if the typed term is used. Also, if the database provides the terms in order of popularity or number of results, the user can be guided to more appropriate searches.

Auto-completion is a very complicated subject with subtleties introduced by different kinds of user interaction. We will craft a working example here, but cannot, in this space, explore all of the advanced concepts such as limiting the rate of requests or multi-term completion. The auto-complete widget in the **jQuery UI** plugin collection is recommended for simple, real-world implementations, and as a starting point for more complex ones. It can be found at `http://ui.jquery.com/`.

The basic idea behind an auto-completion routine is to react to a keystroke, and to send an AJAX request to the server containing the contents of the field in the request. The results will contain a list of possible completions for the field. The script then presents this list as a dropdown below the field.

On the server

We need some server-side code to handle requests. While a real-world implementation will usually rely on a database to produce a list of possible completions, for this example we can use a simple PHP script with the results built in:

```php
<?php
  if (strlen($_REQUEST['search-text']) < 1) {
    print '[]';
    exit;
  }
  $terms = array(
    'access',
    'action',
    // List continues...
    'xaml',
    'xoops',
  );
  $possibilities = array();
  foreach ($terms as $term) {
    if (strpos($term, strtolower($_REQUEST['search-text']))
                                                 === 0) {
      $possibilities[] = "'". str_replace("'", "\\'", $term)
                                                    ."'";
    }
  }
  print ('['. implode(', ', $possibilities) .']');
```

The page compares the provided string against the beginning of each term, and composes a **JSON array** of matches. The string manipulation operations here (such as `str_replace()` and `implode()`) ensure that the output of the script is properly-formatted JSON, so as to avoid JavaScript errors during parsing.

In the browser

Now we can make a request to this PHP script from our JavaScript code:

```
$(document).ready(function() {
  var $autocomplete = $('<ul class="autocomplete"></ul>')
  .hide()
  .insertAfter('#search-text');
  $('#search-text').keyup(function() {
    $.ajax({
      'url': '../search/autocomplete.php',
      'data': {'search-text': $('#search-text').val()},
      'dataType': 'json',
      'type': 'GET',
      'success': function(data) {
        if (data.length) {
          $autocomplete.empty();
          $.each(data, function(index, term) {
            $('<li></li>').text(term).appendTo($autocomplete);
          });
          $autocomplete.show();
        }
      }
    });
  });
});
```

We need to use `keyup`, not `keydown` or `keypress`, as the event that triggers the AJAX request. The latter two events occur during the process of the key press, before the character has actually been entered in the field. If we attempt to act on these events and issue the request, the suggestion list will lag behind the search text. When the third character is entered, for example, the AJAX request will be made using just the first two characters. By acting on `keyup`, we avoid this problem.

In our stylesheet, we position this list of suggestions absolutely, so that it overlaps the text underneath. Now when we type in the search field, we see our possible terms presented to us:

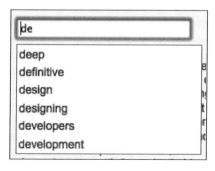

To properly display our list of suggestions, we have to take into account the built-in auto-completion mechanism of some web browsers. Browsers will often remember what users have typed in a form field, and suggest these entries the next time the form is used. This can look confusing when in conjunction with our custom auto-complete suggestions:

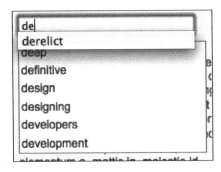

Fortunately, this can be disabled in the browsers that perform autocompletion by setting the `autocomplete` attribute of the form field to `off`. We could do this right in the HTML, but this would not be in keeping with the principle of progressive enhancement because we would be disabling the browser's autocompletion function without offering our own. Instead, we can add this attribute from our script:

```
$('#search-text').attr('autocomplete', 'off')
```

Populating the search field

Our list of suggestions doesn't do us much good if we can't place them in the search box. To begin with, we'll allow a mouse click to confirm a suggestion:

```
'success': function(data) {
  if (data.length) {
    $autocomplete.empty();
    $.each(data, function(index, term) {
      $('<li></li>').text(term)
      .appendTo($autocomplete)
      .click(function() {
        $('#search-text').val(term);
        $autocomplete.hide();
      });
    });
    $autocomplete.show();
  }
}
```

This modification sets the text of the search box to whatever list item was clicked. We also hide the suggestions after this since we are done with them.

Keyboard navigation

Since the user is already at the keyboard, and typing in the search term, it is very convenient to allow the keyboard to control selection from the suggestion list as well. We'll need to keep track of the currently selected item to enable this. First, we can add a helper function that will store the index of the item and perform the necessary visual effects to reveal which item is currently selected:

```
var selectedItem = null;
var setSelectedItem = function(item) {
  selectedItem = item;
  if (selectedItem === null) {
    $autocomplete.hide();
    return;
  }
  if (selectedItem < 0) {
    selectedItem = 0;
  }
  if (selectedItem >= $autocomplete.find('li').length) {
    selectedItem = $autocomplete.find('li').length - 1;
  }
  $autocomplete.find('li').removeClass('selected')
    .eq(selectedItem).addClass('selected');
  $autocomplete.show();
};
```

The selectedItem variable will be set to null whenever no item is selected. By always calling setSelectedItem() to change the value of the variable, we can be sure that the suggestion list is only visible when there is a selected item.

The two tests for the numeric value of selectedItem are present to **clamp** the results to the appropriate range. Without these tests, selectedItem could end up with any value, even negative ones. This function ensures that the current value of selectedItem is always a valid index in the list of suggestions.

We can now revise our existing code to use the new function:

```
$('#search-text').attr('autocomplete', 'off').keyup(function() {
  $.ajax({
    'url': '../search/autocomplete.php',
    'data': {'search-text': $('#search-text').val()},
    'dataType': 'json',
```

```
      'type': 'GET',
      'success': function(data) {
        if (data.length) {
          $autocomplete.empty();
          $.each(data, function(index, term) {
            $('<li></li>').text(term)
            .appendTo($autocomplete)
            .mouseover(function() {
              setSelectedItem(index);
            })
            .click(function() {
              $('#search-text').val(term);
              $autocomplete.hide();
            });
          });

          setSelectedItem(0);
        }
        else {
          setSelectedItem(null);
        }
      }
    });
  });
```

This revision has several immediate benefits. First, the suggestion list is hidden when there are no results for a given search. Second, we are able to add a mouseover handler that highlights the item under the mouse cursor. Third, the first item is highlighted immediately when the suggestion list is shown:

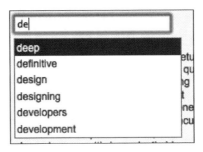

Now we need to allow the keyboard keys to change which item is currently active in the list.

Handling the arrow keys

We can use the `keyCode` attribute of the event object to determine which key was pressed. This will allow us to watch for codes 38 and 40, corresponding to the up and down arrow keys, and react accordingly:

```
$('#search-text').attr('autocomplete', 'off').keyup(function(event) {
  if (event.keyCode > 40 || event.keyCode == 8) {
    // Keys with codes 40 and below are special
    //    (enter, arrow keys, escape, etc.).
    // Key code 8 is backspace.
    $.ajax({
      'url': '../search/autocomplete.php',
      'data': {'search-text': $('#search-text').val()},
      'dataType': 'json',
      'type': 'GET',
      'success': function(data) {
        if (data.length) {
          $autocomplete.empty();
          $.each(data, function(index, term) {
            $('<li></li>').text(term)
            .appendTo($autocomplete)
            .mouseover(function() {
              setSelectedItem(index);
            })
            .click(function() {
              $('#search-text').val(term);
              $autocomplete.hide();
            });
          });

          setSelectedItem(0);
        }
        else {
          setSelectedItem(null);
        }
      }
    });
  }
  else if (event.keyCode == 38 &&
                        selectedItem !== null) {
    // User pressed up arrow.
    setSelectedItem(selectedItem - 1);
    event.preventDefault();
  }
```

```
    else if (event.keyCode == 40 &&
                        selectedItem !== null) {
    // User pressed down arrow.
    setSelectedItem(selectedItem + 1);
    event.preventDefault();
  }
});
```

Our `keyup` handler now checks the `keyCode` that was sent, and performs the corresponding action. The AJAX requests are now skipped if the pressed key was special, such as an *arrow* key or *escape* key. If an *arrow* key is detected and the suggestion list is currently displayed, the handler changes the selected item by 1 in the appropriate direction. Since we wrote `setSelectedItem()` to clamp the values to the range of indices possible for the list, we don't have to worry about the user *stepping off* of either end of the list.

Inserting suggestions in the field

Next, we need to handle the *Enter* key (or *return* key on a Mac). When the suggestion list is displayed, a press of the *Enter* key should populate the field with the currently selected item. Since we are now going to be doing this in two places, we should factor the field population routine (which we coded earlier for the mouse button) out and into a separate function:

```
var populateSearchField = function() {
  $('#search-text').val($autocomplete
     .find('li').eq(selectedItem).text());
  setSelectedItem(null);
};
```

Now our `click` handler can be a simple call to this function. We can call this function when handling the *Enter* key as well:

```
$('#search-text').keypress(function(event) {
  if (event.keyCode == 13 && selectedItem !== null) {
    // User pressed enter key.
    populateSearchField();
    event.preventDefault();
  }
});
```

This handler is attached to the `keypress` event rather than `keyup` as before. We have to make this alteration so that we can prevent the keystroke from submitting the form. If we wait until the `keyup` event is triggered, the submission will already be underway.

Removing the suggestion list

There's one final tweak we will make to our auto-complete behavior. We should hide the suggestion list when the user decides to do something else on the page. First of all, we can react to the *escape* key in our `keyup` handler, and let the user dismiss the list that way:

```
else if (event.keyCode == 27 && selectedItem !== null) {
  // User pressed escape key.
  setSelectedItem(null);
}
```

More importantly, we should hide the list when the search field loses focus. A first attempt at this is quite simple:

```
$('#search-text').blur(function(event) {
  setSelectedItem(null);
});
```

However, this causes an unintended side effect. Since a mouse click on the list removes focus from the field, this handler is called and the list is hidden. That means that our `click` handler defined earlier never gets called, and it becomes impossible to interact with the list using the mouse.

There is no easy solution to this problem. The `blur` handler will always be called before the `click` handler. A workaround is to hide the list when the focus is lost, but to wait a fraction of a second first:

```
$('#search-text').blur(function(event) {
  setTimeout(function() {
    setSelectedItem(null);
  }, 250);
});
```

This gives a chance for the `click` event to get triggered on the list item before the list item is hidden.

Auto-completion versus live search

The earlier example focused on auto-completion of the text field, as it is a technique that applies to many forms. However, for searches in particular, an alternative called **live search** is preferred. This feature actually performs the content searches as the user types.

Functionally, auto-completion and live search are very similar. In both cases, key presses initiate an AJAX submission to the server, passing the current field contents along with the request. The results are then placed in a drop-down box below the field. In the case of auto-completion, as we have seen, the results are possible search terms to use. With live search, the results are the actual pages that contain the search terms that have been typed.

On the JavaScript end, the code to build these two features is nearly identical, so we won't go into detail here. Deciding which to use is a matter of tradeoffs; live search provides more information to the user with less effort, but is typically more resource intensive.

The finished code

Our completed code for the search field's presentation and auto-complete behaviors is as follows:

```
$(document).ready(function() {
  var $search = $('#search').addClass('overlabel');
  var $searchInput = $search.find('input');
  var $searchLabel = $search.find('label');

  if ($searchInput.val()) {
    $searchLabel.hide();
  }

  $searchInput
  .focus(function() {
    $searchLabel.hide();
  })
  .blur(function() {
    if (this.value == '') {
      $searchLabel.show();
    }
  });
  $searchLabel.click(function() {
    $searchInput.trigger('focus');
  });
  var $autocomplete = $('<ul class="autocomplete"></ul>')
  .hide()
  .insertAfter('#search-text');
  var selectedItem = null;

  var setSelectedItem = function(item) {
    selectedItem = item;
```

```javascript
  if (selectedItem === null) {
    $autocomplete.hide();
    return;
  }
  if (selectedItem < 0) {
    selectedItem = 0;
  }
  if (selectedItem >= $autocomplete.find('li').length) {
    selectedItem = $autocomplete.find('li').length - 1;
  }
  $autocomplete.find('li').removeClass('selected')
    .eq(selectedItem).addClass('selected');
  $autocomplete.show();
};
var populateSearchField = function() {
  $('#search-text').val($autocomplete
  .find('li').eq(selectedItem).text());
  setSelectedItem(null);
};
$('#search-text')
.attr('autocomplete', 'off')
.keyup(function(event) {
  if (event.keyCode > 40 || event.keyCode == 8) {
    // Keys with codes 40 and below are special
    // (enter, arrow keys, escape, etc.).
    // Key code 8 is backspace.
    $.ajax({
      'url': '../search/autocomplete.php',
      'data': {'search-text': $('#search-text').val()},
      'dataType': 'json',
      'type': 'GET',
      'success': function(data) {
        if (data.length) {
          $autocomplete.empty();
          $.each(data, function(index, term) {
            $('<li></li>').text(term)
            .appendTo($autocomplete)
            .mouseover(function() {
              setSelectedItem(index);
            }).click(populateSearchField);
          });

          setSelectedItem(0);
```

```
            }
            else {
              setSelectedItem(null);
            }
          }
        });
      }
      else if (event.keyCode == 38 &&
                                selectedItem !== null) {
        // User pressed up arrow.
        setSelectedItem(selectedItem - 1);
        event.preventDefault();
      }
      else if (event.keyCode == 40 &&
                                selectedItem !== null) {
        // User pressed down arrow.
        setSelectedItem(selectedItem + 1);
        event.preventDefault();
      }
      else if (event.keyCode == 27 && selectedItem !== null) {
        // User pressed escape key.
        setSelectedItem(null);
      }
    }).keypress(function(event) {
      if (event.keyCode == 13 && selectedItem !== null) {
        // User pressed enter key.
        populateSearchField();
        event.preventDefault();
      }
    }).blur(function(event) {
      setTimeout(function() {
        setSelectedItem(null);
      }, 250);
    });
  });
```

Working with numeric form data

We've now looked at several form features that apply to textual inputs from the user. Often, though, our forms are primarily numeric in content. There are several more form enhancements we can make when we are dealing with numbers as form values.

In our bookstore site, a prime candidate for a numeric form is the shopping cart. We need to allow the user to update quantities of items being purchased, and we also need to present numeric data back to the user for prices and totals.

Shopping cart table structure

The HTML for the shopping cart will describe one of the more involved table structures we have seen so far:

```
<form action="checkout.php" method="post">
  <table id="cart">
    <thead>
      <tr>
        <th class="item">Item</th>
        <th class="quantity">Quantity</th>
        <th class="price">Price</th>
        <th class="cost">Total</th>
      </tr>
    </thead>
    <tfoot>
      <tr class="subtotal">
        <td class="item">Subtotal</td>
        <td class="quantity"></td>
        <td class="price"></td>
        <td class="cost">$152.95</td>
      </tr>
      <tr class="tax">
        <td class="item">Tax</td>
        <td class="quantity"></td>
        <td class="price">6%</td>
        <td class="cost">$9.18</td>
      </tr>
      <tr class="shipping">
        <td class="item">Shipping</td>
        <td class="quantity">5</td>
        <td class="price">$2 per item</td>
        <td class="cost">$10.00</td>
      </tr>
      <tr class="total">
        <td class="item">Total</td>
        <td class="quantity"></td>
        <td class="price"></td>
        <td class="cost">$172.13</td>
      </tr>
```

```
    <tr class="actions">
      <td></td>
      <td>
        <input type="button" name="recalculate"
                      value="Recalculate" id="recalculate" />
      </td>
      <td></td>
      <td>
        <input type="submit" name="submit"
                          value="Place Order" id="submit" />
      </td>
    </tr>
  </tfoot>
  <tbody>
    <tr>
      <td class="item">
        Building Telephony Systems With Asterisk
      </td>
      <td class="quantity">
        <input type="text" name="quantity-2" value="1"
                          id="quantity-2" maxlength="3" />
      </td>
      <td class="price">$26.99</td>
      <td class="cost">$26.99</td>
    </tr>
    <tr>
      <td class="item">
        Smarty PHP Template Programming and Applications
      </td>
      <td class="quantity">
        <input type="text" name="quantity-1" value="2"
                          id="quantity-1" maxlength="3" />
      </td>
      <td class="price">$35.99</td>
      <td class="cost">$71.98</td>
    </tr>
    <tr>
      <td class="item">
        Creating your MySQL Database
      </td>
      <td class="quantity">
        <input type="text" name="quantity-3" value="1"
                          id="quantity-3" maxlength="3" />
      </td>
```

```
        <td class="price">$17.99</td>
        <td class="cost">$17.99</td>
      </tr>
      <tr>
        <td class="item">
          Drupal: Creating Blogs, Forums, Portals, and
                                      Community Websites
        </td>
        <td class="quantity">
          <input type="text" name="quantity-4" value="1"
                          id="quantity-4" maxlength="3" />
        </td>
        <td class="price">$35.99</td>
        <td class="cost">$35.99</td>
      </tr>
    </tbody>
  </table>
</form>
```

This table introduces another element rarely seen in the wild, `<tfoot>`. Like `<thead>`, this element groups a set of table rows. Note that though the element comes before the table body, it is presented after the body when the page is rendered:

Item	Quantity	Price	Total
Building Telephony Systems With Asterisk	1	$26.99	$26.99
Smarty PHP Template Programming and Applications	2	$35.99	$71.98
Creating your MySQL Database	1	$17.99	$17.99
Drupal: Creating Blogs, Forums, Portals, and Community Websites	1	$35.99	$35.99
Subtotal			$152.95
Tax		6%	$9.18
Shipping	5	$2 per item	$10.00
Total			$172.13
		Recalculate	Place Order

This source code ordering, while non-intuitive to designers thinking visually about the table rendering, is useful to those with visual impairments. When the table is read aloud by assistive devices, the footer is read before the potentially long content, allowing the user to get a summary of what is to come.

We've also placed a class on each cell of the table, identifying which column of the table contains that cell. In the previous chapter, we demonstrated some ways to find cells in a column by looking at the index of the cell within its row. Here, we'll make a tradeoff and allow the JavaScript code to be simpler by making the HTML source a bit more complex. With a class identifying the column of each cell, our selectors can become a bit more straightforward.

Before we proceed with manipulating the form fields, we will apply a standard line of row striping code to spruce up the table's appearance:

```
$(document).ready(function() {
    $('#cart tbody tr:nth-child(even)').addClass('alt');
});
```

Once again, we make sure to only select rows to color if they are in the body of the table:

Item	Quantity	Price	Total
Building Telephony Systems With Asterisk	1	$26.99	$26.99
Smarty PHP Template Programming and Applications	2	$35.99	$71.98
Creating your MySQL Database	1	$17.99	$17.99
Drupal: Creating Blogs, Forums, Portals, and Community Websites	1	$35.99	$35.99
Subtotal			$152.95
Tax		6%	$9.18
Shipping	5	$2 per Item	$10.00
Total			$172.13
		Recalculate	Place Order

Rejecting non-numeric input

When improving the contact form, we discussed some **input validation** techniques. With JavaScript, we verified that what the user typed matched what we were expecting so that we could provide feedback before the form was even sent to the server. Now, we'll examine the counterpart to input validation called **input masking**.

Input validation checks what the user has typed against some criteria for valid inputs. Input masking applies criteria to the entries while they are being typed in the first place, and simply disallows invalid keystrokes. In our shopping-cart form, for example, the input fields must contain only numbers. Input masking code can cause any key that is not a number to do nothing when one of these fields is in focus:

```
$('td.quantity input').keypress(function(event) {
  if (event.which && (event.which < 48 ||
                                   event.which > 57)) {
    event.preventDefault();
  }
});
```

When catching keystrokes for our search field's auto-completion function, we watched the `keyup` event. This allowed us to examine the `.keyCode` property of the event which told us which key on the keyboard was pressed. Here, we observe the `keypress` event instead. This event does not have a `.keyCode` property, but instead offers the `.which` property. This property reports the actual ASCII character that is represented by the keystroke that just occurred.

If the keystroke results in a character (that is, it is not an *arrow* key, *delete*, or some other editing function) and that character is not in the range of ASCII codes that represent numerals, then we call `.preventDefault()` on the event. As we have seen before, this stops the browser from acting on the event; in this case, that means that the character is never inserted into the field. Now, the quantity fields can accept only numbers.

Numeric calculations

Now, we'll move on to some manipulation of the actual numbers the user will enter in the shopping cart form. We have a **Recalculate** button on the form, which would cause the form to be submitted to the server, where new totals can be calculated and the form can be presented again to the user. This requires a round trip that is not necessary, though; all of this work can be done on the browser side using jQuery.

The simplest calculation on this form is for the cell in the **Shipping** row that displays the total quantity of items ordered. When the user modifies a quantity in one of the rows, we want to add up all of the entered values to produce a new total and display this total in the cell:

```
Var $quantities = $('td.quantity input');
$quantities.change(function() {
  var totalQuantity = 0;
  $quantities.each(function() {
    var quantity = parseInt(this.value);
    totalQuantity += quantity;
  });
  $('tr.shipping td.quantity').text(String(totalQuantity));
});
```

We have several choices for which event to watch for this recalculation operation. We could observe the keypress event, and fire the recalculation with each keystroke. We could also observe the blur event, which is triggered each time the user leaves the field. Here, we can be a little more conservative with CPU usage, though, and only perform our calculations when the change event is triggered. This way, we recalculate the totals only if the user leaves the field with a different value than it had before.

The total quantity is calculated using a simple .each() loop. The .value property of a field will report the string representation of the field's value, so we use the built-in parseInt() function to convert this into an integer for our calculation. This practice can avoid strange situations in which addition is interpreted as string concatenation, since the two operations use the same symbol. Conversely, we need a string to pass to jQuery's .text() method when displaying the calculation's result, so we use the String() function to build a new one using our calculated total quantity.

Changing a quantity now updates the total automatically:

Item	Quantity	Price	Total
Building Telephony Systems With Asterisk	11	$26.99	$26.99
Smarty PHP Template Programming and Applications	2	$35.99	$71.98
Creating your MySQL Database	1	$17.99	$17.99
Drupal: Creating Blogs, Forums, Portals, and Community Websites	1	$35.99	$35.99
Subtotal			$152.95
Tax		6%	$9.18
Shipping	15	$2 per item	$10.00
Total			$172.13
	Recalculate		Place Order

Parsing and formatting currency

Now, we can move on to the totals in the right-hand column. Each row's total cost should be calculated by multiplying the quantity entered by the price of that item. Since we're now performing multiple tasks for each row, we can begin by refactoring the quantity calculations a bit to be row-based rather than field-based:

```
$('#cart tbody tr').each(function() {
    var quantity = parseInt($('td.quantity input', this).val());
    totalQuantity += quantity;
});
```

This produces the same result as before, but we now have a convenient place to insert our total cost calculation for each row:

```
$('td.quantity input').change(function() {
  var totalQuantity = 0;
  $('#cart tbody tr').each(function() {
    var price = parseFloat($('td.price', this).text()
                                   .replace(/^[^\d.]*/, ''));
    price = isNaN(price) ? 0 : price;
    var quantity =
               parseInt($('td.quantity input', this).val());
    var cost = quantity * price;
    $('td.cost', this).text('$' + cost);
    totalQuantity += quantity;
  });
  $('tr.shipping td.quantity').text(String(totalQuantity));
});
```

We fetch the price of each item out of the table using the same technique we needed when sorting tables by price earlier. The regular expression first strips the currency symbols off from the front of the value, and the resulting string is then sent to `parseFloat()`, which interprets the value as a floating-point number. Since we will be doing calculations with the result, we need to check that a number was found, and set the price to 0 if not. Finally, we multiply the cost by the quantity, and then place the result in the total column with a $ preceding it. We can now see our total calculations in action:

Item	Quantity	Price	Total
Building Telephony Systems With Asterisk	11	$26.99	$296.89
Smarty PHP Template Programming and Applications	3	$35.99	$107.97
Creating your MySQL Database	1	$17.99	$17.99
Drupal: Creating Blogs, Forums, Portals, and Community Websites	1	$35.99	$35.99
Subtotal			$152.95
Tax		6%	$9.18
Shipping	16	$2 per item	$10.00
Total			$172.13
		Recalculate	Place Order

Dealing with decimal places

Though we have placed dollar signs in front of our totals, JavaScript is not aware that we are dealing with monetary values. As far as the computer is concerned, these are just numbers, and should be displayed as such. This means that if the total ends in a zero after the decimal point, this will be chopped off:

Item	Quantity	Price	Total
Building Telephony Systems With Asterisk	11	$26.99	$296.89
Smarty PHP Template Programming and Applications	30	$35.99	$1079.7
Creating your MySQL Database	1	$17.99	$17.99
Drupal: Creating Blogs, Forums, Portals, and Community Websites	1	$35.99	$35.99
Subtotal			$152.95
Tax		6%	$9.18
Shipping	43	$2 per item	$10.00
Total			$172.13
	Recalculate		Place Order

As we see here, the total that should read **$1079.70** displays as **$1079.7**. Even worse, the precision limitations of JavaScript can sometimes lead to rounding errors. These can make the calculations appear completely broken:

Item	Quantity	Price	Total
Building Telephony Systems With Asterisk	11	$26.99	$296.89
Smarty PHP Template Programming and Applications	30	$35.99	$1079.7
Creating your MySQL Database	10	$17.99	$179.89999999999998
Drupal: Creating Blogs, Forums, Portals, and Community Websites	1	$35.99	$35.99
Subtotal			$152.95
Tax		6%	$9.18
Shipping	52	$2 per item	$10.00
Total			$172.13
	Recalculate		Place Order

Fortunately, the fix for both problems is simple. JavaScript's `Number` class has several methods to deal with this sort of issue, and `.toFixed()` fits the bill here. This method takes a number of decimal places as a parameter, and returns a string representing the floating-point number rounded to that many decimal places:

```
$('#cart tbody tr').each(function() {
  var price = parseFloat($('td.price', this).text()
                                   .replace(/^[^\d.]*/, ''));
  price = isNaN(price) ? 0 : price;
  var quantity = parseInt($('td.quantity input', this).val());
  var cost = quantity * price;
  $('td.cost', this).text('$' + cost.toFixed(2));
  totalQuantity += quantity;
});
```

Now our totals all look like normal monetary values:

Item	Quantity	Price	Total
Building Telephony Systems With Asterisk	11	$26.99	$296.89
Smarty PHP Template Programming and Applications	30	$35.99	$1079.70
Creating your MySQL Database	10	$17.99	$179.90
Drupal: Creating Blogs, Forums, Portals, and Community Websites	1	$35.99	$35.99
Subtotal			$152.95
Tax		6%	$9.18
Shipping	52	$2 per item	$10.00
Total			$172.13

Recalculate   Place Order

After a long series of arithmetic operations, the rounding of floating-point numbers could cause enough error to accumulate that even .toFixed() cannot mask it. The safest way to handle manipulations of currency in larger applications is to store and manipulate all values in cents, as integers; decimal points can be added for display only.

Other calculations

The rest of the calculations on the page follow a similar pattern. For the subtotal, we can add up our totals for each row as they are calculated, and display the result using the same currency formatting as before:

```
$('td.quantity input').change(function() {
  var totalQuantity = 0;
  var totalCost = 0;
  $('#cart tbody tr').each(function() {
    var price = parseFloat($('td.price', this).text()
```

```
                                   .replace(/^[^\d.*/, ''));
   price = isNaN(price) ? 0 : price;
   var quantity =
                parseInt($('td.quantity input', this).val());
   var cost = quantity * price;
   $('td.cost', this).text('$' + cost.toFixed(2));
   totalQuantity += quantity;
   totalCost += cost;
 });
 $('tr.shipping td.quantity').text(String(totalQuantity));
 $('tr.subtotal td.cost').text('$' +
                       totalCost.toFixed(2));
});
```

Item	Quantity	Price	Total
Building Telephony Systems With Asterisk	11	$26.99	$296.89
Smarty PHP Template Programming and Applications	1	$35.99	$35.99
Creating your MySQL Database	10	$17.99	$179.90
Drupal: Creating Blogs, Forums, Portals, and Community Websites	1	$35.99	$35.99
Subtotal			$548.77
Tax		6%	$9.18
Shipping	23	$2 per item	$10.00
Total			$172.13

Recalculate   Place Order

Rounding values

To calculate tax, we need to divide the figure given by 100 and then multiply the
taxRate by the subtotal. As tax is always rounded up, we must ensure that the
correct value is used both for display and for later calculations. JavaScript's Math.
ceil() function can round a number *up* to the nearest integer, but since we are
dealing with dollars and cents we need to be a bit trickier:

```
var taxRate = parseFloat($('tr.tax td.price').text()) / 100;
var tax = Math.ceil(totalCost * taxRate * 100) / 100;
$('tr.tax td.cost').text('$' + tax.toFixed(2));
totalCost += tax;
```

The tax is multiplied by 100 first so that it becomes a value in cents, not dollars. This can then be rounded safely by `Math.ceil()` and then divided by `100` to convert it back into dollars. Finally `.toFixed()` is called as before to produce the correct result:

Item	Quantity	Price	Total
Building Telephony Systems With Asterisk	3	$26.99	$80.97
Smarty PHP Template Programming and Applications	1	$35.99	$35.99
Creating your MySQL Database	2	$17.99	$35.98
Drupal: Creating Blogs, Forums, Portals, and Community Websites	1	$35.99	$35.99
Subtotal			$188.93
Tax		6%	$11.34
Shipping	7	$2 per item	$10.00
Total			$172.13

Recalculate   Place Order

Finishing touches

The shipping calculation is simpler than tax since no rounding is involved in our example. The shipping rate is simply multiplied by the number of items to determine the total:

```
$('tr.shipping td.quantity').text(String(totalQuantity));
var shippingRate = parseFloat($('tr.shipping td.price')
  .text().replace(/^[^\d.]*/, ''));
var shipping = totalQuantity * shippingRate;
$('tr.shipping td.cost').text('$' + shipping.toFixed(2));
totalCost += shipping;
```

We have been keeping track of the grand total as we have gone along, so all we need to do for this last cell is to format `totalCost` appropriately:

```
$('tr.total td.cost').text('$' + totalCost.toFixed(2));
```

Now, we have completely replicated any server-side calculations that would occur so we can safely hide the **Recalculate** button:

```
$('#recalculate').hide();
```

This change once again echoes our **progressive enhancement** principle: First, ensure that the page works properly without JavaScript. Then, use jQuery to perform the same task more elegantly when possible.

Item	Quantity	Price	Total
Building Telephony Systems With Asterisk	3	$26.99	$80.97
Smarty PHP Template Programming and Applications	1	$35.99	$35.99
Creating your MySQL Database	2	$17.99	$35.98
Drupal: Creating Blogs, Forums, Portals, and Community Websites	1	$35.99	$35.99
Subtotal			$188.93
Tax		6%	$11.34
Shipping	7	$2 per item	$14.00
Total			**$214.27**
			Place Order

Deleting items

If shoppers on our site change their minds about items they have added to their carts, they can change the **Quantity** field for those items to **0**. We can provide a more reassuring behavior, though, by adding explicit **Delete** buttons for each item. The actual effect of the button can be the same as changing the **Quantity** field, but the visual feedback can reinforce the fact that the item will not be purchased.

First, we need to add the new buttons. Since they won't function without JavaScript, we won't put them in the HTML. Instead, we'll let jQuery add them to each row:

```
$('<th> </th>')
  .insertAfter('#cart thead th:nth-child(2)');
$('#cart tbody tr').each(function() {
  $deleteButton = $('<img />').attr({
    'width': '16',
    'height': '16',
    'src': '../images/cross.png',
    'alt': 'remove from cart',
    'title': 'remove from cart',
    'class': 'clickable'
  });
  $('<td></td>')
    .insertAfter($('td:nth-child(2)', this))
```

```
      .append($deleteButton);
  });
  $('<td> </td>')
    .insertAfter('#cart tfoot td:nth-child(2)');
```

We need to create empty cells in the header and footer rows as placeholders so that the columns of the table still line up correctly. The buttons are created and added on the body rows only:

Item	Quantity		Price	Total
Building Telephony Systems With Asterisk	3	✖	$26.99	$26.99
Smarty PHP Template Programming and Applications	1	✖	$35.99	$71.98
Creating your MySQL Database	2	✖	$17.99	$17.99
Drupal: Creating Blogs, Forums, Portals, and Community Websites	1	✖	$35.99	$35.99
Subtotal				$152.95
Tax			6%	$9.18
Shipping	5		$2 per item	$10.00
Total				**$172.13**
				Place Order

Now we need to make the buttons do something. We can change the button definition to add a `click` handler:

```
$deleteButton = $('<img />').attr({
  'width': '16',
  'height': '16',
  'src': '../images/cross.png',
  'alt': 'remove from cart',
  'title': 'remove from cart',
  'class': 'clickable'
}).click(function() {
  $(this).parents('tr').find('td.quantity input')
    .val(0);
});
```

The handler finds the `quantity` field in the same row as the button, and sets the value to `0`. Now, the field is updated, but the calculations are out of sync:

Item	Quantity		Price	Total
Building Telephony Systems With Asterisk	3	✖	$26.99	$80.97
Smarty PHP Template Programming and Applications	0	✖	$35.99	$35.99
Creating your MySQL Database	2	✖	$17.99	$35.98
Drupal: Creating Blogs, Forums, Portals, and Community Websites	1	✖	$35.99	$35.99
Subtotal				$188.93
Tax			6%	$11.34
Shipping	7		$2 per item	$14.00
Total				$214.27
				Place Order

We need to trigger the calculation as if the user had manually changed the field value:

```
$deleteButton = $('<img />').attr({
  'width': '16',
  'height': '16',
  'src': '../images/cross.png',
  'alt': 'remove from cart',
  'title': 'remove from cart',
  'class': 'clickable'
}).click(function() {
  $(this).parents('tr').find('td.quantity input')
    .val(0).trigger('change');
});
```

Now the totals update when the button is clicked:

Item	Quantity		Price	Total
Building Telephony Systems With Asterisk	3	✖	$26.99	$80.97
Smarty PHP Template Programming and Applications	0	✖	$35.99	$0.00
Creating your MySQL Database	2	✖	$17.99	$35.98
Drupal: Creating Blogs, Forums, Portals, and Community Websites	1	✖	$35.99	$35.99
Subtotal				$152.94
Tax			6%	$9.18
Shipping	6		$2 per item	$12.00
Total				$174.12
				Place Order

Now for the visual feedback. We'll hide the row that was just clicked, so that the item is clearly removed from the cart:

```
$deleteButton = $('<img />').attr({
   'width': '16',
   'height': '16',
   'src': '../images/cross.png',
   'alt': 'remove from cart',
   'title': 'remove from cart',
   'class': 'clickable'
}).click(function() {
   $(this).parents('tr').find('td.quantity input')
     .val(0).trigger('change')
   .end().hide();
});
```

Item	Quantity		Price	Total
Building Telephony Systems With Asterisk	3	✖	$26.99	$80.97
Creating your MySQL Database	2	✖	$17.99	$35.98
Drupal: Creating Blogs, Forums, Portals, and Community Websites	1	✖	$35.99	$35.99
Subtotal				$152.94
Tax			6%	$9.18
Shipping	6		$2 per item	$12.00
Total				$174.12
				Place Order

While the row is hidden, the field is still present on the form. This means it will be submitted with the rest of the form, and the item will be removed on the server side at that time.

Our row striping has been disturbed by the removal of this row. To correct this, we move our existing striping code into a function so that we can call it again later. At the same time, we need to modify the code to ensure that our alternating row selection ignores any hidden rows. Unfortunately, even if we filter out all of the hidden rows, we still can't use the `:nth-child(even)` selector, because it will apply the `alt` class to all visible rows that are the "eventh" child of their parent. Let's see what happens when we apply the following modified code to four table rows when the second one is hidden:

```
$('#cart tbody tr').removeClass('alt')
   .filter(':visible:nth-child(even)').addClass('alt');
```

We get the following markup [condensed]:

```
<tr> . . . </tr>
<tr style="display: none"> . . . </tr>
<tr> . . . </tr>
<tr class="alt"> . . . </tr>
```

Three rows are visible; only the fourth has the `alt` class applied to it. What we need is the `:visible:odd` selector expression, since it will choose every other row after removing the hidden ones for the selection (and it accounts for the shift from a **one-indexed** to a **zero-indexed** selector). As in Chapter 2, using `:odd` or `:even` could produce unexpected results if we had more than one `<tbody>` element, but in this case we're in good shape. With the selector change in place, our new function looks like this:

```
var stripe = function() {
  $('#cart tbody tr').removeClass('alt')
    .filter(':visible:odd').addClass('alt');
};
stripe();
```

Now we can call this function again after removing a row:

```
$deleteButton = $('<img />').attr({
  'width': '16',
  'height': '16',
  'src': '../images/cross.png',
  'alt': 'remove from cart',
  'title': 'remove from cart',
  'class': 'clickable'
}).click(function() {
  $(this).parents('tr').find('td.quantity input')
    .val(0).trigger('change')
  .end().hide();
  stripe();
});
```

The deleted row has now seamlessly disappeared:

Item	Quantity		Price	Total
Building Telephony Systems With Asterisk	3	✖	$26.99	$80.97
Creating your MySQL Database	2	✖	$17.99	$35.98
Drupal: Creating Blogs, Forums, Portals, and Community Websites	1	✖	$35.99	$35.99
Subtotal				$152.94
Tax			6%	$9.18
Shipping	6		$2 per item	$12.00
Total				**$174.12**
				Place Order

This completes yet another enhancement using jQuery that is completely transparent to the code on the server. As far as the server is concerned, the user just typed a **0** in the input field, but to the user this is a distinct removal operation that is different from changing a quantity.

Editing shipping information

The shopping cart page also has a form for shipping information. Actually, it isn't a form at all when the page loads, and without JavaScript enabled, it remains a little box tucked away on the right side of the content area, containing a link to a page where the user can edit the shipping information:

But with JavaScript available, and with the power of jQuery at our disposal, we can turn this little link into a full-fledged form. We'll do this by requesting the form from a PHP page. Typically the data populating the form would be stored in a database of some sort, but for the purpose of this demonstration, we'll just keep some static data in a PHP array.

To retrieve the form and make it appear inside the **Shipping to** box, we use the `$.get()` method inside the `.click()` event handler:

```
$(document).ready(function() {
  $('#shipping-name').click(function() {
    $.get('shipping.php', function(data) {
      $('#shipping-name').remove();
      $(data).hide().appendTo('#shipping').slideDown();
    });
    return false;
  });
});
```

By testing for the absence of the server variable `$_SERVER['HTTP_X_REQUESTED_WITH']` before printing most of the page, the PHP page (`shipping.php`) returns only a fragment of the full page, the form, when it is requested with the `$.get()` method.

In the callback of the $.get() method, we remove the name that was just clicked and in its place append the form and its data from shipping.php. We then add return false so that the default event for the clicked link (loading the page indicated in the href attribute) does not occur. Now the **Shipping to** box is an editable form:

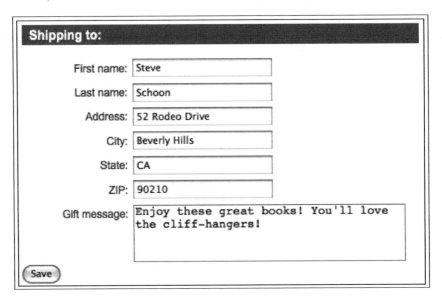

The user can now edit the shipping information without leaving the page.

The next step is to hijack the form submission and post the edited data back to the server with jQuery. We start by serializing the data in the form and storing it in a postData variable. Then we post the data back to the server using shipping.php once again:

```
$(document).ready(function() {
  $('shipping form').submit(function() {
    var postData = $(this).serialize();
    $.post('shipping.php', postData);
    return false;
  };
});
```

The jQuery Form plugin offers a more robust .serialize() method. The plugin, which can be found at http://www.malsup.com/jquery/form/, is recommended for most AJAX form submission scenarios.

It makes sense for the form to be removed at this point and for the **Shipping to** box to return to its original state. We can achieve this in the callback of the $.post() method that we just used:

```
$(document).ready(function() {
  $('#shipping form').submit(function() {
    var postData = $(this).serialize();
    $.post('shipping.php', postData, function(data) {
      $('#shipping form').remove();
      $(data).appendTo('#shipping');
    });
    return false;
  };
});
```

But, this will not work! The way we have it set up now, the .submit() event handler is being bound to the **Shipping to** form as soon as the DOM is loaded, but the form is not in the DOM until the user clicks on the **Shipping to** name. The event can't be bound to something that doesn't exist.

To overcome this problem, we can put the form-creation code into a function called editShipping() and the form-submission or form-removal code into a function called saveShipping(). Then we can bind the saveShipping() function in the callback of $.get(), after the form has been created. Likewise, we can bind the editShipping() function both when the DOM is ready and when the **Edit shipping** link is re-created in the callback of $.post():

```
$(document).ready(function() {
  var editShipping = function() {
    $.get('shipping.php', function(data) {
      $('#shipping-name').remove();
      $(data).hide().appendTo('#shipping').slideDown();
      $('#shipping form').submit(saveShipping);
    });
    return false;
  };
  var saveShipping = function() {
    var postData = $('#shipping :input').serialize();
    $.post('shipping.php', postData, function(data) {
      $('#shipping form').remove();
      $(data).appendTo('#shipping');
      $('#shipping-name').click(editShipping);
    });
    return false;
  };
  $('#shipping-name').click(editShipping);
});
```

The code has formed a circular pattern of sorts, in which one function allows for the other by rebinding their respective event handlers.

The finished code

Taken together, the code for the shopping cart page is a mere 80 lines—quite small considering the functionality it accomplishes, but especially so when we take into account the breezy style that the code has acquired for optimum readability. Many of the lines in jQuery could have been merged, were we particularly concerned with number of lines, because of jQuery's chainability. At any rate, here is the finished code for the shopping cart page, which concludes this chapter on forms:

```
$(document).ready(function() {
  var stripe = function() {
    $('#cart tbody tr').removeClass('alt')
    .filter(':visible:odd').addClass('alt');
  };
  stripe();

  $('#recalculate').hide();

  $('.quantity input').keypress(function(event) {
    if (event.which && (event.which < 48 ||
                                   event.which > 57)) {
      event.preventDefault();
    }
  }).change(function() {
    var totalQuantity = 0;
    var totalCost = 0;
    $('#cart tbody tr').each(function() {
      var price = parseFloat($('.price', this)
                      .text().replace(/^[^\d.]*/, ''));
      price = isNaN(price) ? 0 : price;
      var quantity =
              parseInt($('.quantity input', this).val(), 10);
      var cost = quantity * price;
      $('.cost', this).text('$' + cost.toFixed(2));
      totalQuantity += quantity;
      totalCost += cost;
    });
    $('.subtotal .cost').text('$' + totalCost.toFixed(2));
    var taxRate = parseFloat($('.tax .price').text()) / 100;
    var tax = Math.ceil(totalCost * taxRate * 100) / 100;
    $('.tax .cost').text('$' + tax.toFixed(2));
    totalCost += tax;
```

```
        $('.shipping .quantity').text(String(totalQuantity));
        var shippingRate = parseFloat($('.shipping .price')
                                 .text().replace(/^[^\d.]*/, ''));
        var shipping = totalQuantity * shippingRate;
        $('.shipping .cost').text('$' + shipping.toFixed(2));
        totalCost += shipping;
        $('.total .cost').text('$' + totalCost.toFixed(2));
      });

    $('<th> </th>')
    .insertAfter('#cart thead th:nth-child(2)');
    $('#cart tbody tr').each(function() {
        $deleteButton = $('<img />').attr({
            'width': '16',
            'height': '16',
            'src': '../images/cross.png',
            'alt': 'remove from cart',
            'title': 'remove from cart',
            'class': 'clickable'
        }).click(function() {
            $(this).parents('tr').find('td.quantity input')
                .val(0).trigger('change')
            .end().hide();
            stripe();
        });
        $('<td></td>')
        .insertAfter($('td:nth-child(2)', this))
        .append($deleteButton);
    });
    $('<td> </td>')
    .insertAfter('#cart tfoot td:nth-child(2)');
});

$(document).ready(function() {
  var editShipping = function() {
    $.get('shipping.php', function(data) {
      $('#shipping-name').remove();
      $(data).hide().appendTo('#shipping').slideDown();
      $('#shipping form').submit(saveShipping);
    });
    return false;
  };
  var saveShipping = function() {
    var postData = $(this).serialize();
    $.post('shipping.php', postData, function(data) {
```

```
          $('#shipping form').remove();
          $(data).appendTo('#shipping');
          $('#shipping-name').click(editShipping);
       });
       return false;
     };
     $('#shipping-name').click(editShipping);
   });
```

Summary

In this chapter we have investigated ways to improve the appearance and behavior of common HTML form elements. We have learned about enhancing the styling of forms while leaving the original markup semantic, conditionally hiding and showing fields based on other field values, and validating field contents both before submission and during data entry. We have covered features like AJAX auto-completion for text fields, allowing only specific characters to be entered in a field, and performing calculations on numeric values in fields. We have also learned to submit forms using AJAX rather than a page refresh.

The form element is often the glue that holds an interactive site together. With jQuery, we can easily improve the user's experience in filling out forms while still preserving their utility and flexibility.

9
Shufflers and Rotators

We've seen a few ways to hide information when it's not needed and reveal it on demand, such as collapsible accordions of information. Sometimes, though, we want to move content in and out of view with even more flair. These kinds of animations go by many names: **carousels**, **cyclers**, **shufflers**, and **rotators**. What they have in common is an ability to quickly flip between multiple pieces of data in an eye-catching and impressive way.

In this third and final how-to chapter, we'll explore these advanced animations, combining them with AJAX techniques and CSS subtlety to really make an impression.

We will step through two large examples in this chapter: a headline rotator, and an image carousel. These examples will allow us to learn how to:

- Animate the position of an element
- Parse XML documents
- Prepare advanced styling effect using partial opacity
- Retrieve information from different domains
- Create a user interface element for horizontal scrolling
- Composite layers for badges and overlays
- Zoom into an image

Headline rotator

For our first **rotator** example, we'll take a news feed and scroll the headlines, along with an excerpt of the article, into view one at a time. The stories will flow into view, pause to be read, and then slide up and off the page as if there were an infinite ribbon of information rolling over the page.

Setting up the page

At its most basic level, this feature is not very difficult to implement. But as we will soon see, making it production-ready requires a bit of finesse.

We begin, as usual, with a chunk of HTML. We'll place the news feed in the sidebar of the page:

```
<h3>Recent News</h3>
<div id="news-feed">
  <a href="news/index.html">News Releases</a>
</div>
```

So far, the content area of our news feed contains only a single link to the main news page.

This is our **graceful degradation** scenario, in case the user does not have JavaScript enabled. The content we'll be working with will come from an actual **RSS feed** instead.

The CSS for this `<div>` is important as it will determine not only how much of each news item will be shown at a time, but also where on the page the news items will appear. Together with the style rule for the individual news items, the CSS looks like this:

```
#news-feed {
  position: relative;
  height: 200px;
  width: 17em;
  overflow: hidden;
}
.headline {
  position: absolute;
  height: 200px;
  top: 210px;
  overflow: hidden;
}
```

Notice here that the height of both the individual news items (represented by the `headline` class) and their container is `200px`. Also, since `headline` elements are absolutely positioned relative to `#news-feed`, we're able to line up the top of the news items with the bottom edge of their container. That way, when we set the `overflow` property of `#news-feed` to `hidden`, the headlines are not displayed initially.

Setting the `position` of the headlines to `absolute` is necessary for another reason as well: for any element to have its location animated on the page, it must have either `absolute` or `relative` positioning, rather than the default `static` positioning.

Now that we have the HTML and CSS in place, we can inject the news items from an RSS feed. To start, we'll wrap the code in a `.each()` method, which will act as an `if` statement of sorts and contain the code inside a private **namespace**:

```
$(document).ready(function() {
  $('#news-feed').each(function() {
    var $container = $(this);
    $container.empty();
  });
});
```

Normally when we use the `.each()` method, we are iterating over a possibly large set of elements. Here, though, our selector `#news-feed` is looking for an ID, so there are only two potential outcomes. The factory function could make a jQuery object matching one unique element with the `news-feed` ID, or it could find no elements on the page with that ID and produce an empty jQuery object. The `.each()` call takes care of executing the contained code if, and only if, the jQuery object is non-empty.

At the beginning of our `.each()` loop, the news feed container is emptied to make it ready for its new content.

Retrieving the feed

To retrieve the feed, we'll use the $.get() method, one of jQuery's many AJAX functions for communicating with the server. This method, as we have seen before, allows us to operate on content from a remote source by using a **success handler**. The content of the feed is passed to this handler as an XML structure. We can then use jQuery's selector engine to work with this data.

```
$(document).ready(function() {
  $('#news-feed').each(function() {
    var $container = $(this);
    $container.empty();
    $.get('news/feed.xml', function(data) {
      $('rss item', data).each(function() {
        // Work with the headlines here.
      });
    });
  });
});
```

> For more information on $.get() and other AJAX methods, see Chapter 6.

Now, we need to combine the parts of each item into a usable block of HTML markup. We can use .each() again to go through the items in the feed and build the headline links:

```
$(document).ready(function() {
  $('#news-feed').each(function() {
    var $container = $(this);
    $container.empty();
    $.get('news/feed.xml', function(data) {
      $('rss item', data).each(function() {
        var $link = $('<a></a>')
          .attr('href', $('link', this).text())
          .text($('title', this).text());
        var $headline = $('<h4></h4>').append($link);

        $('<div></div>')
          .append($headline)
          .appendTo($container);
      });
    });
  });
});
```

We get the text of each item's `<title>` and `<link>` elements, and construct the `<a>` element from them. This link is then wrapped in an `<h4>` element. We put each news item into `<div id="news-feed">`, but for now we're omitting the `headline` class on each news item's containing `<div>` so that we can more easily see our work in progress.

Recent News

jQuery, Microsoft, and Nokia

jQuery UI 1.6rc2

jQuery Conference 2008 Agenda

Death to JavaScript Rock Stars!

jQuery Site Redesign - The
Community Speaks

jQuery.com Site Redesign

Registration Open for jQuery
Conference 2008

jQuery UI 1.5.2

In addition to the headlines, we want to display a bit of supporting information about each article. We'll grab the publication date and article summary, and display these as well.

```
$(document).ready(function() {
  $('#news-feed').each(function() {
    var $container = $(this);
    $container.empty();
    $.get('news/feed.xml', function(data) {
      $('rss item', data).each(function() {
        var $link = $('<a></a>')
          .attr('href', $('link', this).text())
          .text($('title', this).text());
        var $headline = $('<h4></h4>').append($link);

        var pubDate = new Date(
          $('pubDate', this).text());
        var pubMonth = pubDate.getMonth() + 1;
        var pubDay = pubDate.getDate();
        var pubYear = pubDate.getFullYear();
        var $publication = $('<div></div>')
          .addClass('publication-date')
          .text(pubMonth + '/' + pubDay + '/'
            + pubYear);
```

```
        var $summary = $('<div></div>')
          .addClass('summary')
          .html($('description', this).text());

      $('<div></div>')
        .append($headline, $publication, $summary)
        .appendTo($container);
    });
   });
  });
 });
```

The date information in an RSS feed is encoded in RFC 822 format, which includes date, time, and time zone information (for example, `Sun, 28 Sep 2008 18:01:55 +0000`). This format is not particularly eye-pleasing, so we use JavaScript's built-in `Date` object to produce a more compact representation of the date (such as `9/28/2008`).

The summary information is easier to retrieve and format. It's worth noting, though, that in our sample feed, some **HTML entities** may exist in the description. To make sure that these are not automatically escaped by jQuery, we need to use the `.html()` method to insert the description into the page, rather than the `.text()` method.

With these new elements created, we insert them into the document using the `.append()` method. Note here that we are using a new feature of the method; if more than one argument is supplied, all of them get appended in sequence.

Recent News

jQuery, Microsoft, and Nokia
9/28/2008

We have two pieces of fantastic, albeit serendipitous, news today: Both Microsoft and Nokia are taking the major step of adopting jQuery as part of their official application development platform.

jQuery UI 1.6rc2
9/19/2008

Hey everyone, I'm glad to announce

As we can see, the title, date, link, and summary of each news item is now in place. All that's left is to add the `headline` class with `.addClass('headline')` (which will hide them from view because of the CSS we defined earlier), and we are ready to proceed with our animation.

Setting up the rotator

Since the visible news item will change over time, we'll need a way to easily keep track of which items are visible and where they are. First, we'll set two variables, one for the currently visible headline and one for the headline that has just scrolled out of view. Initially, both values will be 0.

```
var currentHeadline = 0, oldHeadline = 0;
```

Next, we'll take care of some initial positioning of the headlines. Recall that in the stylesheet we have already set the `top` property of the headlines to be 10 pixels greater than their container's `height`; because the container has an `overflow` property of `hidden`, the headlines are initially not displayed. It'll be helpful later on if we store that property in a variable, so that we can move headlines to this position when needed.

```
var hiddenPosition = $container.height() + 10;
```

We also want the first headline to be visible immediately upon page load. To achieve this, we can set its `top` property to `0`.

```
$('div.headline').eq(currentHeadline).css('top', 0);
```

The rotator area of the page is now in the correct initial state:

Recent News

jQuery, Microsoft, and Nokia
9/28/2008

We have two pieces of fantastic, albeit serendipitous, news today: Both Microsoft and Nokia are taking the major step of adopting jQuery as part of their official application development platform.

Finally, we'll store the total number of headlines for later use and define a timeout variable to be used for the pause mechanism between each rotation.

```
var headlineCount = $('div.headline').length;
var pause;
```

There is no need yet to give `pause` a value at this time; it will be set each time the rotation occurs. Nevertheless, we must always declare **local variables** using `var` to avoid the risk of collisions with **global variables** of the same name.

The headline rotate function

Now we're ready to rotate the headlines, dates, and summaries. We'll define a function for this task so that we can easily repeat the action each time we need it.

First, let's take care of updating the variables that are tracking which headline is active. The **modulus operator** (`%`) will let us easily cycle through the headline numbers. We can add 1 to the `currentHeadline` value each time our function is called, and then take this value modulus the `headlineCount` value to constrain the variable to valid headline numbers.

 Recall that we used this same technique to cycle through row colors when striping tables in Chapter 7.

We should also update the `oldHeadline` value so that we can easily manipulate the headline that is moving out of view.

```
var headlineRotate = function() {
  currentHeadline = (oldHeadline + 1) % headlineCount;
  // Animate the headline positions here.
  oldHeadline = currentHeadline;
};
```

Now we have to fill in the gap with code that actually moves the headlines. First, we'll add an animation that moves the old headline out of the way. Then, we'll insert another animation that slides the new headline into view.

```
var headlineRotate = function() {
  currentHeadline = (oldHeadline + 1) % headlineCount;
  $('div.headline').eq(oldHeadline).animate(
    {top: -hiddenPosition}, 'slow', function() {
      $(this).css('top', hiddenPosition);
    });
  $('div.headline').eq(currentHeadline).animate(
    {top: 0}, 'slow', function() {
      pause = setTimeout(headlineRotate, 5000);
    });
  oldHeadline = currentHeadline;
};
```

In both cases, we're animating the `top` property of the news item. Recall that the items are hidden because they have a `top` value of `hiddenPosition` (which is a number greater than the height of the container). Animating this property to `0` brings an item into view; further animating it to `-hiddenPosition` moves it out of view again.

 Recall from Chapter 4 that `top` is a CSS positioning property, and only has an effect if the `position` of the element is `absolute` or `relative`.

In both cases, we also have a callback function specified to take action when the animation is complete. When the old headline has completely slid out of view, it gets its `top` property reset to `hiddenPosition` so it is ready to return later. When the new headline is finished with its animation, we want to queue up the next transition; this is done with a call to the JavaScript `setTimeout()` function, which registers a function to be invoked after a specified period. In this case, we're causing `headlineRotate()` to be fired again in five seconds (5000 milliseconds).

We now have a cycle of activity; once one animation completes, the next one is ready to activate. It remains to call the function the first time; we'll do this with another call to `setTimeout()`, causing the first transition to happen 5 seconds after the RSS feed has been retrieved. Now we have a functional headline rotator.

```
$(document).ready(function() {
  $('#news-feed').each(function() {
    var $container = $(this);
    $container.empty();
    $.get('news/feed.xml', function(data) {
      $('rss item', data).each(function() {
        var $link = $('<a></a>')
          .attr('href', $('link', this).text())
          .text($('title', this).text());
        var $headline = $('<h4></h4>').append($link);

        var pubDate = new Date($('pubDate', this).text());
        var pubMonth = pubDate.getMonth() + 1;
        var pubDay = pubDate.getDate();
        var pubYear = pubDate.getFullYear();
        var $publication = $('<div></div>')
          .addClass('publication-date')
          .text(pubMonth + '/' + pubDay + '/' + pubYear);

        var $summary = $('<div></div>')
          .addClass('summary')
          .html($('description', this).text());
```

```
        $('<div></div>')
          .addClass('headline')
          .append($headline, $publication, $summary)
          .appendTo($container);
      });
      var currentHeadline = 0, oldHeadline = 0;
      var hiddenPosition = $container.height() + 10;
      $('div.headline').eq(currentHeadline).css('top', 0);
      var headlineCount = $('div.headline').length;
      var pause;
      var headlineRotate = function() {
        currentHeadline = (oldHeadline + 1) % headlineCount;
        $('div.headline').eq(oldHeadline).animate(
          {top: -hiddenPosition}, 'slow', function() {
            $(this).css('top', hiddenPosition);
          });
        $('div.headline').eq(currentHeadline).animate(
          {top: 0}, 'slow', function() {
            pause = setTimeout(headlineRotate, 5000);
          });
        oldHeadline = currentHeadline;
      };
      pause = setTimeout(headlineRotate, 5000);
    });
  });
});
```

Partially through the animation, we can see one headline cropped at the top, and the next coming into view cropped at the bottom:

Pause on hover

Even though the headline rotator is now fully functioning, there is one significant usability issue that we should address—a headline might scroll out of the viewable area before a user is able to click on one of its links. This forces the user to wait until the rotator has cycled through the full set of headlines again before getting a second chance. We can reduce the likelihood of this problem by having the rotator pause when the user's mouse cursor hovers anywhere within the headline.

```
$container.hover(function() {
  clearTimeout(pause);
}, function() {
  pause = setTimeout(headlineRotate, 250);
});
```

When the mouse enters the headline area, the first `.hover()` handler calls JavaScript's `clearTimeout()` function. This cancels the timer in progress, preventing `headlineRotate()` from being called. When the mouse leaves, the second `.hover()` handler reinstates the timer, thereby invoking `headlineRotate()` after a 250 millisecond delay.

This simple code works fine most of the time. However, if the user moves the mouse over and back out of the `<div>` quickly and repeatedly, a very undesirable effect can occur. Multiple headlines will be in motion at a time, layering on top of each other in the visible area.

Unfortunately, we need to perform some serious surgery to remove this cancer. Before the `headlineRotate()` function, we'll introduce one more variable:

```
var rotateInProgress = false;
```

Now, on the very first line of our function, we can check if a rotation is currently in progress. Only if the value of `rotateInProgress` is `false` do we want the code to run again. Therefore, we wrap everything within the function in an `if` statement. Immediately inside this conditional, we set the variable to `true`, and then in the callback of the second `.animate()` method, we set it back to `false`.

```
var headlineRotate = function() {
  if (!rotateInProgress) {
    rotateInProgress = true;
    currentHeadline = (oldHeadline + 1)
      % headlineCount;
    $('div.headline').eq(oldHeadline).animate(
      {top: -hiddenPosition}, 'slow', function() {
        $(this).css('top', hiddenPosition);
      });
    $('div.headline').eq(currentHeadline).animate(
      {top: 0}, 'slow', function() {
        rotateInProgress = false;
        pause = setTimeout(headlineRotate, 5000);
      });
    oldHeadline = currentHeadline;
  }
};
```

These few additional lines improve our headline rotator substantially. Rapid, repeated hovering no longer causes the headlines to pile up on top of each other. Yet this user behavior still leaves us with one nagging problem: the rhythm of the rotator is thrown off with two or three animations immediately following each other, rather than all of them evenly spaced out at five-second intervals.

The problem is that more than one timer can become active concurrently if a user mouses out of the `<div>` before the existing timer completes. We therefore need to put one more safeguard into place, using our `pause` variable as a flag indicating whether another animation is imminent. To do this, we set the variable to `false` when the timeout is cleared or when one completes. Now we can test the variable's value to make sure there is no timeout active before we put a new one in place.

```
var headlineRotate = function() {
  if (!rotateInProgress) {
    rotateInProgress = true;
    pause = false;
    currentHeadline = (oldHeadline + 1)
      % headlineCount;
    $('div.headline').eq(oldHeadline).animate(
      {top: -hiddenPosition}, 'slow', function() {
        $(this).css('top', hiddenPosition);
```

```
      });
    $('div.headline').eq(currentHeadline).animate(
      {top: 0}, 'slow', function() {
         rotateInProgress = false;
         if (!pause) {
            pause = setTimeout(headlineRotate, 5000);
         }
      });
    oldHeadline = currentHeadline;
  }
};
if (!pause) {
  pause = setTimeout(headlineRotate, 5000);
}
$container.hover(function() {
  clearTimeout(pause);
  pause = false;
}, function() {
  if (!pause) {
     pause = setTimeout(headlineRotate, 250);
  }
});
```

At last, our headline rotator can withstand all manner of attempts by the user to thwart it.

Retrieving a feed from a different domain

The news feed that we've been using for our example is a local file, but we might want to retrieve a feed from another site altogether. As we saw in Chapter 6, AJAX requests cannot, as a rule, be made to a different site than the one hosting the page being viewed. There, we discussed the JSONP data format as a method for circumventing this limitation. Here, though, we'll assume we cannot modify the data source, so we need a different solution.

To allow AJAX to fetch this file, we'll use some server-side code as a **proxy** for the request, so that JavaScript believes the XML file is on our server even though it actually resides on a different one. We will write a short PHP script to pull the content of the news feed to our server, and relay that data to the requesting jQuery script. This script, which we'll call **feed.php**, can be called in the same way **feed.xml** was fetched previously:

```
$.get('news/feed.php', function(data) {
  // ...
});
```

Inside the **feed.php** file, we pull in the content of the news feed from the remote site, then print the content as the output of the script.

```php
<?php
  header('Content-Type: text/xml');
  print file_get_contents('http://jquery.com/blog/feed');
?>
```

Note here that we need to explicitly set the content type of the page to text/xml so that jQuery can fetch it and parse it as if it were a normal, static XML document.

 Some web-hosting providers may not allow the use of the PHP file_get_contents() function to fetch remote files because of security concerns. In these cases, alternative solutions, such as using the **cURL** library, may be available. More information on this library can be found at http://wiki.dreamhost.com/CURL.

Adding a loading indicator

Pulling in a remote file like this might take some time, depending on a number of factors, so we should inform the user that loading is in progress. To do this, we'll add a **loading indicator** image to the page before we issue our AJAX request.

```javascript
var $loadingIndicator = $('<img/>')
  .attr({
    'src': 'images/loading.gif',
    'alt': 'Loading. Please wait.'
  })
  .addClass('news-wait')
  .appendTo($container);
```

Then, as the first line of our $.get() function's success callback, we can remove the image from the page with a simple command:

```javascript
$loadingIndicator.remove();
```

Now, when the page first loads, if there is a delay in retrieving the headline content, we'll see a loading image rather than an empty area.

This image is an animated GIF, and in a web browser will spin to signify that activity is taking place.

 We can easily create new animated GIF images for use as AJAX loading indicators by using the service at `http://ajaxload.info/`.

Gradient fade effect

Before we put away our headline rotator example, let's give it a finishing touch, by making the headline text appear to fade in from the bottom of its container. The effect will be a **gradient fade**, appearing as if the text is opaque at the top of the effect area and transparent at the bottom.

A single text element cannot have multiple opacities simultaneously, however. To simulate this, we'll actually cover up the effect area with a series of elements, each of which has a different opacity. These slices with be `<div>` elements with a few style properties in common, which we can declare in our stylesheet:

```
.fade-slice {
  position: absolute;
  width: 20em;
  height: 2px;
  background: #efd;
  z-index: 3;
}
```

They all have the same `width` and `background-color` properties as their containing element, `<div id="news-feed">`. This will fool the user's eye into thinking the text is fading away, rather than being covered up by another element.

Now we can create the `<div class="fade-slice">` elements. To make sure we have the right number of them, first we'll determine a height in pixels for the entire effect area. In this case, we're choosing 25 percent of the `<div id="news-feed">` height. We'll use a `for` loop to iterate across the height of this area, creating a new slice element for each 2-pixel segment of the gradient:

```
$(document).ready(function() {
  $('#news-feed').each(function() {
    var $container = $(this);
    $container.empty();
    var fadeHeight = $container.height() / 4;
    for (var yPos = 0; yPos < fadeHeight; yPos += 2) {
      $('<div></div>')
```

```
          .addClass('fade-slice')
          .appendTo($container);
      }
    });
  });
```

Now we have 25 slices (one for each 2-pixel segment of the 50-pixel gradient area), but they are all piled up at the top of the container. For our trick to work, we need each one to have a different position and opacity. We can use the iteration variable yPos to mathematically determine each element's opacity and top properties:

```
$(document).ready(function() {
  $('#news-feed').each(function() {
    var $container = $(this);
    $container.empty();

    var fadeHeight = $container.height() / 4;
    for (var yPos = 0; yPos < fadeHeight; yPos += 2) {
      $('<div></div>').css({
        opacity: yPos / fadeHeight,
        top: $container.height() - fadeHeight + yPos
      }).addClass('fade-slice').appendTo($container);
    }
  });
});
```

These calculations can be a bit tricky to visualize, so we'll lay out the numbers in a table. The opacity values step up incrementally from transparent to opaque, as the top values begin at the top of the fade area (150) and grow to the container's height:

yPos	opacity	top
0	0	150
2	0.04	152
4	0.08	154
6	0.12	156
8	0.16	158
	...	
40	0.80	190
42	0.84	192
44	0.88	194
46	0.92	196
48	0.96	198

Keep in mind that since the top position of the final `<div class="fade-slice">` is 198, its 2-pixel height will neatly overlay the bottom two pixels of the 200-pixel-tall containing `<div>`.

With our code in place, the text in the headline area of the page now blends beautifully from transparent to opaque as it overlaps the bottom of the container:

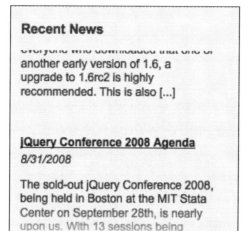

The finished code

Our first rotator is now complete. The news items are now fetched from a remote server, formatted, animated in and out of view on schedule, and beautifully styled:

```
$(document).ready(function() {
  $('#news-feed').each(function() {
    var $container = $(this);
    $container.empty();

    var fadeHeight = $container.height() / 4;
    for (var yPos = 0; yPos < fadeHeight; yPos += 2) {
      $('<div></div>').css({
        opacity: yPos / fadeHeight,
        top: $container.height() - fadeHeight + yPos
      }).addClass('fade-slice').appendTo($container);
    }

    var $loadingIndicator = $('<img/>')
      .attr({
        'src': 'images/loading.gif',
        'alt': 'Loading. Please wait.'
      })
```

```
    .addClass('news-wait')
    .appendTo($container);

$.get('news/feed.php', function(data) {
  $loadingIndicator.remove();
  $('rss item', data).each(function() {
    var $link = $('<a></a>')
      .attr('href', $('link', this).text())
      .text($('title', this).text());
    var $headline = $('<h4></h4>').append($link);

    var pubDate = new Date($('pubDate', this).text());
    var pubMonth = pubDate.getMonth() + 1;
    var pubDay = pubDate.getDate();
    var pubYear = pubDate.getFullYear();
    var $publication = $('<div></div>')
      .addClass('publication-date')
      .text(pubMonth + '/' + pubDay + '/' + pubYear);

    var $summary = $('<div></div>')
      .addClass('summary')
      .html($('description', this).text());

    $('<div></div>')
      .addClass('headline')
      .append($headline, $publication, $summary)
      .appendTo($container);
  });
  var currentHeadline = 0, oldHeadline = 0;
  var hiddenPosition = $container.height() + 10;
  $('div.headline').eq(currentHeadline).css('top', 0);
  var headlineCount = $('div.headline').length;
  var pause;
  var rotateInProgress = false;

  var headlineRotate = function() {
    if (!rotateInProgress) {
      rotateInProgress = true;
      pause = false;
      currentHeadline = (oldHeadline + 1)
        % headlineCount;
      $('div.headline').eq(oldHeadline).animate(
        {top: -hiddenPosition}, 'slow', function() {
          $(this).css('top', hiddenPosition);
        });
      $('div.headline').eq(currentHeadline).animate(
        {top: 0}, 'slow', function() {
```

```
                rotateInProgress = false;
                if (!pause) {
                   pause = setTimeout(headlineRotate, 5000);
                }
             });
             oldHeadline = currentHeadline;
          }
       };
       if (!pause) {
          pause = setTimeout(headlineRotate, 5000);
       }

       $container.hover(function() {
          clearTimeout(pause);
          pause = false;
       }, function() {
          if (!pause) {
             pause = setTimeout(headlineRotate, 250);
          }
       });
     });
   });
});
```

An image carousel

As another example of shuffling around page content, we'll implement an **image gallery** for the front page of the bookstore site. The gallery will present a few featured books for sale, with links to larger cover art for each. Unlike the previous example, where the headlines in our news ticker moved on a set schedule, here we'll use jQuery to slide the images across the screen in response to user interaction.

An alternative mechanism for scrolling through a set of images is implemented by the **jCarousel** plugin for jQuery. Additionally, the highly flexible **SerialScroll** plugin allows for scrolling any type of content. While not identical to the result we'll achieve here, these plugins can produce high-quality shuffling effects with very little code. More information on using plugins can be found in Chapter 10.

Setting up the page

As always, we begin by crafting the HTML and CSS so that users without JavaScript available receive an appealing and functional representation of the information:

```html
<div id="featured-books">
  <div class="covers">
    <a href="images/covers/large/1847190871.jpg"
      title="Community Server Quickly">
      <img src="images/covers/medium/1847190871.jpg"
        width="120" height="148"
        alt="Community Server Quickly" />
      <span class="price">$35.99</span>
    </a>
    <a href="images/covers/large/1847190901.jpg"
      title="Deep Inside osCommerce: The Cookbook">
      <img src="images/covers/medium/1847190901.jpg"
        width="120" height="148"
        alt="Deep Inside osCommerce: The Cookbook" />
      <span class="price">$44.99</span>
    </a>
    <a href="images/covers/large/1847190979.jpg"
      title="Learn OpenOffice.org Spreadsheet Macro
        Programming: OOoBasic and Calc automation">
      <img src="images/covers/medium/1847190979.jpg"
        width="120" height="148"
        alt="Learn OpenOffice.org Spreadsheet Macro
          Programming: OOoBasic and Calc automation" />
      <span class="price">$35.99</span>
    </a>
    <a href="images/covers/large/1847190987.jpg"
      title="Microsoft AJAX C# Essentials: Building
        Responsive ASP.NET 2.0 Applications">
      <img src="images/covers/medium/1847190987.jpg"
        width="120" height="148"
        alt="Microsoft AJAX C# Essentials: Building
          Responsive ASP.NET 2.0 Applications" />
      <span class="price">$31.99</span>
    </a>
    <a href="images/covers/large/1847191002.jpg"
      title="Google Web Toolkit GWT Java AJAX Programming">
      <img src="images/covers/medium/1847191002.jpg"
        width="120" height="148"
        alt="Google Web Toolkit GWT Java AJAX Programming" />
      <span class="price">$40.49</span>
    </a>
    <a href="images/covers/large/1847192386.jpg"
      title="Building Websites with Joomla! 1.5 Beta 1">
```

```
        <img src="images/covers/medium/1847192386.jpg"
          width="120" height="148"
          alt="Building Websites with Joomla! 1.5 Beta 1" />
        <span class="price">$40.49</span>
      </a>
    </div>
  </div>
```

Each image is contained within an anchor tag, pointing to the larger version of the cover. We also have prices given for each cover; these will be hidden for now, and we'll use JavaScript to display them later at an appropriate time.

To save space on the front page, we want to show only three covers at a time. Without JavaScript, we can accomplish this by setting the overflow property of the container to scroll, and adjusting the width appropriately:

```
#featured-books {
  position: relative;
  background: #ddd;
  width: 440px;
  height: 186px;
  overflow: scroll;
  margin: 1em auto;
  padding: 0;
  text-align: center;
  z-index: 2;
}
#featured-books .covers {
  position: relative;
  width: 840px;
  z-index: 1;
}
#featured-books a {
  float: left;
  margin: 10px;
  height: 146px;
}
#featured-books .price {
  display: none;
}
```

These styles bear a bit of discussion. The outermost element needs to have a larger z-index property than the one inside it; this allows Internet Explorer to hide the part of the inner element that stretches beyond its container. We set the width of the outer element to 440px, which accommodates three images, the 10px margin around each, and an extra 20px for the scroll bar.

With these styles in place, the images can be browsed using a standard system scroll bar:

Revising the styles with JavaScript

Now that we have gone to the work of making the image gallery usable without JavaScript, we need to undo some of the niceties. The scroll bar will be redundant when we implement our own scrolling mechanism, and the automatic layout of the covers using the `float` property will get in the way of the positioning we need to do to animate the covers. So our first order of business will be overriding some styles:

```
$(document).ready(function() {
  var spacing = 140;
  $('#featured-books').css({
    'width': spacing * 3,
    'height': '166px',
    'overflow': 'hidden'
  }).find('.covers a').css({
    'float': 'none',
    'position': 'absolute',
    'left': 1000
  });
  var $covers = $('#featured-books .covers a');
  $covers.eq(0).css('left', 0);
  $covers.eq(1).css('left', spacing);
  $covers.eq(2).css('left', spacing * 2);
});
```

The `spacing` variable is going to come in handy throughout many of our calculations. It represents the width of one of the cover images, plus the padding on either side of it. The `width` of the containing element can now be set to exactly what is necessary to contain three of the cover images, since we don't need space for the scroll bar anymore. Indeed, we change the `overflow` property to `hidden`, and bye-bye scroll bar.

The cover images all get positioned absolutely, and start with a left coordinate of `1000`. This places them out of the visible area. Then we move the first three covers into position, one at a time. The `$covers` variable holding all of the anchor elements will also come in handy later.

Now the first three covers are visible, with no scrolling mechanism available:

Shuffling images when clicked

Now, we need to add code to respond to a click on either of the end images, and reorder the covers as necessary. When the left cover is clicked, this means the user wants to see more images to the left, which in turn means we need to shift the covers to the *right*. Similarly, when the right cover is clicked we will have to shift the covers to the *left*. We want the carousel to **wrap around**, so when images fall off the left side, they get appended to the right. To begin, we will just change the image positions without animation.

```
$(document).ready(function() {
  var spacing = 140;

  $('#featured-books').css({
    'width': spacing * 3,
    'height': '166px',
    'overflow': 'hidden'
  }).find('.covers a').css({
```

```
            'float': 'none',
            'position': 'absolute',
            'left': 1000
        });
        var setUpCovers = function() {
          var $covers = $('#featured-books .covers a');

          $covers.unbind('click');

          // Left image; scroll right (to view images on left).
          $covers.eq(0)
            .css('left', 0)
            .click(function(event) {
              $covers.eq(2).css('left', 1000);
              $covers.eq($covers.length - 1)
                .prependTo('#featured-books .covers');
              setUpCovers();

              event.preventDefault();
            });

          // Right image; scroll left (to view images on right).
          $covers.eq(2)
            .css('left', spacing * 2)
            .click(function(event) {
              $covers.eq(0).css('left', 1000);
              $covers.eq(0)
                .appendTo('#featured-books .covers');
              setUpCovers();

              event.preventDefault();
            });

          // Center image.
          $covers.eq(1)
            .css('left', spacing);
        };
        setUpCovers();
      });
```

The new setUpCovers() function incorporates the image positioning code that
we wrote earlier. By encapsulating this in a function, we can repeat the image
positioning after the elements have been reordered; this will be important, as we
shall soon see.

In our example, there are six images in total (which JavaScript will reference with the numbers 0 through 5), and numbers 0, 1, and 2 are visible. When image #0 is clicked, we want to shift all the images to the right by one position. We first move image #2 out of the viewable area (with `.css('left', 1000)`), since we don't want it to be visible after the shift. Then, we move the image at the end of the line (#5) to the front of the queue (using `.prependTo()`). This reorders all of the images so when `setUpCovers()` is called again, the former #5 is now #0, #0 has become #1, and #1 has become #2. The existing positioning code in this function is therefore sufficient to move the covers to their new locations.

Clicking on image #2 performs the process in reverse. This time, it is #0 that gets hidden from view, and then moved to the end of the queue. This shifts #1 to the #0 spot, #2 to #1, and #3 to #2.

There are a couple of details that we have to take care of to avoid user interaction anomalies:

1. We need to call `.preventDefault()` within our `click` handler, since we have made the covers into links to the large version. Without this call, the link will be followed and we would never see our shuffle effect.

2. We need to unbind all of the `click` handlers at the beginning of the `setUpCovers()` function, or we could end up with multiple handlers bound to the same image as the carousel rotates.

Adding sliding animation

It can be difficult to understand what just happened when an image is clicked; since the covers move instantaneously, they can appear to have just changed rather than moved. To mitigate this issue, we can add an animation that causes the covers to slide into place rather than just appearing in their new positions. This requires a revision of the `setUpCovers()` function:

```
var setUpCovers = function() {
  var $covers = $('#featured-books .covers a');
  $covers.unbind('click');
  // Left image; scroll right (to view images on left).
  $covers.eq(0)
    .css('left', 0)
    .click(function(event) {
      $covers.eq(0).animate({'left': spacing}, 'fast');
      $covers.eq(1).animate({'left': spacing * 2}, 'fast');
      $covers.eq(2).animate({'left': spacing * 3}, 'fast');
      $covers.eq($covers.length - 1)
        .css('left', -spacing)
        .animate({'left': 0}, 'fast', function() {
          $(this).prependTo('#featured-books .covers');
          setUpCovers();
        });
      event.preventDefault();
    });
  // Right image; scroll left (to view images on right).
  $covers.eq(2)
    .css('left', spacing * 2)
    .click(function(event) {
      $covers.eq(0)
        .animate({'left': -spacing}, 'fast', function() {
          $(this).appendTo('#featured-books .covers');
          setUpCovers();
        });
      $covers.eq(1).animate({'left': 0}, 'fast');
      $covers.eq(2).animate({'left': spacing}, 'fast');
      $covers.eq(3)
        .css('left', spacing * 3)
        .animate({'left': spacing * 2}, 'fast');
      event.preventDefault();
    });
  // Center image.
  $covers.eq(1)
    .css('left', spacing);
};
```

When the left image is clicked, we can move all three visible images to the right by one image width (reusing the `spacing` variable we defined earlier). This part is straightforward, but we also have to make the new image slide into view. To do this, we grab the image from the end of the queue, and first set its screen position to be just off-screen on the left side (`-spacing`). Then, we slide it into view along with the other items.

Even though the animation takes care of the initial move, we still need to change the cover order by calling `setUpCovers()` again. If we don't, the next click won't work correctly. Since `setUpCovers()` changes the cover positions, we must defer the call until after the animation completes, so we place the call in the animation's callback.

A click on the rightmost image performs a similar set of animations, but in reverse. This time, it's the leftmost image that moves out of view, and must be moved to the end of the queue before we trigger `setUpCovers()` when the animation is complete. The new, rightmost image, on the other hand, must be moved into position (`spacing * 3`) before its animation can begin.

Displaying action icons

Our image carousel now rotates smoothly, but we haven't provided any hint to the user that clicking on the covers will cause them to scroll. We can assist the user by displaying appropriate icons when the mouse hovers over the images.

In this case, we'll place the icons on top of the existing images. By using the opacity property, we can continue to see the cover underneath when the icon is displayed. We'll use simple monochrome icons so that the cover is not too obscured:

We'll need three icons, one each for the left and right covers, which the user will choose to scroll, and one for the middle cover, which the user can click for an enlarged version. We can create HTML elements that reference the icons and store them in variables for later use:

```
var $leftRollover = $('<img/>')
  .attr('src', 'images/left.gif')
  .addClass('control')
  .css('opacity', 0.6)
  .css('display', 'none');
var $rightRollover = $('<img/>')
  .attr('src', 'images/right.gif')
  .addClass('control')
  .css('opacity', 0.6)
  .css('display', 'none');
var $enlargeRollover = $('<img/>')
  .attr('src', 'images/enlarge.gif')
  .addClass('control')
  .css('opacity', 0.6)
  .css('display', 'none');
```

You may notice that we've got a fair amount of repetition here. To minimize this extra code, we can pull this work out into a function that we call for each icon that needs to be created:

```
function createControl(src) {
  return $('<img/>')
    .attr('src', src)
    .addClass('control')
    .css('opacity', 0.6)
    .css('display', 'none');
}
var $leftRollover = createControl('images/left.gif');
var $rightRollover = createControl('images/right.gif');
var $enlargeRollover = createControl('images/enlarge.gif');
```

In the CSS for the page, we set the `z-index` of these controls to be higher than the images', and then position them absolutely so that they can overlap the covers:

```
#featured-books .control {
  position: absolute;
  z-index: 3;
  left: 0;
  top: 0;
}
```

The rollover icons all share the same `control` class, so one might be tempted to place the `opacity` style in the CSS stylesheet. However, **element opacity** is not handled consistently between browsers; in Internet Explorer, the syntax for 60% opacity is `filter: alpha(opacity=60)`. Rather than wrestle with these distinctions, we set the opacity style using jQuery's `.css()` method, which abstracts away these browser inconsistencies.

Now, all we have to do in our `hover` handlers is to place the images in the right DOM location and show them.

```
var setUpCovers = function() {
  var $covers = $('#featured-books .covers a');

  $covers.unbind('click mouseenter mouseleave');

  // Left image; scroll right (to view images on left).
  $covers.eq(0)
    .css('left', 0)
    .click(function(event) {
      $covers.eq(0).animate({'left': spacing}, 'fast');
      $covers.eq(1).animate({'left': spacing * 2}, 'fast');
      $covers.eq(2).animate({'left': spacing * 3}, 'fast');
      $covers.eq($covers.length - 1)
        .css('left', -spacing)
        .animate({'left': 0}, 'fast', function() {
          $(this).prependTo('#featured-books .covers');
          setUpCovers();
        });

      event.preventDefault();
    }).hover(function() {
      $leftRollover.appendTo(this).show();
    }, function() {
      $leftRollover.hide();
    });

  // Right image; scroll left (to view images on right).
```

```
$covers.eq(2)
  .css('left', spacing * 2)
  .click(function(event) {
    $covers.eq(0)
      .animate({'left': -spacing}, 'fast', function() {
        $(this).appendTo('#featured-books .covers');
        setUpCovers();
      });
    $covers.eq(1).animate({'left': 0}, 'fast');
    $covers.eq(2).animate({'left': spacing}, 'fast');
    $covers.eq(3)
      .css('left', spacing * 3)
      .animate({'left': spacing * 2}, 'fast');

    event.preventDefault();
  }).hover(function() {
    $rightRollover.appendTo(this).show();
  }, function() {
    $rightRollover.hide();
  });

// Center image.
$covers.eq(1)
  .css('left', spacing)
  .hover(function() {
    $enlargeRollover.appendTo(this).show();
  }, function() {
    $enlargeRollover.hide();
  });
};
```

Just as we did earlier with `click`, we unbind `mouseenter` and `mouseleave` handlers at the beginning of `setUpCovers()` so that the hover behaviors do not accumulate. Here, we use another feature of the `.unbind()` method: handlers for multiple event types can be unbound at once by separating the event type names with spaces.

Why `mouseenter` and `mouseleave`? When we call the `.hover()` method, internally jQuery translates this into two separate event bindings. The first function we supply is bound as a handler for the `mouseenter` event, and the second is bound to `mouseleave`. So, to remove the handlers bound using `.hover()`, we need to unbind `mouseenter` and `mouseleave`.

Now when the mouse cursor is over a cover, the appropriate rollover image is overlaid on top of the cover:

Image enlargement

Now, our image gallery is fully functional, with a carousel that allows the user to navigate to a desired image. A click on the center image leads to an enlarged view of the cover in question. But, there is more we can do with this image enlargement functionality.

Rather than lead the user to a separate URL when the center image is clicked, we can overlay the enlarged book cover on the page itself.

A number of variations on the theme of displaying information overlaid on the page are available as jQuery plugins. A few of the more popular ones include **FancyBox, ShadowBox, Thickbox, SimpleModal,** and **jqModal.** More information on using plugins can be found in Chapter 10.

This larger cover image will require a new image element, which we can create at the same time that the hover images are instantiated:

```
var $enlargedCover = $('<img/>')
  .addClass('enlarged')
  .hide()
  .appendTo('body');
```

We will apply a set of style rules to this new class that are similar to the ones we have seen before:

```
img.enlarged {
  position: absolute;
  z-index: 5;
  cursor: pointer;
}
```

This absolute positioning will allow the cover to float above the other images we have positioned, because the z-index is higher than the ones we have already used. Now we need to actually position the enlarged image when the center image in the carousel is clicked:

```
// Center image; enlarge cover.
$covers.eq(1)
  .css('left', spacing)
  .click(function(event) {
    $enlargedCover.attr('src', $(this).attr('href'))
      .css({
        'left': ($('body').width() - 360) / 2,
        'top' : 100,
        'width': 360,
        'height': 444
      }).show();
    event.preventDefault();
  })
  .hover(function() {
    $enlargeRollover.appendTo(this).show();
  }, function() {
    $enlargeRollover.hide();
  });
```

We can take advantage of the links already present in the HTML source to know where the larger cover's image file resides on the server. We pluck this from the href attribute of the link, and set it as the src attribute of the enlarged cover image.

Now, we must position the image. The top, width, and height are hard-coded for now, but the left requires a little calculation. We want the enlarged image to be centered on the page, but we can't know in advance what the appropriate coordinate is to achieve this positioning. We can find the halfway mark across the page by measuring the width of the <body> element and dividing this by two. Half of our enlarged image will be on either side of this point, so the left coordinate of the image will be ($('body').width() - 360) / 2, since 360 is the width of the enlarged cover. The cover is now positioned appropriately, centered horizontally across the page:

Hiding the enlarged cover

We need a mechanism for dismissing the cover once it has been enlarged. The simplest way to do this is by making a `click` event on the cover fade it out:

```
// Center image; enlarge cover.
$covers.eq(1)
  .css('left', spacing)
  .click(function(event) {
    $enlargedCover.attr('src', $(this).attr('href'))
      .css({
        'left': ($('body').width() - 360) / 2,
        'top' : 100,
        'width': 360,
        'height': 444
      })
      .show()
      .one('click', function() {
        $enlargedCover.fadeOut();
      });
    event.preventDefault();
  })
  .hover(function() {
    $enlargeRollover.appendTo(this).show();
  }, function() {
    $enlargeRollover.hide();
  });
```

We use the `.one()` method to bind this `click` handler, which sidesteps a couple of potential problems. With a regular `.bind()` of the handler, the user could click on the image again as it was fading out. This would cause the handler to fire again. Also, since we are reusing the same image element every time the cover is enlarged, the binding will occur again for each enlargement. If we do nothing to unbind the handler, they will stack up over time. Using `.one()` ensures that the handlers are removed once used.

Displaying a close button

This behavior is sufficient for removing the large cover, but we've given no indication to the user that clicking the cover will make it go away. We can provide this assistance by **badging** the enlarged image with a **Close** button. Creating the button is similar to defining the other **singleton elements** we've used—the items that are guaranteed to appear only once—and we can call the utility function that we created earlier:

```
var $closeButton = createControl('images/close.gif')
    .addClass('enlarged-control')
    .appendTo('body');
```

When the center cover is clicked, and the enlarged cover is displayed, we need to position and show the button:

```
$closeButton.css({
    'left': ($('body').width() - 360) / 2,
    'top' : 100
}).show();
```

The coordinates of the **Close** button are identical to the enlarged cover, so their top-left corners are aligned:

We already have a behavior bound to the image that hides it when the image is clicked. Typically in this situation we could rely on **event bubbling** to cause a click on the **Close** button to cause the same effect. In this case, however, the **Close** button is not a **descendant element** of the cover, despite appearances. We've absolutely positioned the **Close** button on top of the cover, which means that clicks on the button do not get passed to the enlarged image. Instead, we must handle clicks on the **Close** button ourselves:

```
// Center image; enlarge cover.
$covers.eq(1)
  .css('left', spacing)
  .click(function(event) {
    $enlargedCover.attr('src', $(this).attr('href'))
```

```
    .css({
      'left': ($('body').width() - 360) / 2,
      'top' : 100,
      'width': 360,
      'height': 444
    })
    .show()
    .one('click', function() {
      $closeButton.unbind('click').hide();
      $enlargedCover.fadeOut();
    });
  $closeButton
    .css({
      'left': ($('body').width() - 360) / 2,
      'top' : 100
    })
    .show()
    .click(function() {
      $enlargedCover.click();
    });
  event.preventDefault();
})
.hover(function() {
  $enlargeRollover.appendTo(this).show();
}, function() {
  $enlargeRollover.hide();
});
```

When we show the **Close** button, we bind a `click` event handler for it. All this handler needs to do, though, is to trigger the `click` handler we've already bound to the enlarged cover. We do need to modify that handler, though, and hide the **Close** button there. While we're at it, we unbind the `click` handler to prevent handlers from accumulating over time.

More fun with badging

Since we have the prices for the books available to us in the HTML source, we can display this as additional information when the book cover is enlarged. This time we'll apply the technique we just developed for the **Close** button to textual content rather than an image.

Once again, we create a **singleton element** at the beginning of our JavaScript code:

```
var $priceBadge = $('<div/>')
  .addClass('enlarged-price')
  .css('opacity', 0.6)
  .css('display', 'none')
  .appendTo('body');
```

Since the price will be partially transparent, a high contrast between font color and background will work best:

```
.enlarged-price {
  background-color: #373c40;
  color: #fff;
  width: 80px;
  padding: 5px;
  font-size: 18px;
  font-weight: bold;
  text-align: right;
  position: absolute;
  z-index: 6;
}
```

Before we can display the price badge, we need to populate it with the actual price information from the HTML. Inside the center cover's click handler, the keyword this refers to the link element. Since the price is in a <span> element within the link, obtaining the text is straightforward:

```
var price = $(this).find('.price').text();
```

Now we can display the badge when the cover is enlarged:

```
$priceBadge.css({
  'right': ($('body').width() - 360) / 2,
  'top' : 100
}).text(price).show();
```

This will fix the price at the top-right corner of the enlarged image:

Once we place a `$priceBadge.hide();` within the cover's `click` handler to clean up after ourselves, we're done.

Animating the cover enlargement

When the user clicks on the center cover, the enlarged version currently appears in the center of the page with no flair. To improve on this, we can use the built-in animation capabilities of jQuery to smoothly transition between the thumbnail view of the cover and the full-size version.

To do this, we need to know the starting coordinates of the animation; i.e. the position of the center cover on the page. Calculating this position requires some clever DOM traversal using plain JavaScript, but jQuery gives us a shortcut. The `.offset()` method returns an object containing the `left` and `top` coordinates of an element relative to the page. We can then insert the `width` and `height` of the image into this object, and have the position information contained in a tidy package.

```
var startPos = $(this).offset();
startPos.width = $(this).width();
startPos.height = $(this).height();
```

Our destination coordinates can now be calculated from these quite easily. We'll collect them in a similar object.

```
var endPos = {};
endPos.width = startPos.width * 3;
endPos.height = startPos.height * 3;
endPos.top = 100;
endPos.left = ($('body').width() - endPos.width) / 2;
```

We can now use these two objects as **maps** of CSS attributes, which can be passed to methods such as `.css()` and `.animate()`.

```
$enlargedCover.attr('src', $(this).attr('href'))
  .css(startPos)
  .show()
  .animate(endPos, 'normal', function() {
    $enlargedCover
      .one('click', function() {
        $closeButton.unbind('click').hide();
        $priceBadge.hide();
        $enlargedCover.fadeOut();
      });
    $closeButton
      .css({
        'left': endPos.left,
        'top' : endPos.top
      })
      .show()
      .click(function() {
        $enlargedCover.click();
      });
    $priceBadge
      .css({
        'right': endPos.left,
        'top' : endPos.top
      })
      .text(price)
      .show();
  });
```

Note that the **Close** button and price badge can't be placed until the animation completes, so we have moved their code into the callback of the `.animate()` method. Also, we've taken this opportunity to simplify the `.css()` calls for both of these elements by reusing the positioning information we calculated for the enlarged cover.

Now we have a smooth transition from small to large cover:

Deferring animations until image loads

Our animation is smooth, but depends on a fast connection to the site. If the enlarged cover takes some time to download, then the first moments of the animation might display the red **X** indicating a broken image, or still display the previous image. We can make the transition a bit more elegant by waiting until the image has fully loaded before starting the animation:

```
$enlargedCover.attr('src', $(this).attr('href'))
  .css(startPos)
  .show();
var performAnimation = function() {
  $enlargedCover.animate(endPos, 'normal', function() {
    $enlargedCover.one('click', function() {
      $closeButton.unbind('click').hide();
      $priceBadge.hide();
      $enlargedCover.fadeOut();
    });
    $closeButton
      .css({
        'left': endPos.left,
        'top' : endPos.top
      })
      .show()
      .click(function() {
        $enlargedCover.click();
      });
    $priceBadge
      .css({
        'right': endPos.left,
        'top' : endPos.top
      })
      .text(price)
      .show();
  });
};
if ($enlargedCover[0].complete) {
  performAnimation();
}
else {
  $enlargedCover.bind('load', performAnimation);
}
```

There are two cases we have to consider: either the image is available nearly instantly (perhaps due to caching), or it needs time to load. In the first situation, the image's complete attribute will be true, so we can call our new performAnimation() function immediately. In the second case, we need to wait for the image load to complete before we call performAnimation(). This is a rare instance in which the standard DOM load event is more useful to us than jQuery's custom ready event. Since load is triggered on a window, image, or frame when all of its contents have fully loaded, we can observe the event to make sure that the image is being properly displayed. Only then is the handler executed, and the animation is performed.

We're using the .bind('load') syntax rather than the shorthand .load() method here for clarity since .load() is also an AJAX method; the two syntaxes are interchangeable.

Internet Explorer and Firefox have different interpretations of what to do if the image is already in the browser cache. In this case, Firefox will immediately send the load event to JavaScript, but Internet Explorer will never send the event because no load actually occurred. Our testing of the complete attribute compensates for this variance in implementations.

Adding a loading indicator

But now, we can have an awkward situation on slow network connections when an image takes a few moments to load. Our page appears to do nothing while this download is in progress. As we did when loading the news headlines, we should provide an indication to the user that some activity is occurring by displaying a **loading indicator** in the meantime.

The indicator will be another **singleton** image that will be displayed when appropriate:

```
var $waitThrobber = $('<img/>')
  .attr('src', 'images/wait.gif')
  .addClass('control')
  .css('z-index', 4)
  .hide();
```

For this image, we're actually using an animated GIF, because the motion will reinforce to the user that the activity is taking place:

It will just take two lines to put our loading indicator in place, now that we have the element defined. At the very beginning of our `click` handler for the center image, before we start doing any work, we need to display the indicator:

```
$waitThrobber.appendTo(this).show();
```

And at the beginning of the `performAnimation()` function, when we know the image has been loaded, we remove the indicator from view:

```
$waitThrobber.hide();
```

This is all it takes to badge the cover being enlarged with the loading indicator. The animation appears overlaying the top left corner of the cover:

The finished code

This chapter represents just a small fraction of what can be done on the Web with animated image and text rotators. Taken all together, the code for the image carousel looks like this:

```
$(document).ready(function() {
  var spacing = 140;
  function createControl(src) {
    return $('<img/>')
      .attr('src', src)
      .addClass('control')
      .css('opacity', 0.6)
      .css('display', 'none');
  }
  var $leftRollover = createControl('images/left.gif');
  var $rightRollover = createControl('images/right.gif');
  var $enlargeRollover = createControl('images/enlarge.gif');
  var $enlargedCover = $('<img/>')
    .addClass('enlarged')
    .hide()
    .appendTo('body');
  var $closeButton = createControl('images/close.gif')
    .addClass('enlarged-control')
    .appendTo('body');
  var $priceBadge = $('<div/>')
    .addClass('enlarged-price')
    .css('opacity', 0.6)
    .css('display', 'none')
    .appendTo('body');
  var $waitThrobber = $('<img/>')
    .attr('src', 'images/wait.gif')
    .addClass('control')
    .css('z-index', 4)
    .hide();
  $('#featured-books').css({
    'width': spacing * 3,
    'height': '166px',
    'overflow': 'hidden'
  }).find('.covers a').css({
    'float': 'none',
    'position': 'absolute',
    'left': 1000
  });
```

```
var setUpCovers = function() {
  var $covers = $('#featured-books .covers a');

  $covers.unbind('click mouseenter mouseleave');

  // Left image; scroll right (to view images on left).
  $covers.eq(0)
    .css('left', 0)
    .click(function(event) {
      $covers.eq(0).animate({'left': spacing}, 'fast');
      $covers.eq(1).animate({'left': spacing * 2}, 'fast');
      $covers.eq(2).animate({'left': spacing * 3}, 'fast');
      $covers.eq($covers.length - 1)
        .css('left', -spacing)
        .animate({'left': 0}, 'fast', function() {
          $(this).prependTo('#featured-books .covers');
          setUpCovers();
        });

      event.preventDefault();
    }).hover(function() {
      $leftRollover.appendTo(this).show();
    }, function() {
      $leftRollover.hide();
    });

  // Right image; scroll left (to view images on right).
  $covers.eq(2)
    .css('left', spacing * 2)
    .click(function(event) {
      $covers.eq(0)
        .animate({'left': -spacing}, 'fast', function() {
          $(this).appendTo('#featured-books .covers');
          setUpCovers();
        });
      $covers.eq(1).animate({'left': 0}, 'fast');
      $covers.eq(2).animate({'left': spacing}, 'fast');
      $covers.eq(3)
        .css('left', spacing * 3)
        .animate({'left': spacing * 2}, 'fast');

      event.preventDefault();
    }).hover(function() {
      $rightRollover.appendTo(this).show();
    }, function() {
      $rightRollover.hide();
    });
```

```
// Center image; enlarge cover.
$covers.eq(1)
  .css('left', spacing)
  .click(function(event) {
    $waitThrobber.appendTo(this).show();
    var price = $(this).find('.price').text();
    var startPos = $(this).offset();
    startPos.width = $(this).width();
    startPos.height = $(this).height();
    var endPos = {};
    endPos.width = startPos.width * 3;
    endPos.height = startPos.height * 3;
    endPos.top = 100;
    endPos.left = ($('body').width() - endPos.width) / 2;

    $enlargedCover.attr('src', $(this).attr('href'))
      .css(startPos)
      .show();
    var performAnimation = function() {
      $waitThrobber.hide();
      $enlargedCover.animate(endPos, 'normal',
          function() {
        $enlargedCover.one('click', function() {
          $closeButton.unbind('click').hide();
          $priceBadge.hide();
          $enlargedCover.fadeOut();
        });
        $closeButton
          .css({
            'left': endPos.left,
            'top' : endPos.top
          })
          .show()
          .click(function() {
            $enlargedCover.click();
          });
        $priceBadge
          .css({
            'right': endPos.left,
            'top' : endPos.top
          })
          .text(price)
          .show();
      });
    };
```

```
          if ($enlargedCover[0].complete) {
            performAnimation();
          }
          else {
            $enlargedCover.bind('load', performAnimation);
          }
          event.preventDefault();
        })
        .hover(function() {
          $enlargeRollover.appendTo(this).show();
        }, function() {
          $enlargeRollover.hide();
        });
    };

    setUpCovers();
  });
```

Summary

In this chapter, we have looked into page elements that change over time, either on their own or in response to user intervention. These **shufflers** and **rotators** can really set a modern web presence apart from traditionally designed sites. We have covered presenting an XML feed of information on a page, as well as rotating items in and out of view on a time delay. Along with displaying a set of images in a navigable carousel-style gallery, we have also discussed enlarging an image for a closer view with a smooth animation and presenting user-interface controls in an unobtrusive way.

These techniques can be combined in many ways to breathe life into otherwise stodgy pages, while simultaneously enhancing the usability of our web-based applications. Animations and effects that would be otherwise tedious to achieve can be effortlessly realized thanks to the power of jQuery.

10
Using Plugins

Throughout this book, we have examined many of the ways in which the jQuery library can be used to accomplish a wide variety of tasks. Yet one aspect that has remained relatively unexplored is jQuery's extensibility. As powerful as the library is at its core, its elegant **plugin architecture** has allowed developers to extend jQuery, making it an even more feature-rich library.

The growing jQuery community has created hundreds of plugins—from small selector helpers to full-scale user-interface widgets. We've already discussed the power of plugins and created a simple one in Chapter 7. In this chapter, we'll look at how to find plugins developed by others and incorporate them into our web pages. We'll explore the popular Form plugin and the official jQuery UI plugin library, and then list and briefly describe a number of other popular, "author-recommended" plugins.

Finding plugins and help

The jQuery website provides a large repository of available plugins at `http://plugins.jquery.com/`, with features such as user ratings, versioning, and bug reporting. This **Plugin Repository** is also a great place to start when looking for documentation. Each plugin listed in the repository is downloadable as a `.zip` file, and many of them also have links to demos, example code, and tutorials to help us get started.

Even more plugins can be found in general code repositories such as `http://github.com/` and on plugin developers' weblogs.

If we can't find the answers to all of our questions in the Plugin Repository, the author's website, and the plugin's comments, we can always turn to the jQuery Google Group at `http://groups.google.com/group/jquery-en/`. Many of the plugin authors are frequent contributors to the list, and are always willing to help with any problems that new users might face.

How to use a plugin

Using a jQuery plugin is very straightforward. The first step is to include it in the <head> of the document, making sure that it appears after the main jQuery source file:

```
<head>
  <meta http-equiv="Content-Type"
    content="text/html; charset=utf-8"/>
  <script src="jquery.js" type="text/javascript"></script>
  <script src="jquery.plugin.js"
    type="text/javascript"></script>
  <script src="custom.js" type="text/javascript"></script>
  <title>Example</title>
</head>
```

After that, it's just a matter of including a custom JavaScript file in which we use the methods that the plugin either creates or extends. Often, we can add a single line inside our custom file's $(document).ready() method to invoke some action:

```
$(document).ready(function() {
  $('#myID').somePlugin();
});
```

Many plugins have built-in flexibility as well, providing a number of optional parameters that we can set to modify their behavior. We can customize their operation as much as needed, typically by including a **map** as the method's argument:

```
$(document).ready(function() {
  $('#myID').somePlugin ({
    send: true,
    message: 'This plugin is great!'
  });
});
```

The syntax of jQuery plugins is, typically, quite similar to the syntax of methods within the jQuery core itself. Now that we've seen how to include a plugin in a web page, let's take a look at a couple of popular ones.

The Form plugin

The Form plugin is a terrific example of a script that makes a difficult, complex task dead simple. The plugin file, along with detailed documentation, is available at http://malsup/com/jquery/form/.

At the heart of the plugin is the `.ajaxForm()` method. Converting a conventional form into an AJAX form requires one simple line of code:

```
$(document).ready(function() {
  $('#myForm').ajaxForm();

});
```

This example will prepare `<form id="myForm">` to be submitted without having to refresh the current page. This feature in itself is quite nice, but the real power comes with the map of options that we can pass into the method. For example, the following code calls `.ajaxForm()` with the `target`, `beforeSubmit`, and `success` options:

```
$(document).ready(function() {
  function validateForm() {
    // the form validation code would go here
    // we can return false to abort the submit
  };
  $('#test-form').ajaxForm({
    target: '#log',
    beforeSubmit: validateForm,
    success: function() {
      alert('Thanks for your comment!');
    }
  });
});
```

The `target` option indicates the element(s)—in this case, an element with `id="log"`—that will be updated by the server response.

The `beforeSubmit` option performs tasks before the form is submitted. Here, it references the `validateForm()` function. If the function returns `false`, the form will not be submitted.

The `success` option performs tasks after the form is successfully submitted. In this example it simply provides an alert message to let the user know that the form has been submitted.

Other options available with `.ajaxForm()` and the similar `.ajaxSubmit()` include:

- `url`: The URL to which the form data will be submitted, if different from the form's `action` attribute.

- `type`: The method used to submit the form—either GET or POST. The default is the form's `method` attribute, or if none is provided, GET.

- `dataType`: The expected data-type of the server response. Possible values are `null`, `xml`, `script`, or `json`. The default value is `null` (an HTML response).

- `resetForm`: *Boolean*; default is `false`. If set to `true`, all of the form's field values will be reset to their defaults when the submit is successful.

- `clearForm`: *Boolean*; default is `false`. If set to `true`, all of the form's field values will be cleared when the submit is successful.

The Form plugin provides a number of other methods to assist in handling forms and their data. For a closer look at these methods, as well as more demos and examples, visit `http://www.malsup.com/jquery/form/`.

Tips and tricks

The `.ajaxForm()` method is usually more convenient than the `.ajaxSubmit()` method, at the expense of a little flexibility. When we want the plugin to manage all the event binding for us, as well as invoke the `.ajaxSubmit()` method for us at the appropriate time, we should use `.ajaxForm()`. When we want finer-grained control over the `submit` event handling, `.ajaxSubmit()` is recommended.

Both `.ajaxForm()` and `.ajaxSubmit()` default to using the `action` and `method` values in the form's markup. As long as we use proper markup for the form, the plugin will work exactly as we expect without any need for tweaking. As an additional benefit, we automatically gain the advantages of **progressive enhancement**; the form is fully functional without JavaScript enabled.

Normally when a form is submitted, if the element used to submit the form has a name, its `name` and `value` attributes are submitted along with the rest of the form data. The `.ajaxForm()` method is **proactive** in this regard, adding `click` handlers to all of the `<input type="submit">` elements so it knows which one submitted the form. The `.ajaxSubmit()` method, on the other hand, is **reactive** and has no way of determining this information. It does not capture the submitting element. The same distinction applies to `<input type="image">` elements as well: `.ajaxForm()` handles them, while `.ajaxSubmit()` ignores them.

Unless a file is being uploaded as part of the form submission, the `.ajaxForm()` and `.ajaxSubmit()` methods pass their `options` argument to the `$.ajax()` method that is part of the jQuery core. Therefore, any valid options for `$.ajax()` can be passed in through the Form plugin. With this feature in mind, we can make our AJAX form responses even more robust, like so:

```
$(document).ready(function() {
  $('#myForm').ajaxForm({
    timeout: 2000,
    error: function (xml, status, e) {
```

```
            alert(e.message);
        }
    });
});
```

When less customization is required, the `.ajaxForm()` and `.ajaxSubmit()` methods can be passed a function instead of an options map. Since the function is treated as the success handler, we can get the response text back from the server, like so:

```
$(document).ready(function() {
    $('#myForm').ajaxForm(function(responseText) {
        alert(responseText);
    });
});
```

The jQuery UI plugin library

While the Form plugin does one thing, and does it very well, **jQuery UI** does a wide variety of things (and does them well). In fact, jQuery UI is not so much a plugin, but rather a whole library of plugins.

Led by Paul Bakaus, the jQuery UI team has created a number of core **interaction components** and full-fledged **widgets** to help make the web experience more like that of a desktop application. Interaction components include methods for dragging, dropping, sorting, and resizing items. The current stable of widgets includes an accordion, date picker, dialog, slider, and tabs, with quite a few more in active development. Additionally, jQuery UI provides an extensive set of advanced effects to supplement the core jQuery animations.

Since the full UI library is too extensive to adequately cover within this chapter, we'll limit our exploration to UI effects, the Sortable core interaction component, and the Dialog widget. Downloads, documentation, and demos of all jQuery modules are available at `http://ui.jquery.com/`.

Effects

The effects module of jQuery UI comes with a core file and a set of individual effect files. The core file provides animations for colors and classes, as well as advanced easing.

Color animations

With the core effects file referenced in the document, the `.animate()` method is extended to accept additional style properties, such as `borderTopColor`, `backgroundColor`, and `color`. For example, we can now gradually change an element from black text on white background to white text on black background:

```
$(document).ready(function() {
  $('#mydiv').animate({
    color: '#fff',
    backgroundColor: '#000'
  }, 'slow');
});
```

A little more than halfway through the animation, the `<div>` looks like this:

The element looks exactly as it should, with the text on its way to becoming white and the background color approaching black.

Class animations

The three class methods that we have worked with in previous chapters— `.addClass()`, `.removeClass()`, and `.toggleClass()` —now take an optional second argument for the animation duration. We can now write them as `.addClass('highlight', 'fast')` or `.removeClass('highlight', 'slow')` or `.toggleClass('highlight, 1000)`.

Advanced easing

Advanced **easing** functions vary the speed and distance at which transitions occur at various points along the way. For example, the `easeInQuart` function ends an animation at four times the speed at which it started. We can specify a custom easing function in any of the core jQuery animation methods or jQuery UI effect methods. This can be done by either adding an argument or adding an option to an **options map**, depending on the syntax being used. For example, specifying the `easeInQuart` function for our previous color animation can be done with an additional argument:

```
$(document).ready(function() {
  $('#mydiv').animate({
    color: '#fff',
    backgroundColor: '#000'
  }, 'slow', 'easeInQuart');
});
```

Or, it can be done with an option added to a second options map:

```
$(document).ready(function() {
  $('#mydiv').animate({
    color: '#fff',
    backgroundColor: '#000'
  }, {
    duration: 'slow',
    easing: 'easeInQuart'
  });
});
```

Demonstrations of the full set of easing functions are available at
http://gsgd.co.uk/sandbox/jquery/easing/.

Additional effects

The individual effect files add various transitions, all of which can be implemented
with the `.effect()` method and some of which extend the functionality of jQuery's
`.show()`, `.hide()`, and `.toggle()` methods as well. For example, the explode effect,
which hides elements by exploding them into a given number of pieces, can be
achieved with the `.effect()` method:

```
$(document).ready(function() {
  $('#explode').effect('explode', {pieces: 16}, 800);
});
```

Or, it can be achieved with the `.hide()` method:

```
$(document).ready(function() {
  $('#explode').hide('explode', {pieces: 16}, 800);
});
```

Either way, the effect hides a box that begins like this:

In the middle of the animation, it looks like this:

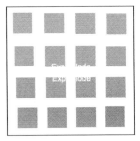

And at the end of the animation, the box is hidden.

Interaction components

Among the jQuery UI **interaction components** is **Sortable**, which can transform just about any group of elements into a drag-and-drop style list. Here, we have an unordered list with some CSS styles applied to each item:

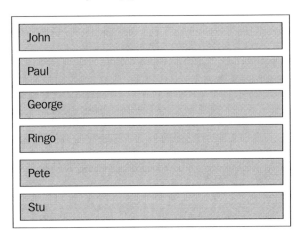

The HTML is pretty straightforward:

```
<ul id="sort-container">
  <li>John</li>
  <li>Paul</li>
  <li>George</li>
  <li>Ringo</li>
  <li>Pete</li>
  <li>Stu</li>
</ul>
```

Now, to make the list sortable, we simply write the following code:

```
$(document).ready(function() {
  $('#sort-container').sortable();
});
```

This single line within the `$(document).ready()` allows us to drag each item and drop it into a different position within the list.

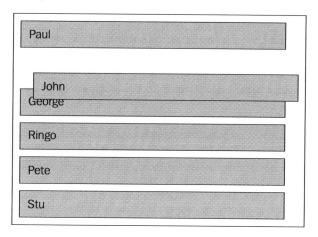

We can enhance the user interaction by adding options to the `.sortable()` method. While this method has over thirty available options, we'll use just a few for our example:

```
$(document).ready(function() {
  $('#sort-container').sortable({
    opacity: .5,
    cursor: 'move',
    axis: 'y'
  });
});
```

The first two options, opacity and cursor, are self-explanatory. The third, axis, limits the element's movement to a particular axis (in this case, the y-axis) while being sorted.

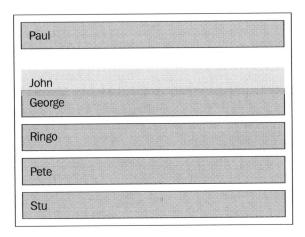

As is evident by the lighter background color of the sorted element, we've also taken advantage of a class that is automatically applied to it, ui-sortable-helper, by applying styles to the class in our stylesheet.

For more information about all of the jQuery UI core interaction components, visit http://docs.jquery.com/UI#Interaction.

Widgets

In addition to building-block components, jQuery UI includes a handful of robust user-interface **widgets** that appear and function "out of the box" like the full-fledged elements we are accustomed to seeing in desktop applications. The **Dialog** widget, for example, uses the *draggable* and *resizable* components to produce a dialog box, so that we don't have to build our own.

As with other UI widgets, Dialog accepts a large number of options. Its aptly named .dialog() method can also take string arguments that alter what the dialog does. At its most basic level, the .dialog() method converts an existing element into a dialog and displays it, along with the element's contents. For instance, we can start with a simple <div> structure.

```
<div id="dlg">My Dialog</div>
```

Unsurprisingly, this `<div>` looks quite plain—a simple text block:

My Dialog

We can invoke the basic dialog in our JavaScript file as soon as the DOM is ready.

```
$(document).ready(function() {
  $('#dlg').dialog();
});
```

The text is now wrapped in a dialog box:

This dialog box can be resized by clicking on one of its borders and dragging. It can be moved by clicking anywhere within the top area of the dialog, just below the top border. And, it can be closed by clicking on the **X** link in the upper-right corner.

We can obviously do a lot better with the styling, though. While jQuery UI provides a minimal set of styles to ensure that widgets are functional, it leaves decisions about look and feel up to us. Here is a dialog with a default **theme** applied:

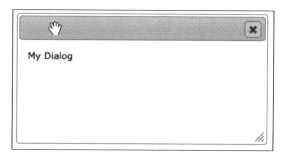

Now, the various areas are clearly indicated, and the mouse cursor changes to provide even more visual feedback on the parts of the dialog enabled for dragging and resizing.

As with the other jQuery UI methods, `.dialog()` comes with a number of options. Some of the options affect the dialog's appearance while others allow events to be triggered. Here is a sampling of these options:

```
$(document).ready(function() {
    var $dlg = $('#dlg');
    var dlgText = $dlg.text();
    $dlg.dialog({
        autoOpen: false,
        title: dlgText,
        open: function() {
            $dlg.empty();
        },
        buttons: {
            'add message': function() {
                $dlg.append('<p>Inserted message</p>');
            },
            'erase messages': function() {
                $('p', $dlg).remove();
            }
        }
    });
    $('#do-dialog').click(function() {
        $dlg.dialog('open');
    });
});
```

We've set the dialog to be initially hidden and to open when the user clicks on a button with `id="do-dialog"`. We've also moved the dialog's initial text content to the title area and added two buttons, one with **add message** as its text and one with **erase messages** as its text. Each button has a function associated with it to append or erase paragraphs when clicked. After clicking the **add message** button three times, the dialog with these options looks like this:

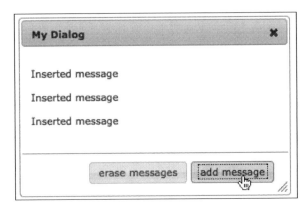

The many other options for configuring the display and behavior of dialogs can be found at `http://docs.jquery.com/UI/Dialog/dialog#options`.

jQuery UI ThemeRoller

A recent addition to the jQuery UI library is the **ThemeRoller**, a web-based interactive theme engine for UI widgets. The ThemeRoller makes creating highly customized, professional-looking elements quick and easy. As we noted, the dialog that we just created has the default theme applied to it; this theme will be output from the ThemeRoller if no custom settings are supplied.

Generating a completely different set of styles is a simple matter of visiting `http://ui.jquery.com/themeroller/`, modifying the various options as desired, and pressing the **Download This Theme** button. A `.zip` file of stylesheets and images can then be placed in the appropriate directory. For example, by choosing a few different colors and textures, we can within a few minutes change our previous dialog to look like this:

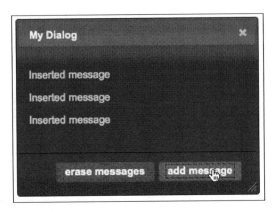

Other recommended plugins

In addition to the plugins described in this chapter, and elsewhere in the book, the plugins listed below are recommended by the authors not only because of their popularity, but also because of their solid code.

Forms

We investigated a few ways to manipulate forms in Chapter 8. These plugins can accomplish related tasks with ease.

Autocomplete

`http://bassistance.de/jquery-plugins/jquery-plugin-autocomplete/`

`http://plugins.jquery.com/project/autocompletex`

Written by jQuery core developer Jörn Zaefferer, the **Autocomplete** plugin provides a list of possible matches as the user types in a text input.

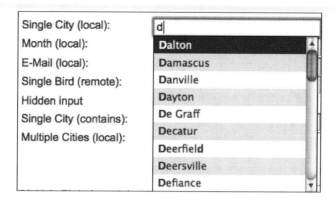

Validation

http://bassistance.de/jquery-plugins/jquery-plugin-validation/

http://plugins.jquery.com/project/validate

Another plugin by Jörn Zaefferer, **Validation** is an enormously flexible tool for validating form inputs based on a wide range of criteria.

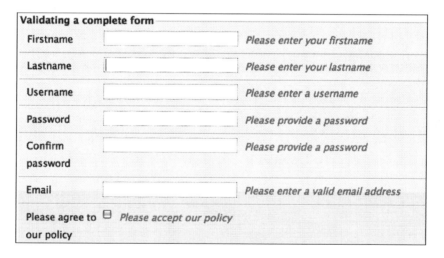

Jeditable

http://www.appelsiini.net/projects/jeditable

http://plugins.jquery.com/project/jeditable

The **Jeditable** plugin converts non-form elements into editable inputs when a user performs some action, such as a click or double-click. Changed content is automatically sent to be stored on the server.

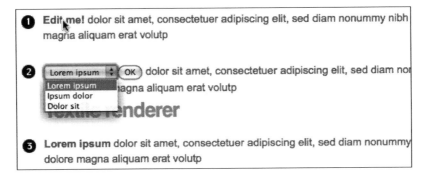

Masked input

http://digitalbush.com/projects/masked-input-plugin/

http://plugins.jquery.com/project/maskedinput

The **Masked Input** plugin offers a way for users to more easily enter data, such as dates, phone numbers, or social-security numbers, in a certain format. It automatically places certain characters (such as a slash for dates) in the field while allowing only a certain set of other characters to be entered, as determined in the plugin options.

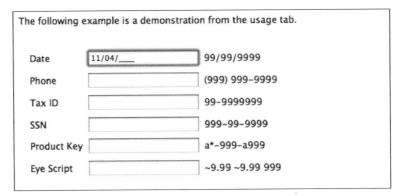

Tables

In Chapter 7, we discussed techniques for arranging, beautifying, and enhancing tabular data. Many plugin developers have packaged together routines to assist us in these tasks.

Tablesorter

`http://tablesorter.com/`

`http://plugins.jquery.com/project/tablesorter`

The **Tablesorter** plugin can turn any table with `<thead>` and `<tbody>` elements into a table that is sortable without page refreshes. Special features include multiple-column sorting, parsers for sorting many different formats (e.g. date, time, currency, URLs), secondary "hidden" sorting, and extensibility through a widget system.

First Name ▲	Last Name ⬍	Age ▲	Total ⬍	Discount ⬍	Difference ⬍	Date ⬍
Bruce	Evans	22	$13.19	11%	-100.9	Jan 18, 2007 9:12 AM
Bruce	Almighty	45	$153.19	44.7%	+77	Jan 18, 2001 9:12 AM
Clark	Kent	18	$15.89	44%	-26	Jan 12, 2003 11:14 AM
John	Hood	33	$19.99	25%	+12	Dec 10, 2002 5:14 AM
Peter	Parker	28	$9.99	20.9%	+12.1	Jul 6, 2006 8:14 AM

jqGrid

`http://www.trirand.com/blog/`

`http://plugins.jquery.com/project/jqGrids`

An AJAX-enabled JavaScript control, **jqGrid** allows developers to dynamically represent and manipulate tabular data on the web. It provides options for inline editing, cell editing, pager navigation, multiple-item selection, sub-grids, and tree grids. The plugin comes with extensive documentation at `http://www.secondpersonplural.ca/jqgriddocs/`

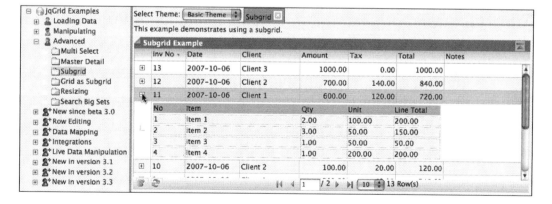

Flexigrid

http://code.google.com/p/flexigrid/

http://plugins.jquery.com/project/flexigrid

Like jqGrid, Flexigrid is a full-featured grid plugin. Some of its many features include JSON support, pagination, quick search, showing and hiding and resizing of columns, and row sorting.

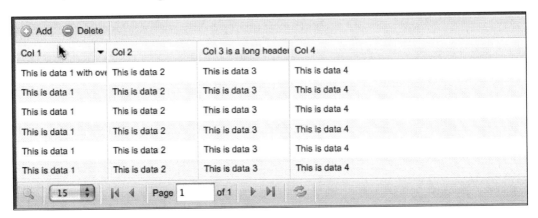

Images

Image manipulation is a task that often requires intense server-side processing. However, some plugin authors have developed ways to do some simple image handling in JavaScript using jQuery as a vehicle.

Jcrop

http://deepliquid.com/content/Jcrop.html

http://plugins.jquery.com/project/Jcrop

Jcrop offers a quick and easy way to add image cropping to web applications. Features include aspect-ratio locking, minimum and maximum size, keyboard nudging support, interaction hooks, and custom styling.

Magnify

http://www.jnathanson.com/index.cfm?page=pages/jquery/magnify/magnify

http://plugins.jquery.com/project/magnify

When provided with a proportionally sized small and large image, the **Magnify** plugin will generate a "magnifier" like those that are commonly used for product detail and close-up images.

Lightboxes and Modal Dialogs

One of our examples in Chapter 9 showed how to overlay detailed information on top of a page without the use of a popup window—a feature often called a **lightbox**. The following plugins assist in the creation of such overlays.

FancyBox

http://fancy.klade.lv/

This lightbox clone emphasizes style, with its Mac-like appearance and elegant drop-shadow effect. In addition to displaying automatically scaled images, the **FancyBox** plugin can show inline or `<iframe>` content.

Thickbox

http://jquery.com/demo/thickbox/

Thickbox is a versatile lightbox plugin that can show a single image, multiple images, inline content, `<iframe>` content, or content served through AJAX in a hybrid modal dialog.

leave blank, or add caption to title attribute
Image 3 of 4 < Prev Next >   close or Esc Key

BlockUI

http://malsup.com/jquery/block/

http://plugins.jquery.com/project/blockUI

The **BlockUI** plugin simulates synchronous behavior, without locking the browser. When activated, it will prevent user interaction with the page (or part of the page) until it is deactivated.

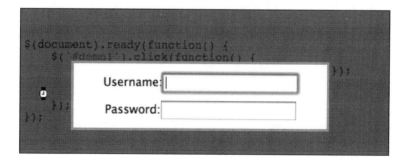

jqModal

http://dev.iceburg.net/jquery/jqModal/

http://plugins.jquery.com/project/jqModal

The **jqModal** plugin is a lightweight modal dialog solution that is also powerful and flexible. With an emphasis on extensibility, it leaves much of the interaction and theming up to web developers who implement it.

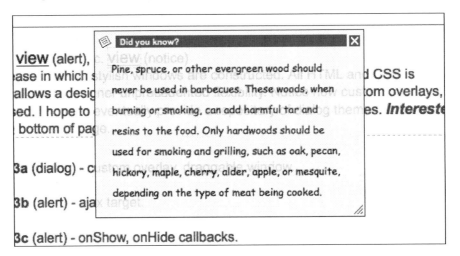

Charting

As with image manipulation, charting has traditionally been a server-side activity requiring significant processing. Inventive programmers have developed several ways to create charts in the browser, and have bundled these techniques into the plugins shown here.

Flot

http://code.google.com/p/flot/

http://plugins.jquery.com/project/flot

The **Flot** plugin uses the `<canvas>` element to produce graphical plots of datasets and optionally modify those plots based on user interaction. With the inclusion of the bundled **Excanvas** translation script, Flot can render graphs in Internet Explorer as well, because Canvas instructions are converted to Internet Explorer's proprietary VML format.

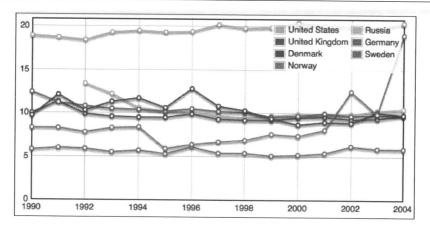

Sparklines

http://omnipotent.net/jquery.sparkline/

http://plugins.jquery.com/project/sparklines

Named after a concept popularized by data visualization expert Edward Tufte, the **Sparklines** plugin generates small and simple inline charts. Like Flot, Sparklines uses the `<canvas>` element to render the charts, but conversion for Internet Explorer is done within the plugin rather than relying on Excanvas.

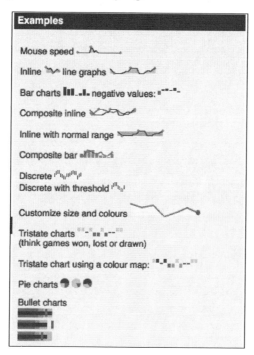

Events

As we have seen time and again, jQuery provides a wealth of tools for intercepting and reacting to user events such as mouse clicks and keystrokes. However, many options are made available in the core library, though, there will always be more advanced techniques to explore. These plugins make some less-common event scenarios easy to implement.

hoverIntent

```
http://cherne.net/brian/resources/jquery.hoverIntent.html
```

```
http://plugins.jquery.com/project/hoverIntent
```

The **hoverIntent** plugin provides a single method to take the place of the `.hover()` method when it's important to prevent the accidental firing of animations when the user moves the mouse over or out of an element. It tries to determine the user's intent by monitoring the change in speed of the user's mouse movement. This plugin is especially effective when used with drop-down navigation.

Live query

```
http://github.com/brandonaaron/livequery/
```

```
http://plugins.jquery.com/project/livequery
```

Like jQuery's built-in `.live()` method, the Live Query plugin dynamically attaches and maintains event bindings to elements in the DOM, no matter when the elements are created. The plugin provides an alternate implementation that may be preferable in some situations.

Summary

In this chapter we have examined ways in which we can incorporate third-party plugins into our web pages. We've looked closely at the Form plugin and jQuery UI and have listed quite a few others. In the next chapter, we'll take advantage of jQuery's plugin architecture to develop a few different types of plugins of our own.

11
Developing plugins

The available third-party plugins provide a bevy of options for enhancing our coding experience, but sometimes we need to reach a bit farther. When we write code that could be reused by others, or even ourselves, we may want to package it up as a new plugin. Fortunately, the process of developing a plugin is not much more involved than writing the code that uses it.

In this chapter, we cover how to create many different kinds of plugins, from the simple to the complex. We'll start with plugins that simply make new global functions available, and move on to cover jQuery object methods of various types. We will also cover extending the jQuery selector engine with new expressions, and conclude with some tips on distributing a plugin for other developers to use.

Adding new global functions

Some of the built-in capabilities of jQuery are provided via what we have been calling **global functions**. As we've seen, these are actually **methods** of the jQuery object, but practically speaking, they are functions within a jQuery **namespace**.

A prime example of this technique is the $.ajax() function. Everything that $.ajax() does could be accomplished with a regular global function called simply ajax(), but this approach would leave us open for function name conflicts. By placing the function within the jQuery namespace, we only have to worry about conflicts with other jQuery methods.

To add a function to the jQuery namespace, we can just assign the new function as a **property** of the jQuery object:

```
jQuery.globalFunction = function() {
  alert('This is a test. This is only a test.');
};
```

Now in any code which uses this plugin, we can write:

```
jQuery.globalFunction();
```

We can also use the $ alias and write:

```
$.globalFunction();
```

This will work just like a basic function call, and the alert will be displayed.

Adding multiple functions

If our plugin needs to provide more than one global function, we could declare them independently:

```
jQuery.functionOne = function() {
  alert('This is a test. This is only a test.');
};
jQuery.functionTwo = function(param) {
  alert('The parameter is "' + param + '".');
};
```

Now both methods are defined, so we can call them in the normal fashion:

```
$.functionOne();
$.functionTwo('test');
```

We can also employ an alternate syntax in defining our functions, using the $.extend() function:

```
jQuery.extend({
  functionOne: function() {
    alert('This is a test. This is only a test.');
  },
  functionTwo: function(param) {
    alert('The parameter is "' + param + '".');
  }
});
```

This produces the same results.

We risk a different kind of namespace pollution here, though. Even though we are shielded from most JavaScript function and variable names by using the jQuery namespace, we could still have a conflict with function names defined in other jQuery plugins. To avoid this, it is best to encapsulate all of the global functions for a plugin into an object:

```
jQuery.myPlugin = {
  functionOne: function() {
    alert('This is a test. This is only a test.');
  },
  functionTwo: function(param) {
    alert('The parameter is "' + param + '".');
  }
};
```

This pattern essentially creates another namespace for our global functions, called `jQuery.myPlugin`. Though we will still informally call these functions "global," they are now methods of the `myPlugin` object, itself a property of the global `jQuery` object. We therefore have to include the plugin name in our function calls:

```
$.myPlugin.functionOne();
$.myPlugin.functionTwo('test');
```

With this technique (and a sufficiently unique plugin name), we are fully protected from namespace collisions in our global functions.

What's the point?

We now have the basics of plugin development in our bag of tricks. After saving our functions in a file called `jquery.myplugin.js`, we can include this script and use the functions from other scripts on the page. But how is this different from any other JavaScript file we could create and include?

We already discussed the namespace benefits of gathering our code inside the `jQuery` object. There is another advantage of writing our function library as a jQuery extension, however: because we know that jQuery will be included, the functions can use jQuery itself.

 Even though jQuery will be included, we shouldn't assume that the `$` shortcut is available. Recall that the `$.noConflict()` method can relinquish control of this shortcut. To account for this, our plugins should always call jQuery methods using `jQuery` or internally define `$` themselves, as described later.

Creating a utility method

Many of the global functions provided by the core jQuery library are **utility methods**; that is, they provide shortcuts for tasks that are frequently needed, but not difficult to do by hand. The array-handling functions `$.each()`, `$.map()`, and `$.grep()` are good examples of these. To illustrate the creation of such utility methods, we'll add a new `$.sum()` function to their number.

Our new method will accept an array, add the values in the array together, and return the result. The code for our plugin is quite brief:

```
jQuery.sum = function(array) {
  var total = 0;
  jQuery.each(array, function(index, value) {
```

```
      total += value;
  });

  return total;
};
```

Note that here, we have used the `$.each()` method to iterate over the array's values. We could certainly use a simple `for()` loop here, but since we can be assured that the jQuery library has been loaded before our plugin, we can use the syntax we've grown comfortable with.

To test our plugin, we'll build a simple page to display the inputs and outputs of the function:

```
<body>
  <p>Array contents:</p>
  <ul id="array-contents"></ul>
  <p>Array sum:</p>
  <div id="array-sum"></div>
</body>
```

Now we'll write a short script that appends the array values and the array sum to the placeholders we've created.

```
$(document).ready(function() {
  var myArray = [52, 97, 0.5, -22];

  $.each(myArray, function(index, value) {
    $('#array-contents').append('<li>' + value + '</li>');
  });

  $('#array-sum').append($.sum(myArray));
});
```

A look at the rendered HTML page verifies that our plugin is working correctly:

Array contents:

- 52
- 97
- 0.5
- -22

Array sum:

127.5

So we've now seen the namespace protection and guaranteed library availability that jQuery plugins grant. These are just organizational benefits, though. To really tap into the power of jQuery plugins, we need to learn how to create new **methods** on individual jQuery object instances.

Adding jQuery Object Methods

Most of jQuery's built-in functionality is provided through its object methods, and this is where plugins shine as well. Whenever we would write a function that acts on part of the DOM, it is probably appropriate instead to create an object method.

We have seen that adding global functions requires extending the jQuery object with new methods. Adding instance methods is similar, but we instead extend the jQuery.fn object:

```
jQuery.fn.myMethod = function() {
  alert('Nothing happens.');
}
```

 The jQuery.fn object is an alias to jQuery.prototype, provided for conciseness.

We can then call this new method from our code after using any selector expression:

```
$('div').myMethod();
```

Our alert is displayed when we invoke the method. We might as well have written a global function, though, as we haven't used the matched DOM nodes in any way. A reasonable method implementation acts on its **context**.

Object Method context

Within any plugin method, the keyword this is set to the current jQuery object. Therefore, we can call any built-in jQuery method on this, or extract its DOM nodes and work on them:

```
jQuery.fn.showAlert = function() {
  alert('You selected ' + this.length + ' elements.');
}
```

To examine what we can do with object context, we'll write a small plugin to manipulate the classes on the matched elements. Our new method will take two class names, and swap which class is applied to each element with every invocation.

```
jQuery.fn.swapClass = function(class1, class2) {
  if (this.hasClass(class1)) {
    this.removeClass(class1).addClass(class2);

  }
  else if (this.hasClass(class2)) {
    this.removeClass(class2).addClass(class1);
  }
};
```

First, we test for the presence of `class1` on the matched element and substitute `class2` if it is found. Otherwise, we test for `class2` and switch in `class1` if necessary. If neither class is currently present, we do nothing.

To test out our method, we need some HTML to play with:

```
<ul>
  <li>Lorem ipsum dolor sit amet</li>
  <li class="this">Consectetur adipisicing elit</li>
  <li>Sed do eiusmod tempor incididunt ut labore</li>
  <li class="that">Magna aliqua</li>
  <li class="this">Ut enim ad minim veniam</li>
  <li>Quis nostrud exercitation ullamco</li>
  <li>Laboris nisi ut aliquip ex ea commodo</li>
  <li class="that">Duis aute irure dolor</li>
</ul>
<input type="button" value="Swap classes" id="swap" />
```

The class `this` is styled as bold text, and the class `that` is styled as italic text:

Now, we can invoke our method whenever the button is clicked:

```
$(document).ready(function() {
  $('#swap').click(function() {
    $('li').swapClass('this', 'that');
    return false;
  });
});
```

But something is wrong. When we click the button, every row gets the that class applied:

```
• Lorem ipsum dolor sit amet
• Consectetur adipisicing elit
• Sed do eiusmod tempor incididunt ut labore
• Magna aliqua
• Ut enim ad minim veniam
• Quis nostrud exercitation ullamco
• Laboris nisi ut aliquip ex ea commodo
• Duis aute irure dolor

( Swap classes )
```

We need to remember that a jQuery selector expression can always match zero, one, or multiple elements. We must allow for any of these scenarios when designing a plugin method. In this case, we are calling .hasClass(), which only examines the first matched element. Instead, we need to check each element independently and act on it.

The easiest way to guarantee proper behavior regardless of the number of matched elements is to always call .each() on the method context; this enforces **implicit iteration**, which is important for maintaining consistency between plugin and built-in methods. Within the .each() call, this refers to each DOM element in turn, so we can adjust our code to separately test for and apply classes to each matched element.

```
jQuery.fn.swapClass = function(class1, class2) {
  this.each(function() {
    var $element = jQuery(this);
    if ($element.hasClass(class1)) {
      $element.removeClass(class1).addClass(class2);
    }
    else if ($element.hasClass(class2)) {
      $element.removeClass(class2).addClass(class1);
    }
  });
};
```

Caution! The keyword this refers to a **jQuery object** within the object method's body, but refers to a **DOM element** within the .each() invocation.

Now when we click the button, the classes are switched without affecting the elements that have neither class applied:

- Lorem ipsum dolor sit amet
- *Consectetur adipisicing elit*
- Sed do eiusmod tempor incididunt ut labore
- **Magna aliqua**
- *Ut enim ad minim veniam*
- Quis nostrud exercitation ullamco
- Laboris nisi ut aliquip ex ea commodo
- **Duis aute irure dolor**

 Swap classes

Method chaining

In addition to implicit iteration, jQuery users should be able to rely on **chaining** behavior. This means that we need to return a jQuery object from all plugin methods, unless the method is clearly intended to retrieve a different piece of information. The returned jQuery object is usually just the one provided as this. If we use .each() to iterate over this, we can just return its result:

```
jQuery.fn.swapClass = function(class1, class2) {
  return this.each(function() {
    var $element = jQuery(this);
    if ($element.hasClass(class1)) {
      $element.removeClass(class1).addClass(class2);
    }
    else if ($element.hasClass(class2)) {
      $element.removeClass(class2).addClass(class1);
    }
  });
};
```

Previously, when we called `.swapClass()` we had to start a new statement to do anything else with the elements. With the `return` statement in place, though, we can freely chain our plugin method with built-in methods:

```
$(document).ready(function() {
  $('#swap').click(function() {
    $('li')
      .swapClass('this', 'that')
      .css('text-decoration', 'underline');
    return false;
  });
});
```

- Lorem ipsum dolor sit amet
- *Consectetur adipisicing elit*
- Sed do eiusmod tempor incididunt ut labore
- **Magna aliqua**
- *Ut enim ad minim veniam*
- Quis nostrud exercitation ullamco
- Laboris nisi ut aliquip ex ea commodo
- **Duis aute irure dolor**

(Swap classes)

DOM traversal methods

In some cases, we may want a plugin method to change which DOM elements are referenced by the jQuery object. For example, suppose we wanted to add a DOM traversal method that found the grandparents of the matched elements:

```
jQuery.fn.grandparent = function() {
  var grandparents = [];
  this.each(function() {
    grandparents.push(this.parentNode.parentNode);
  });
  grandparents = jQuery.unique(grandparents);
  return this.setArray(grandparents);
};
```

This method creates a new `grandparents` array, populating it by iterating over all of the elements currently referenced by the jQuery object. The standard DOM `.parentNode` property is used to find the grandparent elements, which are pushed onto the `grandparents` array. This array is stripped of its duplicates with a call to `$.unique()`. Then the internal jQuery `.setArray()` method changes the set of matched elements to the new array. Now, we can find and operate on the grandparent of an element with a single method call.

To test our method, we'll set up a deeply-nested `<div>` structure:

```
<div>Deserunt mollit anim id est laborum</div>
<div>Ut enim ad minim veniam
  <div>Quis nostrud exercitation
    <div>Ullamco laboris nisi
      <div>Ut aliquip ex ea</div>
        <div class="target">Commodo consequat
          <div>Lorem ipsum dolor sit amet</div>
        </div>
      </div>
    </div>
    <div>Duis aute irure dolor</div>
    <div>In reprehenderit
      <div>In voluptate</div>
      <div>Velit esse
        <div>Cillum dolore</div>
        <div class="target">Fugiat nulla pariatur</div>
      </div>
      <div>Excepteur sint occaecat cupidatat</div>
    </div>
  </div>
  <div>Non proident</div>
</div>
<div>Sunt in culpa qui officia</div>
```

We'll identify the target elements (`<div class="target">`) by styling their text bold:

Now we can locate the items' grandparent elements by using our new method:

```
$(document).ready(function() {
  $('.target').grandparent().addClass('highlight');
});
```

The `highlight` class correctly italicizes both grandparent items on the page:

However, this method is **destructive**. The actual jQuery object is modified as a side effect—one that becomes evident if we store the jQuery object in a variable:

```
$(document).ready(function() {
  var $target = $('.target');
  $target.grandparent().addClass('highlight');
  $target.hide();
});
```

This code should highlight the grandparent elements, and then hide the target elements. However, the actual effect is that the grandparents are hidden instead:

The jQuery object stored in $target has changed to refer to the grandparent. To avoid this, we need to make the method **nondestructive**. This is made possible by the internal **stack** jQuery keeps for each object.

```
jQuery.fn.grandparent = function() {
  var grandparents = [];
  this.each(function() {
    grandparents.push(this.parentNode.parentNode);
  });
  grandparents = jQuery.unique(grandparents);
  return this.pushStack(grandparents);
};
```

By calling .pushStack() instead of .setArray(), we create a new jQuery object, rather than modifying the old one. Now the $target object is not modified, and the original target objects are hidden by our code:

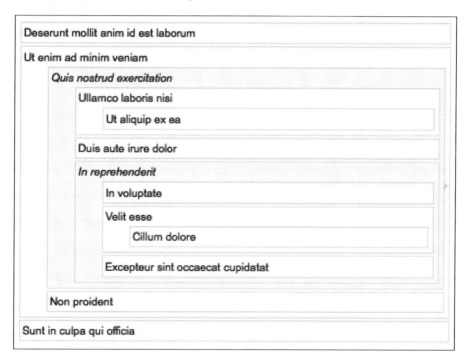

As a side benefit, `.pushStack()` also allows the `.end()` and `.andSelf()` methods to work with our plugin, so we can chain methods together properly:

```
$(document).ready(function() {
  $('.target').grandparent().andSelf().addClass('highlight');
});
```

 DOM traversal methods such as `.children()` were destructive operations in jQuery 1.0, but became non-destructive in 1.1.

Adding new shortcut methods

Many of the methods included in jQuery are **shortcuts** for other underlying methods. For example, most of the **event methods** are shortcuts for calls to `.bind()` or `.trigger()`, and many AJAX methods internally call `$.ajax()`. These shortcuts make it convenient to use features that are otherwise complicated by many options.

The jQuery library must maintain a delicate balance between convenience and complexity. Each method that is added to the library can help developers to write certain pieces of code more quickly, but also adds to the overall size of the code base and can reduce performance. For this reason, many shortcuts for built-in functionality are relegated to plugins, so that we can pick and choose the ones that are useful for each project and omit the irrelevant ones.

When we find ourselves repeating an idiom in our code many times, it may call for the creation of a shortcut method. For example, suppose we frequently animate items using a combination of the built-in "slide" and "fade" techniques. Putting these effects together means animating the `height` and `opacity` of an element simultaneously. The `.animate()` method makes this easy:

```
.animate({height: 'hide', opacity: 'hide'});
```

We can create a trio of shortcut methods to perform this animation when showing and hiding elements:

```
jQuery.fn.slideFadeOut = function() {
  return this.animate({
    height: 'hide',
    opacity: 'hide'
  });
};
jQuery.fn.slideFadeIn = function() {
  return this.animate({
    height: 'show',
    opacity: 'show'
  });
};
jQuery.fn.slideFadeToggle = function() {
  return this.animate({
    height: 'toggle',
    opacity: 'toggle'
  });
};
```

Now we can call `.slideFadeOut()` and trigger the animation whenever it is needed. Because, within a plugin method definition, `this` refers to the current jQuery object, the animation will be performed on all matched elements at once.

For completeness, our new methods should support the same parameters that the built- in shortcuts do. In particular, methods such as `.fadeIn()` can be customized with speeds and callback functions. Since `.animate()` also takes these parameters, allowing this is straightforward. We just accept the parameters and forward them on to `.animate()`.

```
jQuery.fn.slideFadeOut = function(speed, callback) {
  return this.animate({
    height: 'hide',
    opacity: 'hide'
  }, speed, callback);
};
jQuery.fn.slideFadeIn = function(speed, callback) {
  return this.animate({
    height: 'show',
    opacity: 'show'
  }, speed, callback);
};
jQuery.fn.slideFadeToggle = function(speed, callback) {
  return this.animate({
    height: 'toggle',
    opacity: 'toggle'
  }, speed, callback);
};
```

Now, we have custom shortcut methods that function just like their built-in counterparts. To demonstrate this, we'll need a simple HTML page:

```
<body>
  <p>Lorem ipsum dolor sit amet, consectetur adipisicing
    elit, sed do eiusmod tempor incididunt ut labore et
    dolore magna aliqua. Ut enim ad minim veniam, quis
    nostrud exercitation ullamco laboris nisi ut aliquip
    ex ea commodo consequat. Duis aute irure dolor in
    reprehenderit in voluptate velit esse cillum dolore eu
    fugiat nulla pariatur. Excepteur sint occaecat
    cupidatat non proident, sunt in culpa qui officia
    deserunt mollit anim id est laborum.</p>
  <div class="controls">
    <input type="button" value="Slide and fade out"
      id="out" />
    <input type="button" value="Slide and fade in" id="in" />
    <input type="button" value="Toggle" id="toggle" />
  </div>
</body>
```

Our script will simply call our new methods when the buttons are clicked:

```
$(document).ready(function() {
  $('#out').click(function() {
    $('p').slideFadeOut('slow');
    return false;
  });
  $('#in').click(function() {
    $('p').slideFadeIn('slow');
    return false;
  });
  $('#toggle').click(function() {
    $('p').slideFadeToggle('slow');
    return false;
  });
});
```

And the animation occurs as expected.

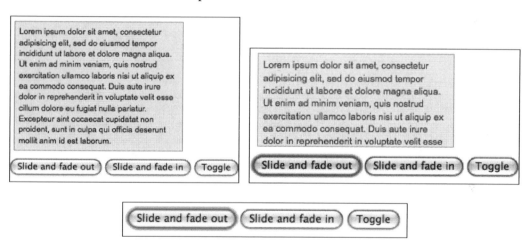

Method parameters

We've now seen several examples of plugin methods, some of which take explicit parameters, and some of which do not. As we have explored, the keyword this is always available to provide context for the method, but we can also supply additional information to influence the method's operation. So far, the parameters have been few, but of course this list could grow large. There are several tricks we can use to manage our method parameters and make life easier for those using our plugins.

As our example, we'll start with a plugin method that provides a shadow on a block of text. Our technique will be similar to that used for the fading effect on the news rotator in Chapter 9: we will use a number of elements that are partially transparent, overlaid in different positions on the page.

```
jQuery.fn.shadow = function() {
  return this.each(function() {
    var $originalElement = jQuery(this);
    for (var i = 0; i < 5; i++) {
      $originalElement
        .clone()
        .css({
          position: 'absolute',
          left: $originalElement.offset().left + i,
          top: $originalElement.offset().top + i,
          margin: 0,
          zIndex: -1,
          opacity: 0.1
        })
        .appendTo('body');
    }
  });
};
```

For each element this method is called on, we make a number of clones of the element, adjusting their opacity. These clones are positioned absolutely, at varying offsets from the original element.

As usual, we'll test our plugin using some simple HTML:

```
<body>
  <h1>The quick brown fox jumps over the lazy dog.</h1>
</body>
```

> **The quick brown fox jumps over the lazy dog.**

For the moment, our plugin takes no parameters, so calling the method is simple:

```
$(document).ready(function() {
  $('h1').shadow();
});
```

> **The quick brown fox jumps over the lazy dog.**

Simple parameters

Now we can introduce some flexibility to the plugin method. The operation of the method relies on several numeric values that the user might want to modify. We can make these into parameters so they can be changed on demand.

```
jQuery.fn.shadow = function(slices, opacity, zIndex) {
  return this.each(function() {
    var $originalElement = jQuery(this);
    for (var i = 0; i < slices; i++) {
      $originalElement
        .clone()
        .css({
          position: 'absolute',
          left: $originalElement.offset().left + i,
          top: $originalElement.offset().top + i,
          margin: 0,
          zIndex: zIndex,
          opacity: opacity
        })
        .appendTo('body');
    }
  });
};
```

Now, when calling our method, we must provide these three values.

```
$(document).ready(function() {
  $('h1').shadow(10, 0.1, -1);
});
```

Our new parameters work as anticipated—the shadow is longer, using twice as many slices as before—but the method interface is less than ideal. These three numbers are easily confused, and their order cannot be logically deduced. It would be an improvement to label the parameters, for the benefit of both the person writing the method call, and anyone who later wishes to read and interpret it.

Parameter maps

We have seen many examples in the jQuery API of **maps** being provided as method parameters. This can be a much friendlier way to expose options to a plugin user than the simple parameter list we just used. A map provides a visual label for each parameter, and also makes the order of the parameters irrelevant. In addition, any time we can mimic the jQuery API in our plugins, we should do so to increase consistency and therefore ease-of-use.

```
jQuery.fn.shadow = function(opts) {
  return this.each(function() {
    var $originalElement = jQuery(this);
    for (var i = 0; i < opts.slices; i++) {
      $originalElement
        .clone()
        .css({
          position: 'absolute',
          left: $originalElement.offset().left + i,
          top: $originalElement.offset().top + i,
          margin: 0,
          zIndex: opts.zIndex,
          opacity: opts.opacity
        })
        .appendTo('body');
    }
  });
};
```

All we have changed to enable our new interface is the way each parameter is referenced; instead of having a separate variable name, each value is accessed as a property of the `opts` argument to the function.

Calling this method now requires a map of values rather than three individual numbers:

```
$(document).ready(function() {
  $('h1').shadow({
    slices: 5,
    opacity: 0.25,
    zIndex: -1
  });
});
```

The quick brown fox jumps over the lazy dog.

The purpose of each parameter is now obvious from a quick glance at the method call.

Default parameter values

As the number of parameters for a method grows, it becomes less likely that we will always want to specify each one. A sensible set of **default values** can make a plugin interface much more usable. Fortunately, using a map for our parameters helps with this task as well; it is simple to omit any item from the map and replace it with a default.

```
jQuery.fn.shadow = function(options) {
  var defaults = {
    slices: 5,
    opacity: 0.1,
    zIndex: -1
  };
  var opts = jQuery.extend(defaults, options);
  return this.each(function() {
    var $originalElement = jQuery(this);
    for (var i = 0; i < opts.slices; i++) {
      $originalElement
        .clone()
        .css({
          position: 'absolute',
          left: $originalElement.offset().left + i,
          top: $originalElement.offset().top + i,
          margin: 0,
          zIndex: opts.zIndex,
          opacity: opts.opacity
        })
        .appendTo('body');
    }
  });
};
```

Here, we have defined a new map, called `defaults`, within our method definition. The utility function `$.extend()` lets us take the `options` map provided as an argument and use it to override the items in `defaults`, leaving omitted items alone.

We still call our method using a map, but now we can specify only the parameters that we want to differ from their defaults:

```
$(document).ready(function() {
  $('h1').shadow({
    opacity: 0.05
  });
});
```

The quick brown fox jumps over the lazy dog.

Unspecified parameters use their default values. The `$.extend()` method even accepts `null` values, so if the default parameters are all acceptable, our method can be called very simply without errors:

```
$(document).ready(function() {
  $('h1').shadow();
});
```

Callback functions

Of course, some method parameters can be quite a bit more complicated than a simple numeric value. One common parameter type we have seen frequently throughout the jQuery API is the **callback function**. Callback functions can lend a large amount of flexibility to a plugin without requiring a great deal of preparation when creating the plugin.

To employ a callback function in our method, we need simply accept the function object as a parameter and call that function where appropriate in our method implementation. As an example, we can extend our text shadow method to allow the user to customize the position of the shadow relative to the text.

```
jQuery.fn.shadow = function(options) {
  var defaults = {
    slices: 5,
    opacity: 0.1,
    zIndex: -1,
    sliceOffset: function(i) {
      return {x: i, y: i};
    }
  };
  var opts = jQuery.extend(defaults, options);

  return this.each(function() {
    var $originalElement = jQuery(this);
    for (var i = 0; i < opts.slices; i++) {
      var offset = opts.sliceOffset(i);
      $originalElement
        .clone()
        .css({
          position: 'absolute',
          left: $originalElement.offset().left
            + offset.x,
          top: $originalElement.offset().top
            + offset.y,
```

```
        margin: 0,
        zIndex: opts.zIndex,
        opacity: opts.opacity
      })
      .appendTo('body');
    }
  });
};
```

Each slice of the shadow has a different offset from the original text. Before, this offset has simply been equal to the index of the slice. Now, though, we're calculating the offset using the `sliceOffset()` function, which is a parameter that the user can override. So, for example, we could provide negative values for the offset in both dimensions:

```
$(document).ready(function() {
  $('h1').shadow({
    sliceOffset: function(i) {
      return {x: -i, y: -2*i};
    }
  });
});
```

This will cause the shadow to be cast up and to the left rather than down and to the right:

The callback allows simple modifications to the shadow's direction, or much more sophisticated positioning if the plugin user supplies the appropriate callback. If the callback is not specified, then the default behavior is once again used.

Customizable defaults

We can improve the experience of using our plugins by providing reasonable default values for our method parameters, as we have seen. However, sometimes it can be difficult to predict what a reasonable default value will be. If a script will be calling our plugin multiple times with a different set of parameters than we set as the defaults, the ability to customize these defaults could significantly reduce the amount of code that needs to be written.

To make the defaults customizable, we need to move them out of our method definition and into a location that is accessible by outside code:

```
jQuery.fn.shadow = function(options) {
  var opts = jQuery.extend({},
    jQuery.fn.shadow.defaults, options);
  return this.each(function() {
    var $originalElement = jQuery(this);
    for (var i = 0; i < opts.slices; i++) {
      var offset = opts.sliceOffset(i);
      $originalElement
        .clone()
        .css({
          position: 'absolute',
          left: $originalElement.offset().left + offset.x,
          top: $originalElement.offset().top + offset.y,
          margin: 0,
          zIndex: opts.zIndex,
          opacity: opts.opacity
        })
        .appendTo('body');
    }
  });
};
jQuery.fn.shadow.defaults = {
  slices: 5,
  opacity: 0.1,
  zIndex: -1,
  sliceOffset: function(i) {
    return {x: i, y: i};
  }
};
```

The defaults are now in the **namespace** of the shadow plugin, and can be directly referred to with $.fn.shadow.defaults. Our call to $.extend() had to change to accommodate this as well. Since we are now reusing the same defaults map for every call to .shadow(), we can't allow $.extend() to modify it. Instead, we provide an empty map {} as the first argument to $.extend(), and it is this new object that gets modified.

Now code that uses our plugin can change the defaults that all subsequent calls to `.shadow()` will use. Options can also still be supplied at the time the method is invoked.

```
$(document).ready(function() {
  $.fn.shadow.defaults.slices = 10;

  $('h1').shadow({
    sliceOffset: function(i) {
      return {x: -i, y: i};
    }
  });
});
```

This script will create a shadow with 10 slices, because that is the new default value, but will also cast the shadow left and down, due to the `sliceOffset` callback that is provided along with the method call.

Adding a selector expression

Built-in parts of jQuery can be extended as well. Rather than adding new methods, we can customize existing ones. A common desire, for example, is to expand on the **selector expressions** provided by jQuery to provide more esoteric options.

The easiest type of selector expression to add is a **pseudo-class**; these are the expressions that start with a colon, such as `:checked` or `:nth-child()`. To illustrate the process of creating a selector expression, we'll build a pseudo-class called `:css()`. This new selector will allow us to locate elements based on the numeric values of their CSS attributes.

When using a selector expression to find elements, jQuery looks for instructions in an internal map called `expr`. This map contains JavaScript code to execute on an element, causing the element to be contained in the result set if the code evaluates to `true`. We can add new expressions to this map using the `$.extend()` function.

```
jQuery.extend(jQuery.expr[':'], {
  'css': function(element, index, matches, set) {
    var parts = /([\w-]+)\s*([<>=]+)\s*(\d+)/
      .exec(matches[3]);
    var value = parseFloat(jQuery(element).css(parts[1]));
    switch (parts[2]) {
```

```
          case '<':
            return value < parseInt(parts[3]);
          case '<=':
            return value <= parseInt(parts[3]);
          case '=':
          case '==':
            return value == parseInt(parts[3]);
          case '>=':
            return value >= parseInt(parts[3]);
          case '>':
            return value > parseInt(parts[3]);
      }
    }
  });
```

This code tells jQuery that `css` is a valid string that can follow a colon in a selector expression, and that when it is encountered, the given function should be called to determine whether the element should be included in the result set.

The function that is evaluated here is passed four parameters:

- `element`: The DOM element under consideration. This is needed for most selectors.

- `index`: The index of the DOM element within the result set. This is helpful for selectors like `:eq()` and `:lt()`.

- `matches`: An array containing the result of the regular expression that was used to parse this selector. Typically, `matches[3]` is the only relevant item in the array; in a selector of the form `:a(b)`, the `matches[3]` item contains `b`, the text within the parentheses.

- `set`: The entire set of DOM elements matched up to this point. This parameter is rarely needed.

Pseudo-class selectors need to use the information contained in these four arguments to determine whether or not the element belongs in the result set. In this case, `element` and `matches` are all that we require.

In our selector function, we first break down the selector into usable parts with a regular expression. We want a selector like `:css(width < 200)` to return all elements with a `width` of less than `200`. So we need to look at the text within the parentheses to pull out the property name (`width`), comparison operator (`<`), and value to compare against (`200`). The regular expression `/([\w-]+)\s*([<>=]+)\s*(\d+)/` performs this search, placing these three portions of the string into the `parts` array for our use.

Next, we need to fetch the current value of the property. We can use jQuery's .css() method to return the value of the property that has been named in the selector. Since this property is returned as a string, we use parseFloat() to turn it into a number.

Finally, we perform the actual comparison. A switch statement determines which type of comparison is done depending on the content of the selector, and the result of the comparison (true or false) is returned.

We now have a new selector expression we can use anywhere in our jQuery code. A simple HTML document can demonstrate this:

```
<body>
  <div>Deserunt mollit anim id est laborum</div>
  <div>Ullamco</div>
  <div>Ut enim ad minim veniam laboris</div>
  <div>Quis nostrud exercitation consequat nisi</div>
  <div>Ut aliquip</div>
  <div>Commodo</div>
  <div>Lorem ipsum dolor sit amet ex ea</div>
</body>
```

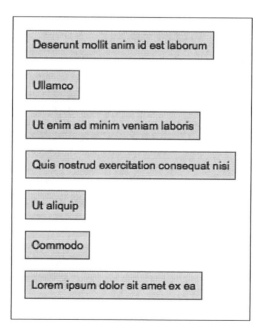

With our new selector, it becomes trivial to highlight the smaller items in this list:

```
$(document).ready(function() {
  $('div:css(width < 100)').addClass('highlight');
});
```

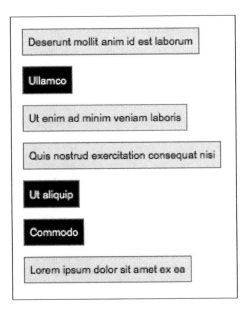

Sharing a plugin with the world

Once a plugin is complete, we may want to publish it so that others can benefit from—and possibly improve—the code. We can do this at the official **jQuery Plugin Repository** at http://plugins.jquery.com/. Here we can log in, or register if we need to, and follow the instructions to describe the plugin and upload a .zip archive of its code. Before this, though, we should make sure the plugin is appropriately polished and prepared for public consumption.

There are a few rules to follow in writing plugins in order to play well with other code. We have covered some of these in passing already, but they are collected again here for convenience.

Naming conventions

All plugin files should be named jQuery.myPlugin.js where myPlugin is the name of the plugin. Within the file, all global functions should be grouped into an object called jQuery.myPlugin, unless there is only one, in which case it may be a function just called jQuery.myPlugin().

Method names are more flexible, but should be kept as unique as possible. If only one method is defined, it should be called `jQuery.fn.myPlugin()`. If more than one is defined, attempt to prefix each method name with the plugin name to prevent confusion. Avoid short, ambiguous method names such as `.load()` or `.get()` that may be confused with methods defined in other plugins.

Use of the $ alias

jQuery plugins may not assume that the `$` alias is available. Instead, the full `jQuery` name must be written out each time.

In longer plugins, many developers find that the lack of the `$` shortcut makes code more difficult to read. To combat this, the shortcut can be locally defined for the scope of the plugin by defining and executing a function. The syntax for defining and executing a function at once looks like this:

```
(function($) {
  // Code goes here
})(jQuery);
```

The wrapping function takes a single parameter, to which we pass the global `jQuery` object. The parameter is named `$`, so within the function we can use the `$` alias with no conflicts.

Method interfaces

All jQuery methods get called within the context of a jQuery object, so `this` refers to an object that may refer to one or more DOM elements. All methods must behave correctly regardless of the number of elements actually matched. In general, methods should call `this.each()` to iterate over the matched elements, operating on each one in turn.

Methods should return the jQuery object to preserve chaining. If the set of matched objects is modified, a new object should be created by calling `.pushStack()` and this object should be returned instead. If something other than a jQuery object is returned, this must be prominently documented.

If methods take several options, it is preferable to use a map as an argument so that the options are labeled and can be specified in any order. Default values should be defined in a map that can be overridden if necessary.

Method definitions must end in a semicolon (`;`) character so that code compressors can properly parse the files. In addition, plugins may begin with a semicolon, so that other poorly-coded scripts do not cause conflicts after compression.

Documentation style

In-file documentation should be prepended to each function or method definition in ScriptDoc format. This format is documented at `http://www.scriptdoc.org/`.

Summary

In this final chapter, we have seen how the functionality that is provided by the jQuery core need not limit the library's capabilities. Plugins that are readily available extend the menu of features substantially, and we can easily create our own that push the boundaries further.

The plugins we've created contain various features, including global functions that use the jQuery library, new methods of the jQuery object for acting on DOM elements, extensible methods that can be easily customized, and enhanced selector expressions for finding DOM elements in new ways.

With these tools at our disposal, we can shape jQuery—and our own JavaScript code—into whatever form we desire.

Online Resources

The following online resources represent a starting point for learning more about jQuery, JavaScript, and web development in general, beyond what is covered in this book. There are far too many sources of quality information on the web for this appendix to approach anything resembling an exhaustive list. Furthermore, while other print publications can also provide valuable information, they are not noted here.

jQuery documentation

These resources offer references and details on the jQuery library itself.

jQuery wiki

The documentation on `jquery.com` is in the form of a wiki, which means that the content is editable by the public. The site includes the full jQuery API, tutorials, getting started guides, and more:

```
http://docs.jquery.com/
```

jQuery API

In addition to the official documentation on `jquery.com`, the API is available at the following location:

```
http://remysharp.com/jquery-api/
```

jQuery API browser

Jörn Zaeferrer has put together a convenient tree-view browser of the jQuery API with a search feature and alphabetical, or categorical sorting:

```
http://jquery.bassistance.de/api-browser-1.2/
```

Visual jQuery

This API browser designed by *Yehuda Katz*, and updated by *Remy Sharp*, is both beautiful and convenient. It also provides quick viewing of methods for a number of jQuery plugins:

```
http://www.visualjquery.com/
```

Adobe AIR jQueryAPI viewer

Remy Sharp has packaged the jQuery API into an Adobe AIR application for off-line viewing:

```
http://remysharp.com/downloads/jquery-api-browser.air.zip
```

JavaScript reference

These sites offer references and guides to JavaScript as a language in general, rather than jQuery in particular.

Mozilla developer center

This site has a comprehensive JavaScript reference, a guide to programming with JavaScript, links to helpful tools, and more:

```
http://developer.mozilla.org/en/docs/JavaScript/
```

Dev.opera

While focused primarily on its own browser platform, Opera's site for web developers includes a number of useful articles on JavaScript:

```
http://dev.opera.com/articles/
```

MSDN JScript Reference

The *Microsoft Developer Network* JScript Reference provides descriptions of the full set of functions, objects, and so on. It's especially helpful for understanding Microsoft's implementation of the ECMAScript standard in Internet Explorer:

```
http://msdn.microsoft.com/en-us/library/x85xxsf4(VS.71).aspx
```

Quirksmode

Peter-Paul Koch's Quirksmode site is a terrific resource for understanding differences in the way browsers implement various JavaScript functions, as well as many CSS properties:

```
http://www.quirksmode.org/
```

JavaScript Toolbox

Matt Kruse's JavaScript Toolbox offers a large assortment of homespun JavaScript libraries, as well as sound advice on JavaScript best practices and a collection of vetted JavaScript resources elsewhere on the Web:

```
http://www.javascripttoolbox.com/
```

JavaScript code compressors

When putting the finishing touches on a site, it is often advisable to compress the JavaScript code. This process reduces download time for all users of the site.

YUI Compressor

This JavaScript compressor from the Yahoo! UI Library is used to reduce the size of the jQuery source code. The Java-based command-line tool is a free download. The resulting code is very efficient in file size and performance, and can be further slimmed down by Gzip compression if desired.

```
http://developer.yahoo.com/yui/compressor/
```

JSMin

Created by *Douglas Crockford*, JSMin is a filter that removes comments and unnecessary white space from JavaScript files. It typically reduces file size by half, resulting in faster downloads, especially when combined with server-based file compression:

```
http://www.crockford.com/javascript/jsmin.html
```

Pretty printer

This tool prettifies JavaScript that has been compressed, restoring line breaks and indentation where possible. It provides a number of options for tailoring the results:

`http://www.prettyprinter.de/`

(X)HTML reference

The jQuery library is at its best when working with properly-formatted, semantic HTML and XHTML documents. The resource below provides assistance with these markup languages.

W3C hypertext markup language home page

The World Wide Web Consortium (W3C) sets the standard for (X)HTML, and the HTML home page is a great launching point for its specifications and guidelines:

`http://www.w3.org/MarkUp/`

CSS reference

The effects and animations we have seen time and again all rely on the power of Cascading Stylesheets. To incorporate the visual flourishes we desire in our sites, we may need to turn to these CSS resources for guidance.

W3C cascading style sheets home page

The W3C's CSS home page provides links to tutorials, specifications, test suites, and other resources:

`http://www.w3.org/Style/CSS/`

Mezzoblue CSS cribsheet

Dave Shea provides this helpful CSS cribsheet in an attempt to make the design process easier, and provides a quick reference to check when you run into trouble:

`http://mezzoblue.com/css/cribsheet/`

Position is everything

This site includes a catalog of CSS browser bugs along with explanations of how to overcome them:

```
http://www.positioniseverything.net/
```

Useful blogs

New techniques and features are always being developed and introduced for any living technology. Staying on top of innovations can be easy by checking in with these sources of web development news from time to time.

The jQuery blog

John Resig and other contributors to the official jQuery blog posts announcements about new versions and other initiatives among the project team, as well as occasional tutorials and editorial pieces.

```
http://jquery.com/blog/
```

Learning jQuery

Karl Swedberg runs this blog for jQuery tutorials, techniques, and announcements. Guest authors include jQuery team members *Mike Alsup* and *Brandon Aaron*:

```
http://www.learningjquery.com/
```

Ajaxian

This frequently updated blog begun by *Dion Almaer* and *Ben Galbraith* provides a tremendous amount of news and features and the occasional tutorial about JavaScript:

```
http://ajaxian.com/
```

John Resig

The creator of jQuery, *John Resig*, discusses advanced JavaScript topics on his personal blog:

```
http://ejohn.org/
```

JavaScript ant

This site contains a repository of articles pertaining to JavaScript and its usage in modern web browsers, as well as an organized list of JavaScript resources found elsewhere on the web:

```
http://javascriptant.com/
```

Robert's talk

Robert Nyman writes about developing for the internet, especially client-side scripting:

```
http://www.robertnyman.com/
```

Web standards with imagination

Dustin Diaz's blog features articles on web design and development, with an emphasis on JavaScript:

```
http://www.dustindiaz.com/
```

Snook

Jonathan Snook's general programming/web-development blog:

```
http://snook.ca/
```

Matt Snider JavaScript resource

Matt Snider's blog is dedicated to the understanding of JavaScript and its many popular frameworks:

```
http://mattsnider.com/
```

I can't

Three sites by *Christian Heilmann* provide blog entries, sample code, and lengthy articles related to JavaScript and web development:

```
http://icant.co.uk/
http://www.wait-till-i.com/
http://www.onlinetools.org/
```

DOM scripting

Jeremy Keith's blog picks up where the popular DOM scripting book leaves off—a fantastic resource for unobtrusive JavaScript:

```
http://domscripting.com/blog/
```

As days pass by

Stuart Langridge experiments with advanced use of the browser DOM:

```
http://www.kryogenix.org/code/browser/
```

A list apart

A List Apart explores the design, development, and meaning of web content, with a special focus on web standards and best practices:

```
http://www.alistapart.com/
```

Web development frameworks using jQuery

As developers of open-source projects become aware of jQuery, many are incorporating the JavaScript library into their own systems. The following is an abbreviated list of these adopters:

Digitalus Site Manager: `http://code.google.com/p/digitalus-site-manager/`

Drupal: `http://drupal.org/`

DutchPIPE: `http://dutchpipe.org/`

Hpricot: `http://code.whytheluckystiff.net/hpricot/`

JobberBase: `http://www.jobberbase.com/`

Laconica: `http://laconi.ca/`

Piwik: `http://piwik.org/`

Pommo: `http://pommo.org/`

simfony: `http://www.symfony-project.org/`

SPIP: `http://www.spip.net/`

Textpattern: `http://www.textpattern.com/`

Trac: `http://trac.edgewall.org/`

WordPress: `http://wordpress.org/`

Z-Blog: `http://www.rainbowsoft.org/zblog`

For a more complete list, visit the *Sites Using jQuery* page at:

`http://docs.jquery.com/Sites_Using_jQuery`

B
Development Tools

Documentation can help in troubleshooting issues with our JavaScript applications, but there is no replacement for a good set of software development tools. Fortunately, there are many software packages available for inspecting and debugging JavaScript code, and most of them are available for free.

Tools for Firefox

Mozilla Firefox is the browser of choice for the lion's share of web developers, and therefore has some of the most extensive and well-respected development tools.

Firebug

The Firebug extension for Firefox is indispensable for jQuery development:

```
http://www.getfirebug.com/
```

Some of the features of Firebug are :

- An excellent DOM inspector for finding names and selectors for pieces of the document
- CSS manipulation tools for finding out why a page looks a certain way and changing it
- An interactive JavaScript console
- A JavaScript debugger that can watch variables and trace code execution

Web developer toolbar

This not only overlaps Firebug in the area of DOM inspection, but also contains tools for common tasks like cookie manipulation, form inspection, and page resizing. You can also use this toolbar to quickly and easily disable JavaScript for a site to ensure that functionality degrades gracefully when the user's browser is less capable:

```
http://chrispederick.com/work/web-developer/
```

Venkman

Venkman is the official JavaScript debugger for the Mozilla project. It provides a troubleshooting environment that is reminiscent of the GDB system for debugging programs that are written in other languages.

```
http://www.mozilla.org/projects/venkman/
```

Regular expressions tester

Regular expressions for matching strings in JavaScript can be tricky to craft. This extension for Firefox allows easy experimentation with regular expressions using an interface for entering search text:

```
http://sebastianzartner.ath.cx/new/downloads/RExT/
```

Tools for Internet Explorer

Sites often behave differently in IE than in other web browsers, so having debugging tools for this platform is important.

Microsoft Internet Explorer Developer Toolbar

The Developer Toolbar primarily provides a view of the DOM tree for a web page. Elements can be located visually, and modified on the fly with new CSS rules. It also provides other miscellaneous development aids, such as a ruler for measuring page elements:

```
http://www.microsoft.com/downloads/details.aspx?FamilyID=e59c3964-
672d-4511-bb3e-2d5e1db91038
```

Microsoft Visual Web Developer

Microsoft's Visual Studio package can be used to inspect and debug JavaScript code:

`http://msdn.microsoft.com/vstudio/express/vwd/`

To run the debugger interactively in the free version (Visual Web Developer Express), follow the process outlined here:

`http://www.berniecode.com/blog/2007/03/08/how-to-debug-javascript-with-visual-web-developer-express/`

DebugBar

The DebugBar provides a DOM inspector as well as a JavaScript console for debugging:

`http://www.debugbar.com/`

Drip

Memory leaks in JavaScript code can cause performance and stability issues for Internet Explorer. Drip helps to detect and isolate these memory issues:

`http://Sourceforge.net/projects/ieleak/`

To learn more about a common cause of Internet Explorer memory leaks, see Appendix C, JavaScript Closures.

Tools for Safari

Safari remains the new kid on the block as a development platform, but there are still tools available for situations in which code behaves differently in this browser than elsewhere.

Develop Menu

As of Safari 3.1, an option in the advanced tab of the Preferences menu provides a special menu called Develop. With this menu enabled, a Web Inspector and JavaScript Console are available.

Web Inspector

Safari 3 includes the ability to inspect individual page elements and collect information especially about the CSS rules that apply to each one.

```
http://trac.webkit.org/wiki/Web%20Inspector
```

Current builds of WebKit have substantially enhanced this web inspector tool, granting it many of Firebug's excellent features such as an integrated JavaScript debugger called Drosera.

```
http://trac.webkit.org/wiki/Drosera
```

Tools for Opera

While it has a limited market share as a desktop browser, Opera is a significant player in embedded systems and mobile devices, and its capabilities should be carefully considered during web development.

Dragonfly

While still in its early stages, Dragonfly is a promising debugging environment for Opera browsers on computers or mobile devices. Dragonfly's feature set is similar to that of Firebug, including JavaScript debugging, as well as CSS and DOM inspection and editing.

Other tools

While the previous tools each focus on a specific browser, these utilities are broader in their scope.

Firebug Lite

Though the Firebug extension itself is limited to the Firefox web browser, some of the features can be replicated by including the Firebug Lite script on the web page. This package simulates the Firebug console, including allowing calls to `console.log()` to work in all browsers and not raise JavaScript errors:

```
http://www.getfirebug.com/lite.html
```

NitobiBug

Like Firebug Lite, NotobiBug is a cross-browser tool that covers some of the same ground as the more robust and refined Firebug. Its strength lies in its DOM and object inspection, though it has a capable console as well. The console and inspector can be invoked by including a reference to the Nitobi JavaScript file and calling `nitobi.Debug.log()`.

`http://www.nitobibug.com/`

TextMate jQuery bundle

This extension for the popular Mac OS X text editor TextMate provides syntax highlighting for jQuery methods and selectors, code completion for methods, and a quick API reference from within your code. The bundle is also compatible with the E text editor for Windows:

`http://github.com/kswedberg/jquery-tmbundle/`

Charles

When developing AJAX-intensive applications, it can be useful to see exactly what data is being sent between the browser and the server. The Charles web debugging proxy displays all HTTP traffic between two points, including normal web requests, HTTPS traffic, Flash remoting, and AJAX responses:

`http://www.xk72.com/charles/`

Fiddler

Fiddler is another useful HTTP debugging proxy with features similar to those in Charles. According to its site, Fiddler "includes a powerful event-based scripting subsystem, and can be extended using any .NET language":

`http://www.fiddlertool.com/fiddler/`

Aptana

This Java-based web development IDE is free and cross-platform. Along with both standard and advanced code editing features, it incorporates a full copy of the jQuery API documentation, and has its own Firebug-based JavaScript debugger.

`http://www.aptana.com/`

C
JavaScript Closures

Throughout this book, we have seen many jQuery methods that take **functions** as parameters. Our examples have thus created, called, and passed around functions time and again. While usually we can do this with only a cursory understanding of the inner JavaScript mechanics at work, at times side effects of our actions can seem strange if we do not have knowledge of the language features. In this appendix, we will study one of the more esoteric (yet prevalent) function-based constructs called **closures**.

Our discussion will involve many small code examples, with which we will want to print out a set of messages. Rather than use a browser-specific logging mechanism (like Firefox's `console.log()`), or create a series of `alert()` dialogs, we will use a small plugin method:

```
jQuery.fn.print = function(message) {
  return this.each(function() {
    $('<div class="result" />')
      .text(String(message))
      .appendTo($(this).find('.results'));
  });
};
```

With this method defined, we can call `$('#example').print('hello')` to add the message "hello" within `<div id="example">`.

Inner functions

JavaScript is fortunate to include itself among the programming languages that support **inner function** declarations. Many traditional programming languages, such as C, collect all functions in a single top-level scope. Languages with inner functions, on the other hand, allow us to gather small utility functions where they are needed, avoiding **namespace pollution**.

An inner function is simply a function that is defined inside of another function. For example:

```
function outerFn() {
   function innerFn() {
   }
}
```

Here, `innerFn()` is an inner function, contained within the scope of `outerFn()`. This means that a call to `innerFn()` is valid within `outerFn()`, but not outside of it. The following code results in a JavaScript error:

```
function outerFn() {
   $('#example-2').print('Outer function');
   function innerFn() {
      $('#example-1').print('Inner Function');
   }
}
$('#example-1').print('innerFn():');
innerFn();
```

We can successfully run the code, though, by calling `innerFn()` from within `outerFn()`:

```
function outerFn() {
   $('#example-2').print('Outer function');
   function innerFn() {
      $('#example-2').print('Inner function');
   }
   innerFn();
}
$('#example-2').print('outerFn():');
outerFn();
```

This results in the output:

```
outerFn():
Outer function
Inner function
```

This technique is especially handy for small, single-purpose functions. For example, algorithms that are **recursive**, but have a non-recursive API wrapper, are often best expressed with an inner function as a helper.

The great escape

The plot thickens when **function references** come into play. Some languages, such as Pascal, allow the use of inner functions for the purpose of **code hiding** only; those functions are forever entombed within their parent functions. JavaScript, on the other hand, allows us to pass functions around just as if they were any other kind of data. This means inner functions can escape their captors.

The escape route can wind in many different directions. For example, suppose the function is assigned to a **global variable**:

```
var globalVar;

function outerFn() {
  $('#example-3').print('Outer function');
  function innerFn() {
    $('#example-3').print('Inner function');
  }
  globalVar = innerFn;
}
$('#example-3').print('outerFn():');
outerFn();
$('#example-3').print('globalVar():');
globalVar();
```

The call to `outerFn()` after the function definition modifies the global variable `globalVar`. It is now a reference to `innerFn()`. This means that the later call to `globalVar()` operates just as an inner call to `innerFn()` would, and the `print` statements are reached:

```
outerFn():
Outer function
globalVar():
Inner function
```

Note that a call to `innerFn()` from outside of `outerFn()` still results in an error! Though the function has escaped by way of the reference stored in the global variable, the function name is still trapped inside the scope of `outerFn()`.

A function reference can also find its way out of a parent function through a **return value**:

```
function outerFn() {
  $('#example-4').print('Outer function');
  function innerFn() {
    $('#example-4').print('Inner function');
  }
```

```
      return innerFn;
    }
    $('#example-4').print('var fnRef = outerFn():');
    var fnRef = outerFn();
    $('#example-4').print(fnRef():');
    fnRef();
```

Here, there is no global variable modified inside `outerFn()`. Instead, `outerFn()` returns a reference to `innerFn()`. The call to `outerFn()` results in this reference, which is stored and called itself in turn, triggering the message again:

```
var fnRef = outerFn():
Outer function
fnRef():
Inner function
```

The fact that inner functions can be invoked through a reference even after the function has gone out of scope means that JavaScript needs to keep referenced functions available as long as they could possibly be called. Each variable that refers to the function is tracked by the JavaScript **runtime**, and once the last has gone away, the JavaScript **garbage collector** comes along and frees up that bit of memory.

Variable scoping

Inner functions can of course have their own variables, which are restricted in scope to the function itself:

```
function outerFn() {
  function innerFn() {
    var innerVar = 0;
    innerVar++;
    $('#example-5').print('innerVar = ' + innerVar);
  }
  return innerFn;
}
var fnRef = outerFn();
fnRef();
fnRef();
var fnRef2 = outerFn();
fnRef2();
fnRef2();
```

Each time the function is called, through a reference or otherwise, a new variable `innerVar` is created, incremented, and displayed:

innerVar = 1
innerVar = 1
innerVar = 1
innerVar = 1

Inner functions can reference global variables in the same way as any other function can:

```
var globalVar = 0;
function outerFn() {
  function innerFn() {
    globalVar++;
    $('#example-6').print('globalVar = ' + globalVar);
  }
  return innerFn;
}
var fnRef = outerFn();
fnRef();
fnRef();
var fnRef2 = outerFn();
fnRef2();
fnRef2();
```

Now our function will consistently increment the variable with each call:

globalVar = 1
globalVar = 2
globalVar = 3
globalVar = 4

But what if the variable is local to the parent function? Since the inner function inherits its parent's scope, this variable can be referenced too:

```
function outerFn() {
  var outerVar = 0;
  function innerFn() {
    outerVar++;
    $('#example-7').print('outerVar = ' + outerVar);
  }
  return innerFn;
}
var fnRef = outerFn();
fnRef();
fnRef();
var fnRef2 = outerFn();
fnRef2();
fnRef2();
```

Now our function calls have more interesting behavior:

```
outerVar = 1
outerVar = 2
outerVar = 1
outerVar = 2
```

We get a mix of the two earlier effects. The calls to `innerFn()` through each reference increment `outerVar` independently. Note that the second call to `outerFn()` is not resetting the value of `outerVar`, but rather creating a new **instance** of `outerVar`, bound to the scope of the second function call. The upshot of this is that after the above calls, another call to `fnRef()` will print the value **3**, and a subsequent call to `fnRef2()` will also print **3**. The two counters are completely separate.

When a reference to an inner function finds its way outside of the scope in which the function was defined, this creates a **closure** on that function. We call variables that are neither parameters nor local to the inner function **free variables**, and the environment of the outer function call **closes** them. Essentially, the fact that the function refers to a local variable in the outer function grants the variable a stay of execution. The memory is not released when the function completes, as it is still needed by the closure.

Interactions between closures

When more than one inner function exists, closures can have effects that are not as easy to anticipate. Suppose we pair our incrementing function with another function, this one incrementing by two:

```
function outerFn() {
  var outerVar = 0;
  function innerFn1() {
    outerVar++;
    $('#example-8').print('(1) outerVar = ' + outerVar);
  }
  function innerFn2() {
    outerVar += 2;
    $('#example-8').print('(2) outerVar = ' + outerVar);
  }
  return {'fn1': innerFn1, 'fn2': innerFn2};
}
var fnRef = outerFn();
fnRef.fn1();
fnRef.fn2();
fnRef.fn1();
```

```
var fnRef2 = outerFn();
fnRef2.fn1();
fnRef2.fn2();
fnRef2.fn1();
```

We return references to both functions, using a **map** to do so (this illustrates another way in which reference to an inner function can escape its parent). Both functions are called through the references:

```
(1) outerVar = 1
(2) outerVar = 3
(1) outerVar = 4
(1) outerVar = 1
(2) outerVar = 3
(1) outerVar = 4
```

The two inner functions refer to the same local variable, so they share the same **closing environment**. When `innerFn1()` increments `outerVar` by 1, this sets the new starting value of `outerVar` when `innerFn2()` is called, and vice versa. Once again, though, we see that any subsequent call to `outerFn()` creates new instances of these closures with a new closing environment to match. Fans of **object-oriented programming** will note that we have in essence created a new **object**, with the free variables acting as **instance variables** and the closures acting as **instance methods**. The variables are also **private**, as they cannot be directly referenced outside of their enclosing scope, enabling true object-oriented data privacy.

Closures in jQuery

The methods we have seen throughout the jQuery library often take at least one function as a parameter. For convenience, we often use **anonymous functions** so that we can define the function behavior right when it is needed. This means that functions are rarely in the top-level namespace; they are usually inner functions, which means they can quite easily create closures.

Arguments to $(document).ready()

Nearly all of the code we write using jQuery ends up getting placed inside a function passed as an argument to `$(document).ready()`. We do this to guarantee that the DOM has loaded before the code is run, which is usually a requirement for interesting jQuery code. When a function is created and passed to `.ready()`, a reference to the function is stored as part of the global jQuery object. This reference is then called at a later time, when the DOM is ready.

We usually place the `$(document).ready()` construct at the top level of the code structure, so this function is not really part of a closure. However, since our code is usually written inside this function, everything *else* is an inner function:

```
$(document).ready(function() {
  var readyVar = 0;
  function innerFn() {
    readyVar++;
    $('#example-9').print('readyVar = ' + readyVar);
  }
  innerFn();
  innerFn();
});
```

This looks like many of our earlier examples, except that in this case, the outer function is the callback passed to `$(document).ready()`. Since `innerFn()` is defined inside of it, and refers to `readyVar` which is in the scope of the callback function, `innerFn()` and its environment create a closure. We can see this by noting that the value of `readyVar` persists between calls to the function:

```
readyVar = 1
readyVar = 2
```

The fact that most jQuery code is inside a function body is useful, because this can protect against some **namespace collisions**. For example, it is this feature that allows us to use `jQuery.noConflict()` to free up the `$` shortcut for other libraries, while still being able to define the shortcut locally for use within `$(document).ready()`.

Event handlers

The `$(document).ready()` construct usually wraps the rest of our code, including the assignment of **event handlers**. Since handlers are functions, they become inner functions. Since those inner functions are stored and called later, they can create closures. A simple `click` handler can illustrate this:

```
$(document).ready(function() {
  var counter = 0;
  $('#example-10 a.add').click(function() {
    counter++;
    $('#example-10').print('counter = ' + counter);
    return false;
  });
});
```

Because the variable `counter` is declared inside of the `.ready()` handler, it is only available to the jQuery code inside this block and not to outside code. It can be referenced by the code in the `click` handler, however, which increments and displays the variable's value. Because a closure is created, the same instance of `counter` is referenced each time the link is clicked. This means that the messages display a continuously incrementing set of values, not just 1 each time:

```
counter = 1
counter = 2
counter = 3
```

Event handlers can share their closing environments, just like other functions can:

```
$(document).ready(function() {
  var counter = 0;
  $('#example-11 a.add').click(function() {
    counter++;
    $('#example-11').print('counter = ' + counter);
    return false;
  });
  $('#example-11 a.subtract').click(function() {
    counter--;
    $('#example-11').print('counter = ' + counter);
    return false;
  });
});
```

Since both of the functions reference the same `counter` variable, the incrementing and decrementing operations of the two links affect the same value rather than being independent:

```
counter = 1
counter = 2
counter = 1
counter = 0
```

These examples have used **anonymous functions**, as has been our custom in jQuery code. This makes no difference in the construction of closures; closures can come from named or anonymous functions. For example, we can write an anonymous function to report the index of an item within a jQuery object:

```
$(document).ready(function() {
  $('#example-12 a').each(function(index) {
    $(this).click(function() {
      $('#example-12').print('index = ' + index);
      return false;
    });
  });
});
```

Because the innermost function is defined within the `.each()` callback, this code actually creates as many functions as there are links. Each of these functions is attached as a `click` handler to one of the links. The functions have `index` in their closing environment, since it is a parameter to the `.each()` callback. This behaves the same way as if the `click` handler were written as a named function:

```
$(document).ready(function() {
  $('#example-13 a').each(function(index) {
    function clickHandler() {
      $('#example-13').print('index = ' + index);
      return false;
    }
    $(this).click(clickHandler);
  });
});
```

The version with the anonymous function is just a bit shorter. The position of this named function is still relevant, however:

```
$(document).ready(function() {
  function clickHandler() {
    $('#example-14').print('index = ' + index);
    return false;
  }
  $('#example-14 a').each(function(index) {
    $(this).click(clickHandler);
  });
});
```

This version will trigger a JavaScript error whenever a link is clicked because `index` is not found in the closing environment of `clickHandler()`. It remains a free variable, and so is undefined in this context.

Memory leak hazards

JavaScript manages its memory using a technique known as **garbage collection**. This is in contrast to low-level languages like C, which require programmers to explicitly **reserve** blocks of memory and free them when they are no longer being used. Other languages such as Objective-C assist the programmer by implementing a **reference counting** system, which allows the user to note how many pieces of the program are using a particular piece of memory so it can be cleaned up when no longer used. JavaScript is a high-level language, on the other hand, and generally takes care of this bookkeeping behind the scenes.

Whenever a new memory-resident item such as an object or function comes into being in JavaScript code, a chunk of memory is set aside for this item. As the object gets passed around to functions and assigned to variables, more pieces of code begin to point to the object. JavaScript keeps track of these **pointers**, and when the last one is gone, the memory taken by the object is released. Consider a chain of pointers:

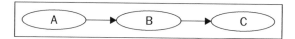

Here object *A* has a property that points to *B*, and *B* has a property that points to *C*. Even if object *A* here is the only one that is a variable in the current scope, all three objects must remain in memory because of the pointers to them. When *A* goes out of scope, however (such as at the end of the function it was declared in), then it can be released by the garbage collector. Now *B* has nothing pointing to it, so can be released, and finally *C* can be released as well.

More complicated arrangements of references can be harder to deal with:

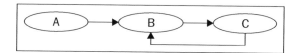

Now we've added a property to object *C* that refers back to *B*. In this case, when *A* is released, *B* still has a pointer to it from *C*. This **reference loop** needs to be handled specially by JavaScript, which must notice that the entire loop is isolated from the variables that are in scope.

Accidental reference loops

Closures can cause reference loops to be inadvertently created. Since functions are objects that must be kept in memory, any variables they have in their closing environment are also kept in memory:

```
function outerFn() {
  var outerVar = {};
  function innerFn() {
    alert(outerVar);
  }
  outerVar.fn = innerFn;
  return innerFnn;
};
```

Here, an object called outerVar is created and referenced from within the inner function innerFn(). Then, a property of outerVar that points to innerFn() is created, and innerFn() is returned. This creates a closure on innerFn() that refers to outerVar, which in turn refers back to innerFn(). But the loop can be more insidious than this:

```
function outerFn() {
  var outerVar = {};
  function innerFn() {
    alert('hello');
  }
  outerVar.fn = innerFn;
  return innerFn;
};
```

Here, we've changed innerFn() so that it no longer refers to outerVar. However, this does not break the loop! Even though outerVar is never referred to from innerFn(), it is still in innerFn()'s **closing environment**. All variables in the scope of outerFn() are *implicitly* referred to by innerFn() due to the closure. So, closures make it easy to accidentally create these loops.

The Internet Explorer memory leak problem

All of this is generally not an issue because JavaScript is able to detect these loops and clean them up when they become orphaned. Internet Explorer, however, has difficulty handling one particular class of reference loops. When a loop contains *both* DOM elements and regular JavaScript objects, IE cannot release either one because they are handled by different memory managers. These loops are never freed until the browser is closed, which can eat up a great deal of memory over time. A common cause of such a loop is a simple event handler:

```
$(document).ready(function() {
  var div = document.getElementById('foo');
  div.onclick = function() {
    alert('hello');
  };
});
```

When the click handler is assigned, this creates a closure with div in the closing environment. But div now contains a reference back to the closure—the onclick property itself. Thus, the resulting loop can't be released by Internet Explorer even when we navigate away from the page.

The good news

Now let's write the same code, but using normal jQuery constructs:

```
$(document).ready(function() {
  var $div = $('#foo');
  $div.click(function() {
    alert('hello');
  });
});
```

Even though a closure is still created, causing the same kind of loop as before, we do not get an IE memory leak from this code. Thankfully, jQuery is aware of the potential for leaks, and manually releases all of the event handlers that it assigns. As long as we faithfully adhere to using jQuery event binding methods for our handlers, we need not fear leaks caused by this particular common idiom.

This doesn't mean we're completely out of the woods; we must continue to take care when we're performing other tasks with DOM elements. Attaching JavaScript objects to DOM elements can still cause memory leaks in Internet Explorer; jQuery just helps make this situation far less prevalent.

Because of this, jQuery gives us another tool to help avoid these leaks. In Chapter 7, we saw that the .data() method allows us to attach information to DOM elements in much the same way as we can with expando properties. Since this data is not stored directly as an expando (jQuery uses an internal map to store the data using IDs it creates), the reference loop is never formed and we sidestep the memory leak issue. Whenever an expando seems like a convenient data storage mechanism, we should consider whether .data() is a safer alternative.

Summary

JavaScript closures are a powerful language feature. They are often quite useful in hiding variables from other code, so that we don't tread on variable names being used elsewhere. Due to jQuery's frequent reliance on functions as method arguments, they can also be inadvertently created quite often. Understanding them allows us to write more efficient and concise code, and with a bit of care and the use of jQuery's built-in safeguards, we can avoid the memory-related pitfalls they can introduce.

D
Quick Reference

This appendix is intended to be a quick reference for the jQuery API, including selector expressions and methods. A more detailed discussion on this topic is available in this book's companion volume, *jQuery Reference Guide*, and on the jQuery documentation site, `http://docs.jquery.com`.

Selector expressions

The jQuery factory function `$()` is used to find elements on the page to work with. This function takes a string composed of CSS-like syntax, called a **selector expression**. Selector expressions are discussed in detail in Chapter 2.

Selector	Matches
`*`	All elements.
`#id`	The element with the given ID.
`element`	All elements of the given type.
`.class`	All elements with the given class.
`a, b`	Elements that are matched by a or b.
`a b`	Elements b that are descendants of a.
`a > b`	Elements b that are children of a.
`a + b`	Elements b that immediately follow a.
`a ~ b`	Elements b that are siblings of a.
`:first`	The first element in the result set.
`:last`	The last element in the result set.
`:not(a)`	All elements in the result set that are not matched by a.
`:even`	Even elements in the result set (0-based).
`:odd`	Odd elements in the result set (0-based).

Selector	Matches
:eq(index)	A numbered element in the result set (0-based).
:gt(index)	All elements in the result set after (greater than) the given index (0-based).
:lt(index)	All elements in the result set before (less than) the given index (0-based).
:header	Header elements (e.g. <h1>, <h2>).
:animated	Elements with an animation in progress.
:contains(text)	Elements containing the given text.
:empty	Elements with no child nodes.
:has(a)	Elements containing a descendant element matching a.
:parent	Elements that have child nodes.
:hidden	Elements that are hidden, either through CSS or because they are <input type="hidden" />.
:visible	The inverse of :hidden.
[attr]	Elements that have the attribute attr.
[attr=value]	Elements whose attr attribute is value.
[attr!=value]	Elements whose attr attribute is not value.
[attr^=value]	Elements whose attr attribute begins with value.
[attr$=value]	Elements whose attr attribute ends with value.
[attr*=value]	Elements whose attr attribute contains the substring value.
:nth-child(index)	Elements which are the indexth child of their parent element (1-based).
:nth-child(even)	Elements which are an even child of their parent element (1-based).
:nth-child(odd)	Elements which are an odd child of their parent element (1-based).
:nth-child(formula)	Elements which are the nth child of their parent element (1-based). Formulas are of the form an+b for integers a and b.
:first-child	Elements which are the first child of their parent.
:last-child	Elements which are the last child of their parent.
:only-child	Elements which are the only child of their parent.
:input	All <input>, <select>, <textarea>, and <button> elements.
:text	<input> elements with type="text".
:password	<input> elements with type="password".
:radio	<input> elements with type="radio".

Selector	Matches
:checkbox	\<input\> elements with type="checkbox".
:submit	\<input\> elements with type="submit".
:image	\<input\> elements with type="image".
:reset	\<input\> elements with type="reset".
:button	\<input\> elements with type="button", and \<button\> elements.
:file	\<input\> elements with type="file".
:enabled	Enabled form elements.
:disabled	Disabled form elements.
:checked	Checked checkboxes and radio buttons.
:selected	Selected \<option\> elements.

DOM traversal methods

After creating a jQuery object using $(), we can alter the set of matched elements we are working with by calling one of these **DOM traversal methods**. DOM traversal methods are discussed in detail in Chapter 2.

Traversal Method	Returns a jQuery object containing...
.filter(selector)	Selected elements that match the given selector.
.filter(callback)	Selected elements for which the callback function returns true.
.eq(index)	The selected element at the given 0-based index.
.slice(start, [end])	Selected elements in the given range of 0-based indices.
.not(selector)	Selected elements that do not match the given selector.
.add(selector)	Selected elements, plus any additional elements that match the given selector.
.find(selector)	Descendant elements that match the selector.
.contents()	Child nodes (including text nodes).
.children([selector])	Child nodes, optionally filtered by a selector.
.next([selector])	The sibling immediately following each selected element, optionally filtered by a selector.
.nextAll([selector])	All siblings following each selected element, optionally filtered by a selector.
.prev([selector])	The sibling immediately preceding each selected element, optionally filtered by a selector.

Traversal Method	Returns a jQuery object containing...
`.prevAll([selector])`	All siblings preceding each selected element, optionally filtered by a selector.
`.siblings([selector])`	All siblings, optionally filtered by a selector.
`.parent([selector])`	The parent of each selected element, optionally filtered by a selector.
`.parents([selector])`	All ancestors, optionally filtered by a selector.
`.closest selector`	The first element that matches the selector, starting at the selected element and moving up through its ancestors in the DOM tree.
`.offsetParent()`	The positioned parent (e.g. `relative`, `absolute`) of the **first** selected element.
`.andSelf()`	The selected elements, plus the previous set of selected elements on the internal jQuery stack.
`.end()`	The previous set of selected elements on the internal jQuery stack.
`.map(callback)`	The result of the `callback` function when called on each selected element.

Event methods

To react to user behavior, we need to register our handlers using these **event methods**. Note that many DOM events only apply to certain element types; these subtleties are not covered here. Event methods are discussed in detail in Chapter 3.

Event Method	Description
`.ready(handler)`	Bind `handler` to be called when the DOM and CSS are fully loaded.
`.bind(type, [data], handler)`	Bind `handler` to be called when the given type of event is sent to the element.
`.one(type, [data], handler)`	Bind `handler` to be called when the given type of event is sent to the element. Removes the binding when the handler is called.
`.unbind([type], [handler])`	Removes the bindings on the element (for an event type, a particular handler, or all bindings).
`.live(type, handler)`	Bind `handler` to be called when the given type of event is sent to the element, using event delegation.
`.die(type, [handler])`	Removes the bindings on the element previously bound with `.live()`.

Event Method	Description
.blur(handler)	Bind handler to be called when the element loses keyboard focus.
.change(handler)	Bind handler to be called when the element's value changes.
.click(handler)	Bind handler to be called when the element is clicked.
.dblclick(handler)	Bind handler to be called when the element is double-clicked.
.error(handler)	Bind handler to be called when the element receives an error event (browser-dependent).
.focus(handler)	Bind handler to be called when the element gains keyboard focus.
.keydown(handler)	Bind handler to be called when a key is pressed and the element has keyboard focus.
.keypress(handler)	Bind handler to be called when a keystroke occurs and the element has keyboard focus.
.keyup(handler)	Bind handler to be called when a key is released and the element has keyboard focus.
.load(handler)	Bind handler to be called when the element finishes loading.
.mousedown(handler)	Bind handler to be called when the mouse button is pressed within the element.
.mouseenter(handler)	Bind handler to be called when the mouse pointer enters the element. Not affected by event bubbling.
.mouseleave(handler)	Bind handler to be called when the mouse pointer leaves the element. Not affected by event bubbling.
.mousemove(handler)	Bind handler to be called when the mouse pointer moves within the element.
.mouseout(handler)	Bind handler to be called when the mouse pointer leaves the element.
.mouseover(handler)	Bind handler to be called when the mouse pointer enters the element.
.mouseup(handler)	Bind handler to be called when the mouse button is released within the element.
.resize(handler)	Bind handler to be called when the element is resized.
.scroll(handler)	Bind handler to be called when the element's scroll position changes.
.select(handler)	Bind handler to be called when text in the element is selected.

Event Method	Description
`.submit(handler)`	Bind `handler` to be called when the form element is submitted.
`.unload(handler)`	Bind `handler` to be called when the element is unloaded from memory.
`.hover(enter, leave)`	Bind `enter` to be called when the mouse enters the element, and `leave` to be called when the mouse leaves it.
`.toggle(handler1, handler2, ...)`	Bind `handler1` to be called when the mouse is clicked on the element, followed by `handler2` and so on for subsequent clicks.
`.trigger(type, [data])`	Trigger handlers for the event on the element, and execute the default action for the event.
`.triggerHandler(type, [data])`	Trigger handlers for the event on the element without executing any default actions.
`.blur()`	Trigger the `blur` event.
`.change()`	Trigger the `change` event.
`.click()`	Trigger the `click` event.
`.dblclick()`	Trigger the `dblclick` event.
`.error()`	Trigger the `error` event.
`.focus()`	Trigger the `focus` event.
`.keydown()`	Trigger the `keydown` event.
`.keypress()`	Trigger the `keypress` event.
`.keyup()`	Trigger the `keyup` event.
`.select()`	Trigger the `select` event.
`.submit()`	Trigger the `submit` event.

Effect methods

These **effect methods** may be used to perform animations on DOM elements. Effect methods are discussed in detail in Chapter 4.

Effect Method	Description
`.show()`	Display the matched elements.
`.hide()`	Hide the matched elements.
`.show(speed, [callback])`	Display the matched elements by animating height, width, and opacity.
`.hide(speed, [callback])`	Hide the matched elements by animating height, width, and opacity.

Effect Method	Description
`.toggle([speed], [callback])`	Display or hide the matched elements.
`.slideDown([speed], [callback])`	Display the matched elements with a sliding motion.
`.slideUp([speed], [callback])`	Hide the matched elements with a sliding motion.
`.slideToggle([speed], [callback])`	Display or hides the matched elements with a sliding motion.
`.fadeIn([speed], [callback])`	Display the matched elements by fading them to opaque.
`.fadeOut([speed], [callback])`	Hide the matched elements by fading them to transparent.
`.fadeTo(speed, opacity, [callback])`	Adjust the opacity of the matched elements.
`.animate(attributes, [speed], [easing], [callback])`	Perform a custom animation of the specified CSS attributes.
`.animate(attributes, options)`	A lower-level interface to `.animate()`, allowing control over the animation queue.
`.stop([clearQueue], [jumpToEnd])`	Stop the currently running animation, then start queued animations, if any.
`.queue()`	Retrieve the queue of animations on the first matched element.
`.queue(callback)`	Add `callback` to the end of the queue.
`.queue(newQueue)`	Replace the queue with a new one.
`.dequeue()`	Execute the next animation on the queue.

DOM manipulation methods

DOM manipulation methods are discussed in detail in Chapter 5.

Method	Description
`.attr(key)`	Get the attribute named `key`.
`.attr(key, value)`	Set the attribute named `key` to `value`.
`.attr(key, fn)`	Set the attribute named `key` to the result of `fn` (called separately on each matched element).
`.attr(map)`	Set attribute values, given as key-value pairs.
`.removeAttr(key)`	Remove the attribute named `key`.

Method	Description
.addClass(class)	Add the given class to each matched element.
.removeClass(class)	Remove the given class from each matched element.
.toggleClass(class)	Remove the given class if present, and adds it if not, for each matched element.
.hasClass(class)	Return true if any of the matched elements has the given class.
.html()	Get the HTML content of the first matched element.
.html(value)	Set the HTML content of each matched element to value.
.text()	Get the textual content of all matched elements as a single string.
.text(value)	Set the textual content of each matched element to value.
.val()	Get the value attribute of the first matched element.
.val(value)	Set the value attribute of each element to value.
.css(key)	Get the CSS attribute named key.
.css(key, value)	Set the CSS attribute named key to value.
.css(map)	Set CSS attribute values, given as key-value pairs.
.offset()	Get the top, and left, pixel coordinates of the first matched element, relative to the viewport.
.position()	Get the top, and left, pixel coordinates of the first matched element, relative to the element returned by .offsetParent().
.scrollTop()	Get the vertical scroll position of the first matched element.
.scrollTop(value)	Set the vertical scroll position of all matched elements to value.
.scrollLeft()	Get the horizontal scroll position of the first matched element.
.scrollLeft(value)	Set the horizontal scroll position of all matched elements to value.
.height()	Get the height of the first matched element.
.height(value)	Set the height of all matched elements to value.
.width()	Get the width of the first matched element.
.width(value)	Set the width of all matched elements to value.
.innerHeight()	Get the height of the first matched element, including padding, but not border.

Method	Description
`.innerWidth()`	Get the width of the first matched element, including padding, but not border.
`.outerHeight (includeMargin)`	Get the height of the first matched element, including padding, border, and optional margin.
`.outerWidth (includeMargin)`	Get the width of the first matched element, including padding, border, and optional margin.
`.append(content)`	Insert `content` at the end of the interior of each matched element.
`.appendTo(selector)`	Insert the matched elements at the end of the interior of the elements matched by `selector`.
`.prepend(content)`	Insert `content` at the beginning of the interior of each matched element.
`.prependTo(selector)`	Insert the matched elements at the beginning of the interior of the elements matched by `selector`.
`.after(content)`	Insert `content` after each matched element.
`.insertAfter(selector)`	Insert the matched elements after each of the elements matched by `selector`.
`.before(content)`	Insert `content` before each matched element.
`.insertBefore(selector)`	Insert the matched elements before each of the elements matched by `selector`.
`.wrap(content)`	Wrap each of the matched elements within `content`.
`.wrapAll(content)`	Wrap all of the matched elements as a single unit within `content`.
`.wrapInner(content)`	Wrap the interior contents of each of the matched elements within `content`.
`.replaceWith(content)`	Replace the matched elements with `content`.
`.replaceAll(selector)`	Replace the elements matched by `selector` with the matched elements.
`.empty()`	Remove the child nodes of each matched element.
`.remove([selector])`	Remove the matched nodes (optionally filtered by `selector`) from the DOM.
`.clone([withHandlers])`	Make a copy of all matched elements, optionally also copying event handlers.
`.data(key)`	Get the data item named `key` associated with the first matched element.
`.data(key, value)`	Set the data item named `key` associated with each matched element to `value`.
`.removeData(key)`	Remove the data item named `key` associated with each matched element.

AJAX methods

We can retrieve information from the server without requiring a page refresh by calling one of these **AJAX methods**. AJAX methods are discussed in detail in Chapter 6.

AJAX Method	Description
`$.ajax(options)`	Make an AJAX request using the provided set of options. This is a low-level method that is usually called via other convenience methods.
`.load(url, [data], [callback])`	Make an AJAX request to `url`, and place the response into the matched elements.
`$.get(url, [data], [callback], [returnType])`	Make an AJAX request to `url` using the GET method.
`$.getJSON(url, [data], [callback])`	Make an AJAX request to `url`, interpreting the response as a JSON data structure.
`$.getScript(url, [callback])`	Make an AJAX request to `url`, executing the response as JavaScript.
`$.post(url, [data], [callback], [returnType])`	Make an AJAX request to `url` using the POST method.
`.ajaxComplete(handler)`	Bind `handler` to be called when any AJAX transaction completes.
`.ajaxError(handler)`	Bind `handler` to be called when any AJAX transaction completes with an error.
`.ajaxSend(handler)`	Bind `handler` to be called when any AJAX transaction begins.
`.ajaxStart(handler)`	Bind handler to be called when any AJAX transaction begins, and no others are active.
`.ajaxStop(handler)`	Bind `handler` to be called when any AJAX transaction ends, and no others are still active.
`.ajaxSuccess(handler)`	Bind `handler` to be called when any AJAX transaction completes successfully.
`$.ajaxSetup(options)`	Set default options for all subsequent AJAX transactions.
`.serialize()`	Encode the values of a set of form controls into a query string.
`.serializeArray()`	Encode the values of a set of form controls into a JSON data structure.
`$.param(map)`	Encode an arbitrary map of values into a query string.

Miscellaneous methods

These utility methods do not fit neatly into the above categories, but are often very useful when writing scripts using jQuery.

Method or Property	Description
`$.support`	Return a map of properties indicating whether the browser supports various features and standards
`$.each(collection, callback)`	Iterate over `collection`, executing `callback` for each item.
`$.extend(target, addition, ...)`	Modify the object `target` by adding properties from the other supplied objects.
`$.grep(array, callback, [invert])`	Filter `array` by using `callback` as a test.
`$.makeArray(object)`	Convert `object` into an array.
`$.map(array, callback)`	Construct a new array consisting of the result of `callback` being called on each item.
`$.inArray(value, array)`	Determine whether `value` is in `array`.
`$.merge(array1, array2)`	Combine the contents of `array1` and `array2`.
`$.unique(array)`	Remove any duplicate DOM elements from `array`.
`$.isFunction(object)`	Determine whether `object` is a function.
`$.trim(string)`	Remove whitespace from the ends of `string`.
`$.noConflict([extreme])`	Revert $ to its pre-jQuery definition.
`.hasClass(className)`	Determine whether any matched element has the given class.
`.is(selector)`	Determine whether any matched element is matched by the given selector expression.
`.each(callback)`	Iterate over the matched elements, executing `callback` for each element.
`.length`	Get the number of matched elements.
`.get()`	Get an array of DOM nodes corresponding to the matched elements.
`.get(index)`	Get the DOM node corresponding to the matched element at the given index.
`.index(element)`	Get the index of the given DOM node within the set of matched elements.

Index

suggestion list, hiding 243
versus live search 244

B

basic alphabetical sorting, JavaScript sorting
comparator, using 157-160
graceful degradation example 159
JavaScript's built in .sort()method, using 157
plugins, modifications 161
sorting behavior, applying 163
blogs
advanced DOM browser, uses 377
Ajaxian 375
A List Apart 377
Christian Heilmann's sites 376
DOM scripting 377
internet developments, by Robert Nyman 376
JavaScript ant 376
John Resig 375
jQuery blog 375
jQuery tutorials 375
Matt Snider JavaScript resource 376
programming/web-development blog 376
web design articles, by Dustin Diaz 376

C

Cascading Style Sheets. *See* **CSS**
charting, plugins
Flot plugin 338
Sparklines plugin 339
client and server communication
form, constructing 137, 138
GET request, performing 132-135
jQuery's AJAX toolkit, using 137
POST request, performing 136
closures 17, 385
anonymous function example 393
argument to $(document).ready(), passing 391, 392
event handlers, assigning 392, 394
in jQuery, anonymous functions used 391
interacting with 390, 391
interacting with, map used 391

code brevity, shortcuts
$() factory function 37
.ready()function 38
compact form
about 232
auto-completion 235
field, labeling 232
label, styling 233
label text, hiding 234
search field code 244-246
solutions, to problems 233-235
compound effects, using 76
compound events
advanced features, hiding 48, 49
advanced features, showing 48, 49
click event 50
DOM elements, hierarchy 51
hover()method 48, 50
toggle() method 48, 49
CSS 19
CSS reference
Mezzoblue CSS cribsheet 374
CSS browser catalog 375
W3C cascading style sheets homepage 374
CSS selectors
about 21
child combinator used 23
list-item levels, styling 23, 24
negation pseudo-class used 24
using 21-23
custom animations, creating
.animate() method 77
.animate() method, first form 77
.animate() method, second form 77
.fadeToggle() method 78
fadeIn() method 78
properties, CSS positions 81
properties, modifying 79, 81
custom selectors
about 26
alternate rows, styling 27-29
CSS pseudo-class syntax 26
form selectors 29, 30
one-based numbering 27
zero-based numbering 26

D

Thank you for buying
Learning jQuery 1.3

Packt Open Source Project Royalties

When we sell a book written on an Open Source project, we pay a royalty directly to that project. Therefore by purchasing Learning jQuery 1.3, Packt will have given some of the money received to the jQuery project.

In the long term, we see ourselves and you—customers and readers of our books—as part of the Open Source ecosystem, providing sustainable revenue for the projects we publish on. Our aim at Packt is to establish publishing royalties as an essential part of the service and support a business model that sustains Open Source.

If you're working with an Open Source project that you would like us to publish on, and subsequently pay royalties to, please get in touch with us.

Writing for Packt

We welcome all inquiries from people who are interested in authoring. Book proposals should be sent to author@packtpub.com. If your book idea is still at an early stage and you would like to discuss it first before writing a formal book proposal, contact us; one of our commissioning editors will get in touch with you.

We're not just looking for published authors; if you have strong technical skills but no writing experience, our experienced editors can help you develop a writing career, or simply get some additional reward for your expertise.

About Packt Publishing

Packt, pronounced 'packed', published its first book "Mastering phpMyAdmin for Effective MySQL Management" in April 2004 and subsequently continued to specialize in publishing highly focused books on specific technologies and solutions.

Our books and publications share the experiences of your fellow IT professionals in adapting and customizing today's systems, applications, and frameworks. Our solution-based books give you the knowledge and power to customize the software and technologies you're using to get the job done. Packt books are more specific and less general than the IT books you have seen in the past. Our unique business model allows us to bring you more focused information, giving you more of what you need to know, and less of what you don't.

Packt is a modern, yet unique publishing company, which focuses on producing quality, cutting-edge books for communities of developers, administrators, and newbies alike. For more information, please visit our website: www.PacktPub.com.

jQuery UI 1.6

ISBN: 978-1-847195-12-8   Paperback: 420 pages

Build highly interactive web applications with ready-to-use widgets of the jQuery user interface library

1. Packed with examples and clear explanations to easily design elegant and powerful front-end interfaces for your web applications

2. Organize your interfaces with reusable widgets like accordions, date pickers, dialogs, sliders, tabs, and more

3. Enhance the interactivity of your pages by making elements drag and droppable, sortable, selectable, and resizable

4. No experience of jQuery UI expected, but familiarity with jQuery is required

jQuery Reference Guide

ISBN: 978-1-847193-81-0   Paperback: 225 pages

A Comprehensive Exploration of the Popular JavaScript Library

1. Organized menu to every method, function, and selector in the jQuery library

2. Quickly look up features of the jQuery library

3. Understand the anatomy of a jQuery script

4. Extend jQuery's built-in capabilities with plug-ins, and even write your own

Please check **www.PacktPub.com** for information on our titles

3400685

Made in the USA